The **Architecture** of **Story**

WILL DUNNE

The **Architecture** of **Story**

A TECHNICAL GUIDE FOR THE DRAMATIC WRITER

THE UNIVERSITY OF CHICAGO PRESS

Chicago and London

Will Dunne is a resident playwright at Chicago Dramatists, where he develops plays and teaches workshops. He is the author of The Dramatic Writer's Companion, *also from the University of Chicago Press.*

The University of Chicago Press, Chicago 60637
The University of Chicago Press, Ltd., London
© 2016 by Will Dunne
All rights reserved. Published 2016.
Printed in the United States of America

25 24 23 22 21 20 19 18 17 16   1 2 3 4 5

ISBN-13: 978-0-226-18188-2   (cloth)
ISBN-13: 978-0-226-18191-2   (paper)
ISBN-13: 978-0-226-18207-0   (e-book)
DOI: 10.7208/chicago/9780226182070.001.0001

Library of Congress Cataloging-in-Publication Data

Dunne, Will, author.
    The architecture of story : a technical guide for the dramatic writer /
Will Dunne.
        pages   cm — (Chicago guides to writing, editing, and publishing)
    ISBN 978-0-226-18188-2 (cloth : alkaline paper)
    ISBN 978-0-226-18191-2 (paperback : alkaline paper)
    ISBN 978-0-226-18207-0 (e-book)
    1. Drama—Technique. 2. Playwriting. I. Title. II. Series: Chicago
guides to writing, editing, and publishing.
PN1661.D858 2016
808.2—dc23

                                                              2015035275

♾ This paper meets the requirements of
ANSI/NISO Z39.48-1992 (Permanence of Paper).

For Jean Shelton,

Stella Adler, and

Corinne Jacker,

who taught me to

analyze scripts

CONTENTS

ABOUT THIS GUIDE

The Architecture of Story: A Technical Guide for the Dramatic Writer can help you build and evaluate your own plays by exploring storytelling tools and techniques that other writers have used. Like *The Dramatic Writer's Companion,*[1] which it complements, this guide has a nonlinear, reference-book structure. Chapters can be read as needed, in any order, any number of times and offer hundreds of questions to help you analyze your work. For best results, please read this introduction, which explains more about the guide and how to use it.

■ A TECHNICAL LOOK AT DRAMATIC STORYTELLING

Dramatic stories are made of parts that work together to draw us in and keep us engaged from beginning to end. These parts, or elements, come in various sizes and shapes and can be used in different ways for different purposes. The job of a dramatic writer is to figure out what elements a story needs and to compose them in a structure that best supports *this* story.

While dramatic works through the ages tend to share certain storytelling elements, there is no formula that can successfully dictate what a play should be. Each new play comes into the world with a set of characters, plot points, and operating rules that must be defined and developed by the writer with the understanding that what works for one play does not necessarily work for another. To learn how to write a play, then, is a goal that can never be fully realized. To learn how to write a *particular* play is a dream that is both manageable and achievable.

The Architecture of Story will help you explore the building blocks of dramatic storytelling by analyzing three successful plays. The approach here is neither to critique these plays nor to assess their social impact or place in theatre history. It is rather to dismantle the stories and examine their key components from a technical point of view so that you can approach your own work with a more informed understanding of dramatic architecture and the possibilities it offers.

The audience for this guide

This guide is addressed to dramatic writers but may also be useful to directors, dramaturgs, theatrical designers, and actors, each of whom must un-

---

1. Will Dunne, *The Dramatic Writer's Companion: Tools to Develop Characters, Cause Scenes, and Build Stories* (Chicago: University of Chicago Press, 2009).

derstand a script thoroughly in order to bring their talents to it. In addition to theatre artists and technicians, the guide may be of interest to anyone who enjoys reading and thinking about dramatic stories.

Three award-winning plays

The analytical focus of this guide is reflected in the criteria I used to select three plays to examine. First, each would be a play by an American playwright that had received its world premiere after the start of the new millennium. Second, each would be a play that had enjoyed widespread critical and commercial success. Third, each would be a play that had moved me personally. In addition, the plays would have to be significantly different from one another both in subject matter and in their approach to dramatic storytelling. The plays I chose are:

- *Doubt: A Parable* by John Patrick Shanley, which received the 2005 Pulitzer Prize for Drama and the 2005 Tony Award for Best Play;
- *Topdog/Underdog* by Suzan-Lori Parks, which received the 2002 Pulitzer Prize for Drama and a 2002 Tony Award nomination for Best Play; and
- *The Clean House* by Sarah Ruhl, which received the 2004 Susan Smith Blackburn Prize and was a finalist for the 2005 Pulitzer Prize for Drama.

SCRIPTS FOR ANALYSIS

Title and author	Genre	Style	Format	Characters	Focus
Doubt: A Parable by John Patrick Shanley	Drama	Realism	One act, 9 scenes	Four	Single protagonist
Topdog/Underdog by Suzan-Lori Parks	Tragicomedy	Hyperrealism	Two acts,* 6 scenes	Two	Dual protagonist
The Clean House by Sarah Ruhl	Comedy	Magic realism	Two acts, 28 scenes	Five	Group protagonist

*While the term "act" is not used in the script, the story is the equivalent of a two-act play since it divides into two major units of action.

Each of these plays is summarized in the next chapter, "The Plays and Playwrights," and again in more detail in "The Big Picture" section of this guide under "Plot." However, you will gain the most from this guide if you have read the plays on your own and are familiar with them. At the time of this writing, one of the plays (*Doubt: A Parable*) has been made into a major film. The analysis in this guide addresses the original stage version, not the film adaptation.

Chapter introductions briefly reference more than a hundred other plays as well, including some from other eras and cultures. These references illustrate that, although the three main plays analyzed in this guide provide a rich sample of contemporary American playwriting, they often employ storytelling components that are not exclusively contemporary or American. Many are principles that dramatic writers around the world have used for centuries.

The underlying importance of character

Woven throughout the analyses in this guide is the idea that character is the foundation of story. To evaluate a play is to examine its characters: who they are, what they want, why they want it, and how they deal with the obstacles standing in their way. Each analysis in this guide, therefore, is a character exploration. Whether the focus is on the whole story or a specific aspect of it, the dramatic elements that emerge are keys to understanding who this story is about and why this story exists. In the end, the character and the story are the same thing.

By establishing character as the context for script analysis, you can approach story from a perspective that is emotional as well as intellectual. An emotional dimension enables you to understand the dramatic elements of a story at a gut level. As a result, you may be able to see connections between story events that are not readily apparent or to grasp why a character acts in a way that at first seems illogical or even contradictory to a previous course of action.

Drama is primarily an emotional experience. By keeping character foremost in mind and adding an emotional dimension to script reading, you can meet dramatic stories on their own terms and gain a fuller understanding of how they work.

■ HOW TO USE THIS GUIDE

A practical reference tool to help you explore principles of dramatic storytelling, *The Architecture of Story* offers easy-to-find information and examples, a wealth of questions to support your own script analysis, and a flexible design that lets you adapt the guide to your current needs.

Organization for ease of use

Each chapter focuses on a storytelling component and how it has been adapted in each of the three analyzed plays. These components are organized into four sections:

- **Technical Considerations** covers fundamental decisions that a writer makes about how to develop a story for the stage. Components for analysis include genre, style, dramatic focus, and other basic ingredients of dramatic storytelling.
- **The Big Picture** looks at the whole story and what it aims to accomplish. Components for analysis include the play's title, characters, plot, and theme, as well the dialogue and visual images woven throughout the script.
- **World of the Characters** explores the specific realm where the story takes place. Components for analysis include the physical, emotional, social, economic, political, and spiritual dimensions of this world as well as its backstory.
- **Steps of the Journey** focuses on the details of the main character's quest and how it unfolds from beginning to end. Components for analysis include the basic elements of dramatic action and the key events that comprise the dramatic journey.

Hundreds of questions to help you evaluate your work

To support your analysis of the story you are developing now, each chapter concludes with a set of questions related to the principles discussed and illustrated in the chapter. These questions are geared toward analyzing a rough draft of a script but may also be used to explore possibilities for a first draft in progress. Altogether, the guide features thirty-three sets of questions, adding up to hundreds of analytical tools. You can address these sets of questions in any order and repeat any of them, as needed, to obtain new results as your understanding of a script evolves.

Flexible design to fit your needs

You can use this guide at any stage of script development. During the early stages, the examples and questions may trigger your creativity as you define characters and flesh out story ideas. During later stages, the guide can help you through the revision process as you evaluate your work and target aspects of it that you wish to develop further. Regardless of when you use the guide, you can approach it in a number of ways. For example:

- **Nonlinear approach: information as needed.** Chapters are self-contained so that you can read them in any order or in any combination. This approach reflects the idea that there is no one way to construct or analyze a dramatic story, and that individual needs may vary, not only from writer to writer but also from project to project and from step to step within a project. Like any reference tool, the guide enables you to review its contents and select the specific information you need. A nonlinear approach may be the best use of the guide if you are an experienced dramatist working on a script or about to begin one.

- **Linear approach: comparative analysis of three plays.** By reading the guide straight through, from cover to cover, you can get a structured look at common elements of dramatic storytelling, see how these elements have been used in three successful plays, and compare the results. This linear approach may be best if you are a beginning playwright or just want an overview of dramatic storytelling principles.

- **Nonlinear or linear approach: analysis of one play at a time.** Within each chapter, the discussion of each play is presented separately under the play's title so you can find the analysis quickly and easily. This gives you the option to focus on one play at a time as you explore storytelling principles. This approach may be best if you wish to streamline your use of the guide.

- **Nonlinear or linear approach: analysis of your work only.** Each chapter concludes with a discrete set of questions about the script you are developing now. Going directly to the questions may be best if you are already familiar with the examples in the chapter and want help with specific dramatic elements as you write or revise.

Analysis is the process of a breaking down any whole into its parts to learn what they are, what they do, and how they relate to one another. The following pages present a detailed, technical analysis of three dramatic stories, but, in the end, the guide is not about these stories. It is about the dramatic principles that they reflect and that can be adapted in countless ways to the scripts you develop.

THE PLAYS AND PLAYWRIGHTS

The Architecture of Story analyzes three successful contemporary American plays to highlight how they are made and how they may inform your own writing decisions.

■ DOUBT: A PARABLE

Set in a Catholic elementary school in the Bronx in 1964, *Doubt: A Parable* depicts the efforts of a principal determined to expose and drive away a priest whom she suspects of child abuse even though she has no factual evidence of his guilt.

The play received its world premiere at the Manhattan Theatre Club in 2004 and was transferred to the Walter Kerr Theatre in 2005—the playwright's Broadway debut. Directed by Doug Hughes, *Doubt* received uniformly rave reviews and won just about every award it could, including the Pulitzer Prize for Drama, the Tony Award for Best Play, and the Drama Desk Award for Outstanding New Play.

Playwright: John Patrick Shanley

A writer and director for both stage and screen, John Patrick Shanley has established himself as a major American dramatist of his time. His plays include: *Danny and the Deep Blue Sea, Savage in Limbo, The Dreamer Examines His Pillow, Italian American Reconciliation, Women of Manhattan, Beggars in the House of Plenty, Four Dogs and a Bone, Psychopathia Sexualis, Cellini, Dirty Story, Sailor's Song, Defiance, Storefront Church,* and *Outside Mullinger.*

In addition to his Oscar-nominated screenplay adaptation for *Doubt,* Shanley's screenplays include *Moonstruck,* which in 1988 won both the Writer's Guild of America Award and the Academy Award for Best Original Screenplay, and *Five Corners,* which in 1987 won the Independent Spirit Award for Best Screenplay. Other film scripts include *The January Man, Joe vs. the Volcano,* and adaptations of *Congo* and *Alive.* His teleplay *Live from Baghdad* received a Primetime Emmy Award for Outstanding Writing for a Miniseries, Movie, or Dramatic Special.

Shanley grew up in an Italian-Irish neighborhood in the Bronx in the 1960s and was himself a product of the Catholic school system. An influential teacher at his grade school, St. Anthony's, inspired the character of Sister James in *Doubt* and attended the world premiere of the play as his guest. While Shanley says that *Doubt* is not autobiographical, his experience at

St. Anthony's was a key source of material for the play. In an interview with the *Houston Chronicle*, he explained: "I've always remembered that church school, the way the Sisters of Charity dressed, the way people behaved, the demarcation between men and women, between the convent and the rectory, and where the power was."[1]

■ TOPDOG/UNDERDOG

Topdog/Underdog explores the competitive relationship of two African-American brothers living in poverty with different visions of the American dream. One is a thief who wants to launch a lucrative three-card monte scam even though he has no skill at card hustling. The other is a reformed three-card monte dealer who wants to work within the system and earn an honest living even if the job is demeaning and underpaid.

The play received its world premiere at the Joseph Papp Public Theater/New York Shakespeare Festival in 2001 and moved to the Ambassador Theater on Broadway in 2002. Both productions were directed by George C. Wolfe. In 2002, the play received the Pulitzer Prize for Drama and was nominated for a Tony Award for Best Play and Drama Desk Award for Outstanding New Play.

Playwright: Suzan-Lori Parks

A playwright, screenwriter, and novelist, Suzan-Lori Parks is the first African-American woman to receive a Pulitzer Prize for Drama and in 2001 was named one of *Time* magazine's "Time 100: Next Wave/Innovators." Her plays include *In the Blood*, which was a finalist for the 2000 Pulitzer Prize for Drama; *Imperceptible Mutabilities in the Third Kingdom*, which received a 1990 Obie Award for Best New American Play; and *Venus*, which in 1996 also received an Obie. Other full-length plays include *The Death of the Last Black Man in the Whole Entire World*, *Devotees in the Garden of Love*, *The America Play*, *Fucking A*, *Father Comes Home from the War*, and *The Book of Grace*. She also authored *365 Days/365 Plays*, the result of a year-long project in which she wrote a play a day. Her screenplay credits include the Spike Lee film *Girl 6*.

Parks is the recipient of a MacArthur Foundation Genius Grant as well as grants from the National Endowment for the Arts, Rockefeller Foundation, Ford Foundation, Guggenheim Foundation, and others.

---

1. Everett Evans, "Shanley's Award-Winning Play Is Opening Doors," *Houston Chronicle*, May 22, 2005.

Talking with the Academy of Achievement about her writing process, Parks explained, "My writing all comes from listening. The more I can listen, the more I can write."[2] And, though she sometimes spends months or years developing a play, she found herself writing and completing *Topdog/ Underdog* in only a weekend, an experience she described as magical. "I wrote for three days, or 72 hours," she said. "Wrote, wrote, wrote, wrote, and I thought if I looked up, I would see someone pouring silver liquid into the back of my head. That's what it felt like. It was just like 'I know.'"

■ THE CLEAN HOUSE

Set in a "metaphysical Connecticut," *The Clean House* centers on three women from different walks of life: a married doctor, a maid who would rather be a comedian, and a restless housewife. Things get messy when the doctor discovers that her maid has stopped cleaning, her husband has fallen in love with another woman, and her sister has been secretly cleaning her house so that the maid can have more time to think up jokes.

The Clean House received its world premiere at the Yale Repertory Theatre in New Haven, Connecticut, in 2004, and its New York premiere at the Mitzi E. Newhouse Theater at Lincoln Center in 2006. Both productions were directed by Bill Rauch. Among other honors, the play earned the 2004 Susan Smith Blackburn Prize and was a finalist for the 2005 Pulitzer Prize for Drama.

Playwright: Sarah Ruhl

Sarah Ruhl's work has been produced across the country and around the world. In addition to *The Clean House*, her plays include *In the Next Room or the vibrator play*, which in 2010 was a Pulitzer Prize finalist and Tony Award nominee for Best Play; *Passion Play: a cycle*, which earned the Pen American Award and the Fourth Freedom Forum Playwriting Award from the Kennedy Center; *Dead Man's Cell Phone*, which received the Helen Hayes Award; and *Demeter in the City*, which received an NAACP Image Award nomination. Other full-length plays include *Melancholy Play*, *Eurydice*, *Orlando*, *Late: A Cowboy Song*, *Three Sisters*, *Stage Kiss*, *Dear Elizabeth*, and *The Oldest Boy*. In 2003, she received the Helen Merrill Emerging Playwrights Award and the Whiting Writers' Award and, in 2006, a MacArthur Foundation Genius Grant.

A poet turned playwright, Ruhl has described her plays as "three-dimensional poems," which often draw from ancient Greek tragedy and

2. "Interview: Suzan-Lori Parks," Academy of Achievement, Washington, DC, June 22, 2007, http://www.achievement.org/autodoc/page/par1int-1.

other mythic sources to explore "the interplay of the actual and the magical." In an interview with playwright Paula Vogel, she explained, "I come into the theater wanting to feel and think at the same time, to have the thought affect the emotion and the emotion affect the thought. That is the pinnacle of a great night at the theater."[3]

Her inspiration for *The Clean House* was a conversation she overheard at a cocktail party. A doctor was complaining about her cleaning woman, who had become too depressed to clean. The doctor medicated the woman in hopes of reviving her interest in her job, but the woman still refused to work. The doctor's comment on the situation became one of the most memorable lines in Ruhl's play: "I'm sorry, but I did not go to medical school to clean my own house."

3. Paula Vogel, "Interview: Sarah Ruhl," *BOMB Magazine*, no. 99 (Spring 2007), http:// bombmagazine.org/article/2902/.

Technical Considerations

A dramatic script reflects certain technical decisions that the writer makes about how to present the story. Such decisions center on genre, style, and dramatic focus, as well as the rules governing how this particular story will be revealed to the audience. Other considerations include the play's framework—its division into acts and scenes—and the stage directions that run throughout the script to communicate the writer's vision of the play to those who will be involved in its production.

Theatrical works can be organized into different genres, or categories, that reflect the writer's point of view about the story being presented. Knowing the genre can help the writer make more informed writing and marketing decisions. Genre can also help producers and audiences find the types of plays they prefer. There are two basic theatrical genres:

Comedy, a humorous story about a normal person in laughable circumstances or a laughable person in normal circumstances who experiences a significant rise in fortune. The story typically moves from unhappiness to happiness. Common characteristics: fast pace, funny situations, exaggeration, incongruity, and matters of rebirth and renewal. Examples: *The Odd Couple* by Neil Simon, *Chinglish* by David Henry Hwang, *Becky Shaw* by Gina Gionfriddo.

Tragedy, a serious story about a good person, usually an important and powerful one, who suffers a significant downfall due to his or her own flaws and missteps. The story typically moves from happiness to unhappiness. Common characteristics: extreme and sometimes dangerous situations, painful emotions, inevitability of failure, catharsis, and a moral lesson. Examples: *Hamlet* by William Shakespeare, *Fences* by August Wilson, *Death of a Salesman* by Arthur Miller.

Through the ages, other theatrical genres and subgenres have evolved as blends or subsets of these two basic types of plays. For example, while the term "drama" is used broadly to describe works written for the stage, it is also used more narrowly to indicate a genre of play:

Drama in this sense is neither a comedy nor a tragedy. It is a serious story about one or more characters at a time of flux and crisis in their lives. Common characteristics: intense conflict, strong emotions, and personal themes. Examples: *A Raisin in the Sun* by Lorraine Hansberry, *Buried Child* by Sam Shepard, *The Night Alive* by Conor McPherson.

Other common genres include:

Tragicomedy, as the name suggests, is a mix of sad and funny story elements. It may be a series of tragic events with a happy ending or a series of comedic events with an unhappy ending. Examples: *Uncle Vanya* by Anton Chekhov, *Angels in America* by Tony Kushner, *Between Riverside and Crazy* by Stephen Adly Guirgis.

Farce, a form of comedy, is designed to evoke laughter but relies more on buffoonery, physical humor, and ludicrously improbable situations. Common characteristics: extreme exaggeration, repetition, and two-dimensional characters entangled in frequent and elaborate plot twists. Examples: *The Miser* by Molière, *What the Butler Saw* by Joe Orton, *Noises Off* by Michael Frayn.

Melodrama is a story about good triumphing over evil. The story typically moves from happiness to unhappiness to happiness again. Common characteristics: strong plot, archetypal characters, exaggerated conflict, sensational elements, and a protagonist who is a victim of circumstances. Examples: *Desire under the Elms* by Eugene O'Neill, *The Mousetrap* by Agatha Christie, *The Bells* by Theresa Rebeck.

Issue play is a story organized around a social or political issue and the author's ideas about how to address it. The purpose is to arouse the audience emotionally, teach them a lesson, and provoke them to take certain new actions in their lives. Examples: *Keely and Du* by Jane Martin, *The Laramie Project* by Moises Kaufman, *Fires in the Mirror* by Anna Deavere Smith.

These genres can be adapted in various ways to create countless other genres and subgenres, such as black comedy, romantic comedy, satire, docudrama, historical drama, courtroom drama, fable, science fiction, fantasy, mystery/thriller, experimental drama, and more.

■ **DOUBT: A PARABLE**
Genre: Drama
Doubt depicts the efforts of a Catholic elementary school principal to expose and expel a suspected pedophile priest. Because of the serious subject matter, intense conflict, emotional themes, and mixed outcome, the play can be classified as drama.

■ **TOPDOG/UNDERDOG**
Genre: Tragicomedy
Topdog/Underdog explores the competition between two brothers who have been forced by social isolation and poverty to share a single furnished room. Because it combines humor with a serious theme and unhappy ending, the play can be classified as tragicomedy. According to playwright Parks, "Comedy and tragedy can exist side by side, and can exist in the same moment, which is what this play is all about."[1]

---

1. *The Topdog Diaries*, a documentary film produced and directed by Oren Jacoby (Storyville Films, 2002).

■ THE CLEAN HOUSE
Genre: Comedy
The Clean House introduces us to a pair of married doctors who met in anatomy class over a dead body, a Brazilian cleaning woman who would rather be a comedian, a restless housewife who secretly cleans her sister's house, and an exotic older cancer patient who falls in love with her surgeon. Because of the play's light approach to serious issues, humorous characters, and uplifting ending, *The Clean House* can be classified as comedy.

ANALYZING YOUR STORY
Define and explore the genre of a play that you are writing or have already written.

STORY CHARACTERISTICS
- How serious is the subject matter and theme of your story?
- How simple or complex are your characters? For example, do they consistently display the same dominant traits or do they undergo changes and embody contradictions?
- How simple or complex is the plot?
- What primary emotional response do you want from the audience?
- Does the story have a happy ending, unhappy ending, or mixed ending?
- How would you define the genre of your play?

GENRE
- How closely does your play match common characteristics of your genre? If you are writing tragedy, for example, are the characters fleshed out enough for the audience to empathize with their plight? If you are writing comedy, is it funny?
- Think about the type of producer and audience your genre will attract. What expectations might they have? Does your play work toward or against those expectations, and how?
- Think about the desired audience for your play. Do you need to target your characters or story more to this audience? If so, how?
- Are there any "rules" of your genre that you wish to break? If so, how and why?
- In promoting your play to theatre producers or audiences, what elements of your story will you stress to stir their interest? How do these elements fit your genre?

Style is the manner in which characters and story events are depicted in both the writing and the staging of a play. Style encompasses all of the play's elements, including sets, props, costumes, light design, sound design, and acting. There are two basic types of style:

Realistic, or representational, style uses empathetic characters, everyday speech, "slice of life" situations, and emotional themes to create the illusion of real life without acknowledging the audience, as in most plays by Henrik Ibsen, Lynne Nottage, and David Mamet. Writers who favor this approach need to decide how lifelike their plays will be. For example, *'Night, Mother* by Marsha Norman closely mirrors the real world by setting the story in one place, a country home, and by letting the dramatic action unfold in real time. As a result, there are no set changes or scene breaks to undercut the illusion of real life in progress. *Edmond* by David Mamet also strives to imitate real life but does so more selectively. Because the play spans a period of months and unfolds in more than twenty different settings, the storytelling has been compressed and composed to fit a playing time of less than ninety minutes on a single stage.

Nonrealistic, or presentational, style may use archetypal characters, exaggeration, distortion, fragmentation, repetition, symbolism, or other imaginative devices to create an artificial reality that—in its contrast to the real world—illuminates the human condition. Such techniques are often designed to keep the audience emotionally detached enough to remember they are watching a play. Settings may be strange or otherworldly, with lighting and sound designs that enhance the unreal atmosphere. The events of the story also may be unusual and the speech of the characters stylized. Characters may speak directly to the audience. For example, plays by Bertolt Brecht, Eugène Ionesco, and José Rivera tend to be presentational.

Nonrealism can take many forms, such as magic realism, expressionism, surrealism, impressionism, romanticism, postmodernism, verse drama, musical theatre, and more. Writers who favor a presentational approach need to decide how nonrealistic their plays will be. In some cases, an ordinary world gives rise to supernatural, dreamlike, or other fantastic beings or events, as in Caryl Churchill's *Cloud 9*, where time shifting and gender bending are routine matters, or Rajiv Joseph's *Bengal Tiger at the Baghdad Zoo*, where Baghdad during the Iraq war is transformed into an unpredictable realm of ghosts. In other cases, objective reality is replaced by a new world, often an absurd one, as in Samuel Beckett's *Endgame*, where the last survivors of an apocalypse live out their last days in a bleak shelter at the end of time.

While a play may be fully realistic or nonrealistic, many writers combine elements of the two styles. Arthur Miller, for example, in *After the Fall* combines the representational—emotional depictions of real-life events—and the presentational—a character who addresses the audience directly and a setting composed of three platforms without walls or conventional furniture except for a chair. Whether a play is realistic, nonrealistic, or a mix of both, it has its own specific style created for it by the writer and reinforced by the theatrical artists who bring their talents to a production.

■ **DOUBT: A PARABLE**
Style: Realism
The style of *Doubt* is realistic in that it depicts settings, characters, language, and story events that mirror everyday life. There are no presentational elements.

■ **TOPDOG/UNDERDOG**
Style: Hyperrealism
The style of *Topdog/Underdog* is hyperrealism in that it depicts real-life settings, characters, language, and story events, but does so in a heightened manner. While everything that happens could conceivably occur in the natural world, the story features extremely unusual elements, for example, an African-American man named Lincoln whose job is to dress up as Abraham Lincoln and be shot at in an arcade by would-be assassins with phony pistols. References to this job include strange details, such as a "Best Customer" who shows up regularly and whispers profundities into Honest Abe's right ear before shooting him on the left. The play also includes presentational elements, such as inner-life monologues that let us hear a character's thoughts.

■ **THE CLEAN HOUSE**
Style: Magic realism
Though much of the plot centers on the mundane tasks of housekeeping, *The Clean House* presents a world where the boundaries of time and space are occasionally blurred so that an apple tossed off a balcony overlooking the sea, for example, can drop down into a white living room far away. It is also a realm in which characters can speak directly to the audience and share visual images from their imaginations, where it may snow in a living room, and where a perfect joke can cause someone literally to die laughing.

Because it weaves fantastic elements into an otherwise ordinary environment, the style of the play is magic realism, which has roots in Latin American fiction. This style choice may explain why two of the play's characters are from South America and why they sometimes speak in untranslated Portuguese. In keeping with common characteristics of magic realism, the play explores the mysteries of everyday life, but tends to do so in a matter-of-fact way, implying that the magical is normal and does not, therefore, require special attention or explanation.

ANALYZING YOUR STORY

Identify the style of your play. Is it realistic, nonrealistic, or a mix of both?

IF THE STYLE IS REALISTIC . . .

- Ideally, your characters appear to be real-life people with whom an audience can empathize. For each principal character, what are his or her most empathetic traits?
- The most lifelike set is three-dimensional and fully rendered. If your story takes place in multiple locations, it may not be feasible to build a full set for each one. Do you need to eliminate or combine any locations so that sets can be more realistic?
- Would the addition of any particular props or costumes enhance the realism of the story?
- Are there lighting or sound directions that can be added to, or removed from, the script to make it feel more realistic?
- Uninterrupted action most closely resembles how everyday life happens. Can any scenes be combined or eliminated to reduce the number of scene breaks?
- Realistic dialogue has the form and feel of everyday speech. How realistic is your dialogue now?
- Are there any events in the script that work against realism because of how or when they occur?
- Do you need to do further research to flesh out an unusual or complicated event that the audience may find hard to believe or understand?

IF THE STYLE IS NONREALISTIC . . .

- Are your characters ordinary people in an extraordinary world, extraordinary people in an ordinary world, or extraordinary people in an extraordinary world?
  - If the characters are extraordinary: review their nonrealistic traits. How and when are these traits established in the script? Why are they important to the story?

- If the world is extraordinary: review the nonrealistic properties of the setting. Does anything need to be changed, added, or removed to make this world more unique?
- For any nonrealistic events in your story, have you established clear rules for how and why how such events occur? Do you need to impose any limitations on what is possible?
- Have you found the right props and costumes for the world you are creating? Do you see opportunities to enhance the nonrealism of this world by adding any unusual objects or attire?
- Do any lighting or sound directions need to be added to the script to enhance its nonrealism?
- Distortion, symbolism, and repetition are among many techniques you can use to create artificial reality. Have you missed any opportunities to use such tools?
- In a nonrealistic play, scenes need not occur in chronological order or have rational connections. Look at how your story divides into scenes. Would it work better if the scenes were organized differently? If scenes were added, removed, or combined?
- The dialogue in a nonrealistic play may be stylized—structured around language rhythms, rhyming schemes, music, ersatz vocabulary, or other artificial modes of expression. How does your dialogue fit the level of nonrealism you are after?

IF THE STYLE IS A MIX . . .

- Review the preceding two sets of questions. What elements of your story are realistic? What elements are nonrealistic?
- Which style dominates, and is this the best balance for the story you want to tell?
- How would the story be different if it were more realistic? Less realistic?

DRAMATIC FOCUS

The dramatic focus of a play determines two basic but critical elements: whose story it is and how this story will be revealed to the audience.

Character focus. In most plays throughout the ages, the protagonist, or main character, has been one individual, such as Hamlet, who drives the story and makes it happen. Everything revolves around this character's dramatic journey. However, the role of protagonist may also be played by more than one character, as in Anton Chekhov's *The Cherry Orchard*, where the protagonist is not an individual but a group, the Ranevskaya family, representing the Russian upper class.

Point of view. Whether the role of protagonist is filled by one character or many, the story reflects a point of view that dictates what we in the audience may see and not see as the dramatic action unfolds. Our vantage point is usually objective: it allows us to observe the characters in the external world they inhabit. The view of this world may be broad or narrow. Its limitations determine whom we may meet onstage, which characters must be present for a scene to occur, where we can observe them, and when we are able to do so.

Because it provides a "fly on the wall" perspective, an objective point of view enables us to observe the facts of certain situations and draw our own conclusions about what we have seen. These conclusions may not always be accurate, however, since the characters can intentionally or unintentionally mislead us.

In some cases, the point of view in a play is subjective. This enables us to experience the inner world of one or more characters. We literally enter someone's mind, hearing and sometimes seeing his or her thoughts, perceptions, and memories. Such events may take the form of inner-life monologues, flashbacks, hallucinations, or other internal visualizations.

Since the subjective point of view creates a deeper contact with characters, it gives us more information about who they really are, how they perceive the world, and why they act the way they do. However, this inner world may distract us from what is real and true in the external world. In some cases, such as Tennessee Williams's *The Glass Menagerie*, the story is told from one character's perspective. As a result, the events we witness are filtered through a narrator's memory and not necessarily reliable.

■ DOUBT: A PARABLE
Character focus: Single protagonist
Point of view: Objective

Doubt is centered on a single protagonist: Sister Aloysius. We enter the world of St. Nicholas church and school to follow her dramatic journey, and we experience the story primarily through her. Our access to this world is objective but restricted to four areas: the pulpit in the church, the principal's office, the garden between the convent and rectory, and the school gym.

Within each of these areas, our view of the dramatic action is unlimited: we can see any combination of characters there. For example, we watch Aloysius conduct school business in her office in scenes 2, 5, and 8 and tend to other matters in the garden in scenes 4 and 9. However, we also are privy to some events that occur when Aloysius is not present, such as Father Flynn in the garden trying to reassure Sister James of his innocence in scene 7. While Aloysius is the main character of the play, therefore, we sometimes observe the story from a vantage point beyond her knowledge and direct experience.

Sometimes the most important part of a story is what is *not* shown to the audience. In Shanley's play, for example, we never gain access to the rectory where Flynn's private meetings with students occur. This restriction in point of view is vital to the play's exploration of doubt and the unanswered questions about Flynn's actions. Neither Aloysius nor we in the audience have tangible proof of his innocence or guilt.

It is also significant that we never meet Donald Muller, the alleged victim of Flynn's abuse. This limitation prevents us from observing the boy first-hand so that we can interpret his mood and behavior in light of the abuse allegations. We must rely instead on the hearsay of people around him. All of this contributes to the doubts we experience as we watch the play.

On a more practical level, we are excluded from many areas where students and staff members interact—such as classrooms, school hallways, and the playground. We can only imagine the other inhabitants and activities of this busy school. Even in scene 3, when Flynn addresses the school basketball team, we see only Flynn and not the boys he is with.

Doubt is a realistic story that presents its characters objectively. We observe them in action and interpret their thoughts and feelings, but we cannot literally enter anyone's mind, so we cannot hear or see what anyone is thinking. There are no inner-life monologues, flashbacks, or other internal visualizations.

■ **TOPDOG/UNDERDOG**
Character focus: Dual protagonist
Point of view: Objective and subjective

In *Topdog/Underdog*, Booth and Lincoln share the role of main character, which allows us to observe their power struggle from both sides. Our access to their lives is both objective and subjective, but limited to the rooming-house room they share. We never see the other areas of their world, such as the place where Booth's ex-girlfriend Grace lives or the shooting arcade where Lincoln works. By limiting our dramatic view to their single room, the play creates a claustrophobic atmosphere that accentuates the brothers' feeling of entrapment and emphasizes their reliance on each other. In effect, they have little outside of this room and no one else to comfort them. All of this heightens the tragedy of the play's ending, when Booth ends up alone.

Our objective view of the room is, however, unlimited. We see not only what the brothers do here together, but also what they do here alone, whether it's Booth hiding his girlie magazines under the bed in scene 5 or Lincoln counting his money in scene 6.

We also at times gain access to their hearts and minds and can listen to them "thinking aloud" in monologues. This subjective point of view enables us in scene 4 to hear Lincoln wrestling with his personal demons and in scene 6 to experience the torment that floods Booth's mind after he kills his brother.

■ **THE CLEAN HOUSE**
Character focus: Group protagonist
Point of view: Objective and subjective

The role of protagonist in *The Clean House* is shared by three characters—Lane, Matilde, and Virginia—each of whom has an individual quest in addition to their collective one. Each character in this group represents a different type of woman: the upper-class professional who rules the world around her (Lane), the working-class housekeeper who dreams of a better life but has limited social and economic opportunities (Matilde), and the middle-class housewife who is bored by her marriage and the person she has become (Virginia). It is through this group of disparate women that we enter the world of the story and observe most of the events of the dramatic journey.

As the story unfolds, each protagonist must deal in some way with loss: the end of a marriage (Lane), the death of parents (Matilde), the erosion of a meaningful life (Virginia). Each finds herself isolated from those she loves and faced with the task of redefining herself and making new connections.

It is the collective quest for new connections that drives most of the dramatic action and makes the play happen.

In act one, the characters of Charles and Ana appear briefly in an imagining in Lane's mind, but they do not enter the play as flesh-and-blood characters until act two. For the first half of the play, therefore, the focus is almost exclusively on Lane, Matilde, and Virginia and how they relate across class lines. In act two, life becomes more complicated with the appearance of Charles and Ana and the impact of their love on Lane's marriage, Matilde's future, and Virginia's relationship with her sister.

We access the world of the story through all five characters objectively and subjectively. Our objective view is confined mostly to the white living room of Lane's house and to a lesser degree the balcony of Ana's seaside home. Though Lane is a successful doctor who works at an important hospital, we never see her in that context. This restriction emphasizes the thematic importance of the house and all it represents to Lane: achievement, social status, and a happy marriage.

Our access to the two main playing areas is unlimited: we can witness any combination of characters there. In the living room, for example, we may see Virginia and Matilde making a secret pact (act one, scene 7) or Ana and Matilde negotiating Ana's death by laughter (act two, scene 12). As a result, we know more than some characters do at certain points in the story. The objective view also includes glimpses of other places, such as the hospital where Charles falls in love with his patient Ana and the Alaskan wilderness he later traverses in search of a yew tree.

A key limitation imposed by the objective view is our inability to hear the perfect joke that Matilde uses to kill Ana. As Matilde whispers the deadly joke into her ear, we hear only sublime music and see a subtitle that reads "The funniest joke in the world." We then witness the joke's impact: Ana laughing intensely and dying. By preventing us from hearing the joke, Ruhl frees us from evaluating its humor—we may or may not have found the joke funny—and enables us simply to accept it as a powerful force in the world of the story. Many in an American audience are likewise excluded from understanding Matilde's other jokes, which are told in Portuguese. As a result, our focus is not on the jokes' quality but on the fact that something funny is happening.

Our subjective view of the characters enables us at certain times to hear their true thoughts and feelings without the other characters listening. This private vantage point gives us a greater opportunity to learn who each of them really is. In the case of Matilde and Lane, we also have opportunities to watch their minds at work, as in act one, scene 6, when we see what Matilde imagines: her parents dancing and kissing in the Brazilian village where she grew up.

Literal access to characters' minds is, however, selective and limited. We never hear or observe Matilde's imagination when she is trying to think up jokes. Nor are we privy to Lane's inner world when she is thinking about anything other than Charles and Ana making love. At no time do we literally enter the imaginations of Virginia, Ana, or Charles.

ANALYZING YOUR STORY

Define the dramatic focus of your story.

CHARACTER FOCUS

- Your story may center on the dramatic journey of one main character or more. Whose story is it? Identify your protagonist(s).
- After the protagonist, who is the most important character in the story?
- Onstage or off, what is the most important relationship between characters? How do you reveal that importance to the audience?

POINT OF VIEW

- Think about the vantage point from which the audience will observe story events. Is this point of view objective (external), subjective (internal), or a combination of the two?
- Whether objective or subjective, an *unlimited* point of view allows the audience to see any combination of characters onstage. A *limited* point of view requires that a certain character or characters be present for a scene to occur. How broad or narrow is the point of view now? If limited, who gives the audience access to story events? Why is that character the best choice for the job?
- In what locations will the audience be able to observe dramatic action? During what time periods?
- Does the point of view provide enough access to story events for the audience to understand and participate in what is happening? If not, how can you expand the point of view, and how would that affect the story?
- What important parts of the dramatic journey will the audience not be able to see? Identify any limitations that influence the audience's experience of the story.
- Are the limitations in point of view sufficient to generate suspense?

If not, what other limitations might be imposed? How would they affect the story?

- Do any scenes in the script violate the point of view that you have established? If so, how might you either redefine the point of view or change a scene that doesn't fit it?
- If we are able to see or hear inside of a character's mind, whose inner world will we enter? Why that character? How will his or her inner world be presented dramatically?

For any dramatic story, the writer needs to understand the nature of the world the characters inhabit and to define the basic operating rules that determine how things usually work here, what is possible under unusual circumstances, and what is never possible under any circumstances. These are the "rules of the game" that cannot be broken by anyone—not even the most rebellious of characters—once the writer has established them.

In a realistic story, the rules of the game simply mirror the laws of nature in the real world. If a cat has been accidentally killed, for example, it cannot be brought back to life (*The Lieutenant of Inishmore* by Martin McDonagh). When dramatic events are rare or technically complicated, the writer may need to do research to ensure that the story's operating rules have been correctly defined. If a woman has been diagnosed with ovarian cancer, for example, the writer may need to understand how the disease affects the body as it progresses (*Wit* by Margaret Edson).

In a nonrealistic story, special operating rules can be established in addition to, or instead of, the usual laws of nature. These alternative facts of life may make it possible for a man to grow the ears of a jackass (*A Midsummer Night's Dream* by William Shakespeare), for a woman to stir the souls of her dead ancestors by playing the piano (*The Piano Lesson* by August Wilson), or for a GI Joe doll to come to life (*God's Ear* by Jenny Schwartz). When a world has nonrealistic elements, it is especially important for the writer to know how this world is unique and how its unusual features can affect characters in both positive and negative ways.

■ **DOUBT: A PARABLE**

Since *Doubt* is a realistic play, the world of the story operates according to the same laws of nature that govern life in the real world.

■ **TOPDOG/UNDERDOG**

Though certain story elements are unusual, *Topdog/Underdog* is grounded in realism. Its world operates according to the same laws of nature that govern life in the real world.

■ **THE CLEAN HOUSE**

The world of *The Clean House* differs in many ways from the world outside the theatre. Most of these differences stem from the play's magic realism, which combines the fantastic and the ordinary. The following are special operating rules integral to the storytelling approach:

- Any character can speak directly to the audience. Example: Matilde tells us a long joke in Portuguese (act one, scene 1).
- Certain figments of a character's imagination can be seen by the audience. Example: as Matilde imagines her parents dancing and laughing, we watch them act out the events she describes (act one, scene 6).
- Certain figments of a character's imagination can be seen by another character. Example: when Lane imagines Charles and Ana making love, Matilde also sees them in Lane's mind and asks who they are (act one, scene 14).
- Magical events are commonplace. Example: Charles and Ana sing exotic songs while he performs surgery on her. When the operation ends, she emerges from her hospital sheet in a lovely dress (act two, scene 1).
- A sequence of events does not need to be depicted in chronological order. Example: after Charles and Ana arrive at Lane's front door to announce that they are soul mates, the story skips back and forth through the recent past to show how they fell in love (act two, scenes 1–4).
- Past and present can exist at the same time. Example: while Matilde tells Lane and Virginia about a fight yesterday between Charles and Ana, we see it happening now on Ana's balcony.
- Two distinct physical locations can merge. Example: as Charles hikes through Alaska in search of a yew tree, it snows in Lane's living room (act two, scene 10).
- Ordinary objects can gain mystical qualities. Example: when Matilde and Ana toss apples off of a balcony into the sea, they land miles away in Lane's living room (act two, scene 6). Later, when Ana hurls a spice jar into the sea, a cloud of yellow spice descends upon the living room (act two, scene 7).
- A character can die from hearing a perfect joke. Example: Matilde uses the perfect joke to kill Ana, who literally dies laughing (act two, scene 13).

ANALYZING YOUR STORY

Review how the world of your story works.

IF THE WORLD IS REALISTIC . . .

Its physical operating rules have been set by nature. However, you may need to flesh out specific rules for any natural phenomenon that is rare or complicated.

- Is additional research necessary to understand any specific character traits or story developments? If so, what topics do you need to address?
- If technical information is important to the story, how much of it does the audience really need to know in order to understand and believe story events?
- Where in the script is this technical information stated, who tells it to whom, and what is the "here and now" dramatic reason for doing so? Can any of this information be integrated more seamlessly into the dramatic action? If so, how?
- Have you included all of the technical facts needed for the audience to understand story events? If not, what information is missing and how can you integrate it into the script?
- Can any technical information be condensed or removed without significantly weakening the story?

IF THE WORLD IS NONREALISTIC . . .

Think about how the world of the story differs from the real world.

- What special rules, if any, enable characters to do things they would not normally be able to do in the real world? State each rule and what it allows.
- What special rules, if any, limit or prevent characters from doing things they would normally be able to do in the real world? State each rule and the limits it imposes.
- Do any of these special rules apply to some characters but not to others? If so, whom do these rules affect, whom don't they affect, and why?
- What special operating rules, if any, govern time, space, and physical phenomena? State each rule and what it encompasses.
- When and how is each special operating rule introduced in the story? Is the rule established early enough for the audience to accept it as credible?
- Are there any special rules that some characters know and others don't? If so, what is the reason for these differences?

- Are there any special operating rules that come into effect only after the story begins? If so, what empowers these rules and when does this happen?
- Are there any special operating rules that change or end during the story? If so, what causes this development?
- Do any special rules have roots in the backstory that need to be revealed? If so, what happened in the past and how much of this backstory does the audience need to know?
- How do most characters in the world of the story view its special rules?
- Do these special rules affect who has physical, social, or political power over others? If so, how?
- Would the story work better if the rules of the game were different? If so, what rules would you add, change, or eliminate and how would that affect the story?

A play is made up of acts and scenes. These basic divisions in the dramatic action, or lack of them, create a framework that gives the story a certain size and shape. There is no formula for how many acts or scenes a play should have or how long each should be. The framework depends on the complexity of its characters, plot, and theme.

Act. An act is a major unit of action triggered by a turning-point experience, positive or negative, and driven by the need of one or more characters to accomplish something important as a result of what happened. The ensuing activity triggers a sequence of events that may unfold in any number of settings over any period of time and leads through rising conflict to a greater turning point, or reversal, that either launches a new act or ends the story. In a play with more than one act, each act has a separate focus, as in Edward Albee's *Who's Afraid of Virginia Woolf?*, where act titles suggest clearly different stages of the story: "One Act: Fun and Games," "Act Two: Walpurgisnacht," and "Act Three: The Exorcism."

Scene. A scene is a division of an act driven by one character's need to achieve an immediate objective in spite of obstacles that stand in the way. Each scene typically unfolds in one setting in real time and adds up to one main event that changes the world of the story in either a good or bad way.

French scene. Some scenes divide into French scenes, which are demarcated by the entrance or exit of an important character. Each time someone comes or goes, a different combination of characters forms onstage and something new happens. Ideally, each French scene contributes in an essential way to the scenic event.

■ DOUBT: A PARABLE
Act structure

Doubt unfolds in one act with a run time of about ninety minutes. This framework supports a single story line that focuses on Sister Aloysius's attempts to expose and expel Father Flynn, whom she suspects of child abuse. During the play, there is no reversal big enough to change the forward direction of the quest and thus trigger a second act focused on a different topic or activity. The steps of the journey always reflect the same quest, even when Aloysius is not onstage. In scene 7, for example, when Flynn tries to convince James of his innocence, his primary tactic is to try to turn her against Aloysius, who remains the focal point of activity.

Scene structure

The one act divides into nine scenes. Each scene break occurs because a change of place and/or time is needed. In scene 2, for example, Aloysius and James discuss the sermon Flynn delivered in scene 1. The scene break is necessary so that the nuns can talk alone outside of church after they have had time to ponder Flynn's words.

French scenes. Two scenes divide into French scenes so that different combinations of characters can appear within the same setting and timeframe. In scene 5, for example, Aloysius confronts Flynn about his relationship with Donald Muller, an eighth grader who may have had wine on his breath after visiting the rectory. This event breaks down into four French scenes:

- **A (Aloysius).** Alone on the phone, Aloysius asks the caretaker, Mr. McGinn, to remove from the church courtyard a fallen tree limb that caused the nearly blind Sister Veronica to trip and fall. This unit of action portrays Aloysius as a problem solver and introduces McGinn, an offstage character who will play a key role in the backstory. We also learn that a tree limb has fallen, a fact that will soon explain why Sister James is late for today's meeting: she couldn't cross the courtyard as usual to get here.

- **B (Aloysius, Flynn).** Flynn arrives for the meeting but has to wait outside the office door since no third party is yet present. He questions Aloysius about Sister Veronica's accident. Worried that the elderly nun might be sent away for being infirm, Aloysius defends her. This unit shows her and Flynn alone for the first time, introduces the third-party rule, and portrays Aloysius as who one protects those who cannot protect themselves.

- **C (Aloysius, Flynn, James).** James arrives, Flynn enters the office with her, and the meeting begins. After being appalled by Flynn's personal habits, such as his use of a ballpoint pen, Aloysius clashes with him over music choices for the Christmas pageant. The tension leads to the real subject: Flynn's relationship with Donald. The priest denies any wrongdoing and storms out. This unit establishes Aloysius and Flynn as overt adversaries and reveals key traits about all three characters.

- **D (Aloysius, James).** After Flynn leaves, James defends him and rebels briefly against her superior, but Aloysius is now determined to bring Flynn down. She calls Donald's mother and asks her to come in for a talk. This unit shows that Aloysius's campaign against Flynn will escalate and foreshadows trouble ahead, including Mrs. Muller's visit to the school.

■ TOPDOG/UNDERDOG

Act structure

The story has a run time of about two hours and fifteen minutes. While the term "act" is not used in the script, the story divides into two major units of action and is thus the equivalent of a two-act play. The first unit (scenes 1–4) focuses on the pursuit of dreams. For Booth, this means winning back his ex-girlfriend Grace by becoming a rich card hustler. For Lincoln, it means keeping his job as an Abraham Lincoln impersonator by improving his performance.

The second unit of action (scenes 5–6) focuses on what happens when dreams are deferred. After Grace stands him up for dinner, Booth is forced to acknowledge that he will never win her back. Meanwhile Lincoln loses his job due to cutbacks. The loss of their dreams gradually pits the brothers against each other and leads to their final showdown.

The two "acts" are separated by a reversal at the end of scene 4, when Lincoln succumbs to the temptation of the cards. With this, his dream of an honest life begins to fade. He has taken the first step on a path that will lead ultimately to his own death at his brother's hands.

Scene structure

The play divides into six scenes. Since the action takes place in one location—the rooming-house room that the brothers share—scene breaks are due to time shifts only. The purpose of these shifts is to allow certain offstage events to occur. As scene 2 ends, for example, Booth is leaving for a date with Grace. Scene 3 begins later that night as he returns from the date with tales of "Amazing Grace" and "an evening to remember."

French scenes. Since the play has only two onstage characters, French scenes are created by showing one brother home alone before the other arrives or after the other leaves. This occurs in four scenes. In scene 1, for example, Booth tries to entice Lincoln to be his partner in a three-card monte scam, but Lincoln declines. The scene breaks down into two French scenes:

- **A (Booth).** Booth alone practices dealing three-card monte. Though he's not good at it, he imagines himself easily winning $500 from a sucker on the street. This unit of action introduces Booth and shows his interest in card hustling as well as lack of talent for it, factors that will soon motivate him to enlist his brother's help.
- **B (Booth, Lincoln).** Booth nearly shoots Lincoln when he arrives home from work in his Abraham Lincoln regalia. After a takeout meal, including a power struggle over who gets which dish, Booth reveals his scheme to win back Grace. The proposal is a three-card

monte scam with Lincoln as the dealer and Booth as his accomplice. Lincoln has sworn off the cards, however, and turns him down. Booth threatens to evict him, but the evening ends peacefully after Lincoln sings about the bad luck in his life. This unit introduces Lincoln, reveals key differences between the brothers, rekindles their sibling rivalry—the central conflict of the play—and foreshadows the violent ending.

■ **THE CLEAN HOUSE**
Act structure
The play unfolds in two acts with a run time of about two hours. Act one presents the three protagonists: Lane, Matilde, and Virginia. Most of the action occurs in Lane's living room, but we sometimes leave it to enter a character's imagination. The focus of this act is on physical cleaning, such as polishing silver and doing laundry. The characters meanwhile journey toward emotional messiness, with Lane's marriage failing, her relationship with Virginia becoming strained, and her relationship with Matilde being severed.

Act two adds Lane's husband, Charles, and his new soul mate, Ana, to the mix. The action is primarily divided between Lane's living room and Ana's balcony at the sea, but also includes glimpses of Charles and Ana at the hospital, Charles in Alaska, and Matilde's imagination. The focus of this act is on spiritual cleaning. As they grapple with personal shortcomings and sins of the past, the characters now journey toward emotional healing, with most finding solutions for the problems that beset them in act one.

The acts are separated by a reversal that begins in act one, scene 13, where Lane reveals that her husband has been unfaithful, finds out that it is Virginia, not Matilde, who has been cleaning her house, and fires Matilde. The reversal is completed in the next scene with the offstage arrival of Charles and Ana at the front door.

As a result of this reversal, the lives of all five characters will be different in act two. Lane will have to let go of her illusion of having a perfect life and acknowledge that her relationship with her husband has been lacking. Matilde will have to look for a new job and will consequently become Ana's part-time housekeeper and friend. Virginia will rise above her cleaning obsession to become a more active participant in her sister's life. Charles and Ana will make their relationship public and begin to live openly as lovers.

Scene structure
Each act divides into fourteen scenes, for a total of twenty-eight. Scene breaks occur so that we can move between the interior worlds of the char-

acters and the exterior settings of the story, such as Lane's living room and Ana's balcony. A few scene breaks occur to allow a passage of time, such as the break in act one between scenes 7 and 8. It is during this break that Virginia cleans Lane's house for the first time so that Lane can return home from work in the next scene and believe that Matilde is doing her job again.

French scenes. To accommodate the active comings and goings of five characters, several scenes divide into French scenes. In act one, scene 13, for example, Lane's life falls apart, Virginia's secret cleaning is exposed, and Matilde gets fired. The scene breaks down into four French scenes:

- **A (Virginia, Matilde).** While sorting laundry, Virginia comes across a pair of women's underwear that does not belong to Lane. This unit of action foreshadows the revelation of Charles's infidelity and strengthens the conspiratorial friendship between Matilde and Virginia.
- **B (Virginia, Matilde, Lane).** Lane returns home from work early and is surprised to find Virginia here. Lane says she is going to shoot herself and goes into the kitchen. This unit foreshadows our discovery that Lane has had bad news, raises concerns about her mental health, and escalates the tension in the house.
- **C (Virginia, Matilde).** Anxious about the underwear in the laundry and her sister's strange announcement, Virginia impulsively rearranges objects on the coffee table. This unit reinforces Virginia's compulsive personality and paves the way for Lane's discovery in the next French scene of the secret pact between Virginia and Matilde.
- **D (Virginia, Matilde, Lane).** Lane returns with a bleeding wrist, claiming that she cut herself accidentally, and reveals that Charles is in love with a patient. Noticing the rearranged objects on the coffee table, Lane figures out that Virginia has been cleaning her house. The sisters fight, and Lane fires Matilde. This unit introduces a major turning point for all three women, reveals the depth of Lane's distress and denial, escalates the conflict between her and the other women, and opens the door to the new territory of act two.

ANALYZING YOUR STORY

A dramatic story may unfold in one act, two acts, or more, divided into any number of scenes.

FOR ANY PLAY . . .

- Think about the current framework. How many acts does it include? How many scenes?

- What is the focus—the main topic or activity—of each act?
- What is the turning point that triggers each act?
- Think about the complexity of your characters and the magnitude of the dramatic journey. Do you have the right number of acts for the story you want to tell? If not, what changes will you make?
- Does each scene center on a main event that changes the world of the characters and moves the dramatic journey forward?
- Too many scenes can make the dramatic action feel choppy. Look at how your play breaks into scenes. How necessary is each break? Can any scenes be combined or eliminated?
- If a scene divides into French scenes, what is the event in each one? How necessary is this smaller event to the whole scene and to the play?
- What is your play's estimated run time? How does this match the substance and scope of the story? If the play feels too long or too short, what changes will you make?

FOR A PLAY WITH MORE THAN ONE ACT . . .

- Ideally, the act break occurs after a major turning point, or reversal, in the story. Where in your script is the act break now?
- Is this the best place for the act break? If so, why? If not, what would work better?
- In general, how does the second act differ from the first? How does the third act, if there is one, differ from the second, and so on?
- If two acts feel similar, the turning point at the end of the first act may not have caused a big enough change in the dramatic journey. To create two distinct units of action, can you heighten the impact of this turning point or find another one that is more powerful?
- Will the script play best with or without an intermission between acts, and why?

STAGE DIRECTIONS

Stage directions are instructions from the playwright to the director, designers, and actors about the play in production. Such directions can strengthen or weaken a script and contribute greatly to a reader's impression of the story and the writer.

Some directions describe production elements, such as characters, settings, props, costumes, lighting, and sound. Other directions tell actors when to enter or exit a scene and may include individual notes to them about their roles. Ideally, all of the nondialogue elements of the script are important, but some can be critical to the story. At the end of Henrik Ibsen's *A Doll's House*, for example, it is a stage direction that indicates Nora has left her husband and family: "The sound of a door shutting is heard from below."

Some plays have almost no stage directions. In the opening scene of Shakespeare's *Hamlet*, the only actor instructions are entrances and exits and the only production information is a six-word set description: "Elsinore. A platform before the castle." Other plays have voluminous directions, as in the opening of Eugene O'Neill's *Long Day's Journey into Night* where pages are devoted to describing the set and the characters who enter it. A writer's approach to stage directions is often influenced by the time period in which he or she lives. In theatre today, less is more when it comes to explaining how to stage a play or telling actors how to act.

Whether sparse or plentiful, stage directions all have one thing in common: they are not read by the audience. They do not need to be literary or entertaining, therefore, unless—as in *The Clean House*—there is a stylistic reason for doing so. Since their purpose is to instruct production members, stage directions tend to work best when they focus on essential physical elements, such as what should be seen or heard onstage, and leave to the director such issues as blocking, that is, the movement and positioning of the actors in a scene.

■ DOUBT: A PARABLE

Scene introductions. As with most plays, each scene begins with directions that identify where the scene takes place, who is present, and what is happening. For most scenes in *Doubt*, this introduction is three sentences or less. In scene 2, for example, the setting is described as "a corner office in a Catholic school in the Bronx." Aloysius is described briefly with a focus on her nun's habit and her manner: "She is watchful, reserved, unsentimental."

The directions also state that she "sits at her desk, writing in a ledger with a fountain pen." Each detail of this introduction, from her attire to her choice of writing instrument, is key to the story.

Physical action. Stage directions are used regularly throughout the play to indicate physical action. These directions are not extraneous suggestions about how to block the scene. Instead they focus on storytelling. In scene 7, for example, a stage direction reminds us that the meeting between Father Flynn and Sister James is a forbidden one because no third party is present. As she cries about her loss of joy, the direction states, "He pats her uneasily, looking around."

Emotional life. Stage directions in *Doubt* often imply emotional life but rarely tell the actor how a deliver a line. In scene 8, for example, after the tense meeting between Aloysius and Mrs. Muller, a direction highlights its emotional impact: "Sister Aloysius is shaken."

Breaks in dialogue. Dramatic writers often use stage directions to indicate breaks in the dialogue. Shanley finds different ways to express such breaks. In some cases, he simply uses the word "pause" or "silence." At other times, he implies the break, as in scene 8, just before the final showdown between Flynn and Aloysius, when a stage direction suggests a lull before the storm: "He comes in and slams the door behind him. They face each other."

Dialogue delivery. While the playwright refrains from telling actors how to say their lines, he occasionally uses typography to suggest dialogue delivery, such as italics to emphasize words that should be stressed ("Your *bond* with your fellow human beings was your *despair*"), ellipses to suggest pauses within a line ("She suggested I be more ... formal"), ellipses to indicate that a line trails off to silence ("Of course, not, but ..."), and exclamation points to suggest lines that should be spoken with emotional intensity ("You have to stop this campaign against me!").

Technical effects. There are no special effects in the play, but stage directions do specify a few lighting and sound cues. For example, directions call for a "crossfade" between most scenes, that is, a gradual shift in lighting from one setting to another so that the action can flow from scene to scene without a blackout. Sound cues are less frequent but important when they occur. In scene 7, the cawing of a crow begins and ends the meeting between Flynn and James in the garden and adds an ominous quality to his plea of innocence.

Commentary. Occasionally Shanley uses stage directions to insert special notes about a character or scenic development. In scene 5, for example, when the disagreement between Aloysius and Flynn about the school Christmas pageant prompts James to intervene, a stage direction states her objective: "Sister James tries to break a bit of tension."

■ TOPDOG/UNDERDOG

Scene introductions. Since the play takes place in a single room, the setting is described only in scene 1, when we first see it, and in scene 5, when it has been transformed into a romantic setting for a dinner date. The opening description is brief: "Thursday evening. A seedily furnished rooming house room. A bed, a reclining chair, a small wooden chair, some other stuff but not much else." There is also a reference to the play's most important scenic element: a three-card monte setup. Booth is described as "a black man in his early 30s." The focus is on his "studied and awkward" attempts to practice card hustling.

The opening directions for the other scenes specify time shifts—for example, "Much later that same Friday evening"—and who is doing what as the action begins. This description is sometimes detailed, as in scene 2, when more than two hundred words are devoted to how Booth enters and removes layers of clothing and other items that he has shoplifted and worn home.

Physical action. In addition to character entrances and exits, directions are used throughout the play to indicate important physical action. In scene 2, for example, Lincoln in his Abraham Lincoln costume rehearses getting assassinated for his job at the arcade: "He pretends to get shot, flings himself on the floor and thrashes around."

Emotional life. Stage directions seldom define a character's emotional life, but often imply it through physical action. In scene 1, for example, when he is startled by his brother's unexpected entrance, Booth's state of alarm is suggested by the direction: "Booth, sensing someone behind him, whirls around, pulling a gun from his pants."

Breaks in dialogue. The playwright has created an original system to communicate breaks in dialogue. A short pause is indicated by the term "Rest" in parentheses. A longer break, or "Spell," is indicated by repeating the character's name with no dialogue after it. In scene 1, for example, after Lincoln warns Booth not to antagonize him, there is a silence that leads to Booth evicting him:

LINCOLN
Don't push me.

BOOTH
LINCOLN

BOOTH
You gonna have to leave.

Dialogue delivery. There are no explicit stage directions to actors about how to say lines, but the playwright frequently uses typographical elements to suggest dialogue delivery, such as spelling throughout the script to imply dialect pronunciation ("Ima give you back yr stocking, man"), dashes to suggest pauses within a line ("She's—she's late"), dashes to indicate lines that are interrupted ("She was once—"), and hyphenation to imply a wooden tone ("I-see-thuh-red-card").

Emotional intensity is indicated through a variety of elements, such as exclamation points ("You pull that one more time I'll shoot you!"), italics (*"I am Booth!"*), capitalization ("YOU STANDING IN MY WAY, LINK!"), and occasionally, at moments of utmost passion, a combination of typographical devices (*"OPEN IT!!!"*).

In addition, the playwright uniquely uses parentheses to indicate that the enclosed line is to be spoken softly, as when a character makes an aside or speaks sotto voce. The number of parentheses suggests the sound level, from (( )), meaning quietly, to ((((((( ))))))), meaning very quietly.

Technical effects. There are no special effects in the play and almost no use of directions to indicate light or sound cues. The only lighting instructions occur at the end of scenes 1 and 3 as the brothers end their day and a direction states that "lights fade." The only sound indication is the implied gunshot that must be heard in scene 6 when Booth shoots Lincoln.

Commentary. In *Topdog/Underdog*, brackets uniquely function as stage directions to indicate that the enclosed words can be cut. In scene 6, for example, when Booth describes how Lincoln's wife once seduced him, several lines are bracketed so that a director has the option to remove them for a production.

■ **THE CLEAN HOUSE**

Stage directions are woven extensively throughout the script and contribute to its unconventional storytelling approach. They often look like lines of poetry, with descriptions of dramatic action that are lyrical and line breaks that emphasize important details or suggest rhythms, as in these directions from one act, scene 11, describing a tense moment between Lane and Virginia:

A pause.
For a moment,
Lane and Virginia experience
a primal moment during which they
are seven and nine years old,
inside the mind, respectively.

They are mad.
Then they return quite naturally
to language, as adults do.

Ruhl explains: "I wanted the stage directions to feel like part of the world of the play. And I think in this play, in particular, I was interested in giving little love notes to the actors, like saying, 'Oh, this is something between you and me, actor, that I'll share with you that maybe no one else will know, like you have a deep impulse to order the universe now, or right now you're going to fall in love very suddenly.'"[1]

Scene introductions. Since most of the action takes place in Lane's living room, introductory scene directions seldom address the setting, which has already been described at the front of the script. The setting is mentioned only when it has significantly changed, as in act two, scene 1, where the opening directions state, "The white living room has become a hospital."

Introductory directions tend to be minimal and usually identify who is present and what they are doing, as in act one, scene 13: "Virginia irons. / Matilde watches." Sometimes characters are briefly described, as in act two, scene 6, when we learn that Matilde and Ana are wearing sunglasses and sunhats as they sit on the balcony surrounded by apples. Two scenes have no introductory directions and simply begin with dialogue.

Physical action. One of the most common uses of stage directions in the play is to indicate physical action during a scene. These doings may be big events, as when Virginia, in act two, scene 9, messes up Lane's living room. More often, however, they are small actions that reveal character or suggest mood. In act one, scene 13, Virginia gets stressed out after finding another woman's underwear in her sister's laundry and then hearing Lane threaten to shoot herself. The mounting tension is expressed in physical directions: "Virginia sits. / Virginia stands. / Virginia sits. / Virginia stands. / Virginia has a deep impulse to order the universe. / Virginia arranges objects on the coffee table."

Emotional life. In some cases, the script spells out how a character feels, as in act one, scene 5, when "Lane is on the verge of tears." Compared to physical action, however, emotional life is a less common topic for directions and typically implied by what the characters say and do.

Breaks in dialogue. The terms "pause" and "silence" are used occasion-

1. "Sarah Ruhl & Blair Brown," Platform Series, Lincoln Center Theater, New York, November 15, 2006.

ally, but breaks in dialogue are usually indicated by physical action, such as "Charles examines the bandage on Lane's wrist. / She pulls away." The most common substitute for "silence" is the direction that one character "looks at" another. In act two, scene 5, for example, after Virginia makes a hypothetical statement about being in love with Charles, the directions read: "Virginia looks at Charles. / Lane looks at Virginia."

Dialogue delivery. In act one, scene 13, as Matilde and Virginia speculate on whether or not Charles wears women's underwear, stage directions explain how Matilde's one-word responses are to be delivered. First she says "No," with the direction "as in—he wouldn't dare." Then she says "But," with the direction "as in—he might dare." These are among the rare explicit instructions to the actors about how to say their lines.

Most dialogue delivery is implied only through typography, such as dashes to indicate pauses within lines ("He's—charismatic"), dashes to indicate interrupted lines ("I just thought—"), ellipses to indicate lines that trail off to silence ("I'm sorry. I was just trying to say . . ."), and italics to stress important words ("I'm *paying* her to clean my house!"). Emotional intensity is implied by exclamation points ("Stop cleaning!") and by capitalization ("I DO NOT WANT TO BE TAKEN CARE OF.").

Technical effects. Lighting, sound, and special effects are occasionally suggested but rarely specified. The term "Blackout" is used only once (at the end of act one), and one of the few lighting cues is a poetic description: "Night turns to day." Sound directions occur more often and are usually simple music cues. Key special effects include snow falling in Lane's living room as Charles traipses through Alaska and the use of projected subtitles at certain times in the story, as in act two, scene 1,when the subtitle reads "Charles Performs Surgery on the Woman He Loves."

Commentary. The playwright's unique voice is evident throughout the stage directions as she makes comments about the dramatic action, suggests staging possibilities, and poses questions. Act two begins, for example, with a surrealistic scene in which Charles performs surgery on Ana. The directions state, "If the actor who plays Charles is a good singer, / it would be nice if he could sing / an ethereal medieval love song in Latin / about being medically cured by love." Another example of this flexible approach to staging is found at the end of act one, when Lane imagines Charles making love to his new wife. The directions state, "Charles and Ana appear. / Charles undoes Ana's gown. / Is it a hospital gown or a ball gown?"

ANALYZING YOUR STORY

Review your use of stage directions in the script.

FOR EACH SCENE . . .

- Do the opening stage directions identify where and when the scene takes place? Have you described only what matters most about this place at this time?
- Do the opening directions identify who is present now and what they are doing?
- During the scene, have you clearly indicated when characters enter and exit?
- Do you need to add or remove any information about costumes or props?
- Are there any critical physical directions during the scene—for example, "He takes out a gun"—that need to be added? Any unnecessary directions that can be eliminated?
- If a direction tells an actor how to say a line—for example, "Nervously"—can you render it unnecessary by strengthening the dialogue?
- If you tell actors when to pause during the dialogue, are you doing so judiciously? Are there specified dialogue breaks that can be eliminated?
- Think about your general use in dialogue of typographical elements— such as italics, dashes, ellipses, exclamation points, and capitalization. Do these elements strengthen the dialogue by clarifying or heightening it? Or do they weaken the dialogue by taking the place of effective word choices or by cluttering the lines with too many intrusions?
- Do you need to add directions related to lighting, sound, or special effects? Could any now present be deleted?
- Do you need to add any directions to clarify what is happening in a scene?
- Have you removed any directions that are not essential to the dramatic action and would be better left to the director, actors, and designers as they work on your script?
- What impact do stage directions add, if any, to the end of each scene?

OTHER SCRIPT ELEMENTS

The front matter of a script is introductory material that appears before the play itself, such as a list of characters and general description of the setting. In some cases, the front matter may also include a scene breakdown, dedication, inspirational quotes, or special notes about the play or its staging. Notes may also appear at the end of the script after the last scene.

■ DOUBT: A PARABLE

Dedication. In response to popular satires about nuns, Shanley dedicates *Doubt* to Catholic nuns who have devoted their lives to service and poses this question: "Though they have been much maligned and ridiculed, who among us has been so generous?"

Preface. This essay introduces some of Shanley's thoughts on the play: what it's about, why he wrote it, how it grew out of his own experience as a Catholic school student in the 1960s. Most importantly, the preface explores his views on doubt as a catalyst for growth that requires courage and the recognition that "there is no last word" in defining truth.

Character list. The four characters are listed in order of appearance and by their full names, for example, "Sister Aloysius Beauvier." There is no character description here except for each character's age, such as: "fifties/sixties."

Setting description. The general setting for the play is simply identified as "St. Nicholas, a Catholic church and school in the Bronx, New York, 1964."

Inspirational quotes. Quotes from Akira Kurosawa, the book of Ecclesiastes, and Ptolemy suggest themes central to Aloysius's dramatic journey from the comfort of certainty to the growing pains of doubt. For example, "'Everything that is hard to attain is easily assailed by the mob.' (Ptolemy)."

■ TOPDOG/UNDERDOG

Dedication. Parks dedicates the play to her husband while making reference to three-card monte, the shell game that dominates the story: "4 Paul Oscher who taught me how 2 throw the cards." The use of digits for words reflects her often phonetic approach to dialogue.

Introduction. The playwright reveals how *Topdog/Underdog* evolved from an earlier work called *The America Play* and how she first got interested in three-card monte. She also states the play's subject: "This is a play about family wounds and healing. Welcome to the family."

Author's note. In this "Elements of Style," Parks explains her unique system for identifying pauses and silences during the dialogue. She also explains her use of parentheses to indicate lines that should be spoken softly and brackets to indicate lines that can be cut.

Character list. The two characters are listed by their first names: "Lincoln" and "Booth (aka 3 Card)." No ages are given here, but a character descriptor accompanies each name, with Lincoln indentified as "the topdog" and Booth, "the underdog."

Setting description. The general setting for the play is summed up in only two words: "Here" and "Now."

Inspirational quote. The front matter includes a quote from Ralph Waldo Emerson that metaphorically suggests the topdog/underdog relationship that runs through the play: "I am God in nature; I am a weed by the wall."

■ THE CLEAN HOUSE

Dedication. For a play that features two doctors married to each other, the dedication reads, "This play is dedicated to the doctors in my life, Tony and Kate."

Character list. The five characters are listed in order of importance. Their descriptions are brief and highlight gender and age—for example: "Lane, a doctor, a woman in her early fifties. She wears white." Information about double casting is included, with the direction that the actors who play Charles and Ana also play Matilde's father and mother. The playwright also adds a special note about casting: "Everyone in this play should be able to tell a really good joke."

Setting description. The two distinct worlds of the play are suggested by the fact that there are two different "Place" descriptions. One describes the white living room and the other something more magical: "A metaphysical Connecticut. Or, a house that is not far from the city and not far from the sea."

Production notes. After the text of the play, the script includes detailed notes by the author about double casting, the optional use of subtitles, and the pronunciation of Matilde's name, as well as sample jokes—in both Portuguese and English—that Matilde can tell during the play.

ANALYZING YOUR STORY

Review your title page, character list, setting description, and any other elements that appear in the script before or after the play.

OTHER SCRIPT ELEMENTS

- Does the title page include your complete contact information, the date of the draft, and a copyright notice?

- A character list features each character's name and usually his or her gender and/or age. A brief character description may also be included. Is your character list complete?
- A setting description sums up where and when the story takes place. Is your setting description complete?
- If you wish to include a list of scenes, how has each scene been identified?
- If you wish to dedicate the play to someone, how will the dedication read?
- If you wish to include an inspirational quote that suggests the play's subject or theme, what is the exact wording of the quote? What is the source?
- Should you include any special notes about the staging of the play? If so, what instructions are essential and how economically can they be stated?
- Should you include a preface that explains why you wrote the play or what it's about? If so, what information do you wish to share with the script reader?

The Big Picture

While juggling the many, often complicated details of a dramatic story, the writer can easily lose track of what matters most. By keeping the big picture in mind—who the story is about, what it's about, and where it ends in relation to where it begins—the writer can make more informed writing decisions at the scenic level, where the path of the dramatic journey is forged.

The title of a dramatic story is important not only because it suggests what the story is about but also because it contributes to our initial impression of the story concept and has the power to raise expectations or questions that will draw us into the world of the characters.

Some titles state the subject of the story either literally (*The Curious Incident of the Dog in the Night-Time*) or figuratively (*Blackbird*). Some identify important characters by name (*Macbeth*) or by description (*The Whale*). Titles can make statements (*Joe Turner's Come and Gone*) or ask questions (*Whose Life Is It Anyway?*). They can highlight settings (*Clybourne Park*), timelines (*Twilight: Los Angeles, 1992*), physical life (*The Chairs*), main events (*Death of a Salesman*), and more.

■ DOUBT: A PARABLE

Shanley's title tells us the subject of the story—doubt—and thus steers us away from the more sensational aspects of the script, such as allegations of pedophilia and corruption in the Catholic Church. In interviews, Shanley has said that the idea to write a play about doubt was triggered by the US invasion of Iraq in 2003, when political leaders appeared to be so certain about the need for war that they left no room for doubt in their justifications for a preemptive strike. Shanley contends that leaders today are reluctant to express doubt because it is perceived as a symptom of weakness rather than a hallmark of wisdom.

These thoughts about the impetus for the play help explain why the title is not simply *Doubt* but *Doubt: A Parable*. Like the stories in Father Flynn's sermons, the play itself is a parable about certainty and doubt in modern life. Webster defines "parable" as a short, simple story from which a moral or religious lesson may be learned. In this case, the moral of the story is that doubt can be a good thing. Or, as Father Flynn tells us in his opening sermon: "Doubt can be a bond as powerful and sustaining as certainty. When you are alone, you are not lost."

■ TOPDOG/UNDERDOG

Parks's title describes the two brothers whom we will meet in the story and their ongoing competition for power and control. The allusion to dog fighting suggests that this contest is a vicious one. The older brother, Lincoln, is identified in the script's front matter as the "topdog" in the contest—the one most likely to succeed—while the younger brother, Booth, is the "underdog." However, these roles keep changing as the balance of power shifts back and forth. Each word in the title could thus refer to either brother at different times in the course of the story.

The slash in the title typographically joins the two terms, suggesting that "topdog" and "underdog" are halves of the same whole, with their opposition binding them together. For one to succeed, the other must fail.

■ **THE CLEAN HOUSE**

Literally, Ruhl's title refers to the main setting of the play: the all-white living room that will become progressively dirtier and messier as the dramatic action unfolds. The title thus prepares us for a play about cleaning and different people's perspectives on it. Of the three protagonists, two do not like to clean and one is obsessed with it. Woven into this concept is the history of women as housewives whose traditional task is to keep the premises clean and, in doing so, to play a subservient role in the lives of their husbands.

Figuratively, the title suggests a different type of cleanliness: a perfect life without flaws, complications, or disappointments. The definite article "the" in the title suggests that this clean house is the ultimate realization of such perfection, an ideal state that can never actually be attained because, just as dust and dirt keep accumulating in the physical house, personal problems and challenges keep disrupting the lives of its inhabitants.

The use of the term "house" rather than "home" suggests the sterile environment that can result when one tries relentlessly to control life and avoid the messy emotions of love, friendship, and loss. It is not until such entanglements are allowed and embraced that real relationships can develop and the "house" can become a "home."

ANALYZING YOUR STORY

The title for a dramatic story might be the first thing or last thing you decide when developing a script. Or it might emerge during the writing or revision process as you discover what matters most. Analyzing a story's title can sometimes be a good way to analyze the story itself.

TITLE AND STORY
- What is the title of your story?
- What does the title communicate about the plot? About the theme?
- Does the title fit the story's genre and style? If it is a comedy, for example, does it sound like one?
- How well does your title fit the story's dramatic focus? If the story

centers on the dramatic journey of one character, does the title support this?

- A title may have a metaphorical meaning as well as a literal one. Can your title be interpreted in more than one way? If so, how do each of its meanings relate to the story?
- Does the title capture the gist of the story without giving away the ending?
- Why is this title the best choice for the story you want to tell?
- If you had to use a different title, what would it be?

TITLE AND AUDIENCE

- Are there other works in the marketplace with similar titles? If so, how might that affect the success of your work?
- How well will the title work as a marketing tool to stir up interest in your play and draw an audience to the theatre? What about the title is most appealing?
- How easy is the title to say and remember?
- What might this title suggest to someone who knows little about the story? Is that the kind of response you want to evoke, and why?
- How might your title affect an audience's perception of the story as they are watching it? Is that the response you want, and why?

CHARACTERS

To think of great plays is to think of great characters: Hamlet, Macbeth, and Richard III in the Shakespearean plays that bear their names; Nora Helmer in *A Doll's House*; Blanche Dubois and Stanley Kowalski in *A Streetcar Named Desire*; Willy Loman in *Death of a Salesman*; Vladimir and Estragon in *Waiting for Godot*; James and Mary Tyrone in *Long Day's Journey into Night*; Walter Lee Younger in *A Raisin in the Sun*; George and Lennie in *Of Mice and Men*; Babe, Meg, and Lenny in *Crimes of the Heart*; George and Martha in *Who's Afraid of Virginia Woolf?*; Mama Nadi in *Ruined*. Memorable figures like these illustrate the principle that character and story are virtually the same thing: the character *is* the story.

Dramatic characters often give us insights into ourselves and the people around us, but they are not themselves human beings. Rather, they are metaphors for human beings with heightened traits, histories, and behaviors that enable us, usually in one sitting, to grasp certain truths about them and why they act the way they do. Ideally, most of the events that occur in a dramatic story are shaped by character needs and reveal not only who the characters are, but also how they change and don't change under stress.

One key to understanding any character is to know what he or she wants most. This burning desire helps drive the story, create rising conflict, and keep us engaged as we wait to see whether the character will succeed.

From a technical perspective, each character has a dramatic function that is essential to the story. One might act as a protagonist, or main character. Another might act as an antagonist, or opponent of the main character. Some might perform other roles in advancing or thwarting the main character's dramatic journey or in illuminating the story's theme. Ideally, each character has a reason to be in the play and a distinct role in how it unfolds.

■ DOUBT: A PARABLE

While Shanley's play brings us into the world of a Catholic elementary school with 372 students and a full staff, we meet only four characters onstage: Sister Aloysius, Father Flynn, Sister James, and Mrs. Muller. Each has a title—"Sister," "Father," or "Mrs."—that not only pinpoints his or her status but also reinforces the formal nature of this world, where characters keep an emotional distance from one another and personal matters are rarely discussed.

Sister Aloysius Beauvier

Personal description. Sister Aloysius is a Sister of Charity named after St. Aloysius Gonzaga, a Jesuit student who died while caring for victims of a plague in sixteenth-century Rome and was later canonized as the patron saint of young students. This namesake is an apt match for Aloysius, who attempts to protect young students from a different type of peril. Her last name, Beauvier, appears in the list of characters at the front of the script but is never spoken in dialogue. The name has no special significance in the Catholic Church and may have been her surname before entering the convent.

The oldest character in the play, "in her fifties or sixties," Aloysius is a seasoned nun and teacher who has become the principal of St. Nicholas school. It's a small pond, but she's a big fish in it. She's in charge. Most notably, Aloysius is firm in her beliefs and fast in her determination to prove them right. She is an avid proponent of the Catholic school system, strict discipline, true fountain pens, and good penmanship. She is an avid opponent of restless minds, art and dance classes, and ballpoint pens. Aloysius was once married to a soldier who fought against Hitler in World War II, and so comes to the convent with a more worldly early life than those of the other nuns.

Burning desire. What Aloysius wants most in the story is to expose Flynn as a child predator and drive him out of her school. She sums up this goal in scene 5 when, in reference to Flynn, she tells James, "I'll bring him down. With or without your help."

Dramatic function. Aloysius is the play's main character, or protagonist. Her quest creates the throughline of the story by causing a certain sequence of dramatic events to occur. From a thematic perspective, the other characters in the play exist to shape this quest and affect its outcome. Such dynamics keep Aloysius at the center of everything that happens onstage. As a result, she is not only essential to the story. She *is* the story.

Doubt is a play that puts certainty on a collision course with doubt. In this scenario, Aloysius embodies certainty that has no doubt to balance it. As she attempts to fulfill her duties as a school principal, her approach reflects an assumption of perfect knowledge that precludes error and eliminates the need for self-reflection. It is such certainty that the playwright seeks first to establish and then to shatter. The power of this certainty is so strong that it is not until the final moments of the play that it finally comes undone.

Father Brendan Flynn

Personal description. A Roman Catholic priest in his late thirties, Father Flynn comes from an Irish working-class family in the northeast and has been at St. Nicholas for about a year. This is his third parish in five years, a transience that Aloysius finds alarming. Popular and charismatic, he coaches schoolboys at basketball and counsels them in the rectory over cookies and Kool-Aid.

Like most priests, Flynn is a sermonizer. He delivers two sermons during the play and, like the playwright, uses parables to make his points. Flynn is also a note taker. He always carries a small notebook and uses a ballpoint pen to jot down ideas for sermons.

Flynn is the only onstage character in scenes 1, 3, and 6, a fact that literally isolates him from the other characters and adds to his mystery. It is not until halfway through the play—scene 5—that he interacts with Aloysius and James. His first name is uttered only once: in scene 8, when he calls the bishop's office to request an appointment and identifies himself as "Father Brendan Flynn." He is otherwise referred to as "Father," a constant reminder of his clerical status and leadership position.

Burning desire. What Flynn wants most is to protect his reputation so he can continue his activities as a priest. He refers to this goal in scene 8, when he asks Aloysius to end her campaign against him: "If you say these things, I won't be able to do my work in the community."

Dramatic function. Flynn occasionally acts as a *raisonneur*, a character who states the story's thematic ideas. His primary role, however, is that of the antagonist, Aloysius's chief opponent. His dramatic purpose as the antagonist is to incite Aloysius's quest by delivering a sermon that disturbs her and then to provide the conflict for that quest by resisting her efforts to force him out of the parish after she suspects him of child abuse. Without Flynn, business at St. Nicholas would be conducted as usual and there would be no reason for a play.

While his background is unknown, Flynn may be one who, like the shipwrecked sailor in his opening sermon, has questioned the direction of his life and experienced a crisis of faith. In thematic terms, he embodies the forces of doubt that are pitted against the forces of certainty and cause the conflict to rise to a crisis.

In the realm of character possibilities, Flynn could have been a nonclerical member of the staff. Instead Shanley developed him as the parish priest. This status makes Flynn a more formidable foe for Aloysius, due to the aura of holiness it confers—in the 1960s, it was difficult to question a priest's moral character—and to the power of the Church it puts behind him: Flynn outranks Aloysius and is well protected by the patriarchal system.

The playwright fuels the conflict between Aloysius and Flynn by emphasizing the generational gap between them. Flynn is a young priest inspired by the modern views of the Second Ecumenical Council. This character choice impels him to challenge Aloysius's rigid and old-fashioned beliefs on many levels, especially those that affect her approach to students.

Sister James

Personal description. Like Aloysius, Sister James is a Sister of Charity and named after a male saint, a choice that reflects the male-dominated system in which the nuns operate. Her low status in the world of St. Nicholas is suggested by the fact that she is the only character without a surname. In her twenties, James is the youngest, most innocent onstage character, far less experienced than Aloysius as a teacher, as a nun, and as a woman. James is new to St. Nicholas. She loves teaching, especially history, but feels insecure about managing forty-eight eighth graders. She also feels intimidated by her new boss, Aloysius. To describe James, the stage directions state: "There's a bit of sunshine in her heart, though she's reserved as well."

Burning desire. What James wants most is to restore the peace of mind she lost when she entered Aloysius's domain. James states this explicitly in scene 4 when she tells Aloysius, "I want to be guided by you and responsible to the children, but I want my peace of mind."

Dramatic function. James is the opposite of Aloysius in almost every way, and this distinction makes her important to the play. It is through the contrast James provides that we get to know Aloysius, just as the young nun's weaknesses help us see the older nun's strengths. James starts out a confidant of Aloysius and ends up as a confidant of Flynn. In both roles, she enables the other character to share thoughts and feelings that we might not otherwise have known. Due to her lack of confidence, she also creates the opportunity for Aloysius to preach the principles by which she runs her school and her life. This enables the playwright to integrate exposition about Aloysius that is critical to our understanding of her and the quest she launches.

In thematic terms, James is an embodiment of doubt. "Everything seems uncertain to me," she tells Aloysius near the end of the play. Even when James first reports her suspicions about Flynn, she feels unsure of what she is reporting: "But maybe it's nothing." Because she has no certainty to balance her doubt, James gains not a powerful and sustaining bond with others, as promised by Flynn in his sermon, but rather a loss of joy and sleep plagued by nightmares.

Mrs. Muller

Personal description. While eighth grader Donald Muller is at the center of the plot, it is not Donald but his mother whom we meet onstage. A black woman of about thirty-eight, Mrs. Muller is a complex but pragmatic person who comes from a "hard place" and has learned to work with how things are. She moved her son to St. Nicholas because she feared for his safety at the public school due to his race and his sexual orientation. Donald is gay. Mrs. Muller appears only in scene 8, when she arrives at the principal's office to discuss Aloysius's concerns about her son and Flynn. She proves to be a strong and surprising challenger to the principal's campaign against the priest. That she keeps a guarded distance from Aloysius is reflected in her character name: *Mrs. Muller.* Her first name is never revealed.

Burning desire. What Mrs. Muller wants most is to make sure her son graduates from St. Nicholas so he can get into a good high school. She is willing to put up with almost anything to make this happen because, as she says more than once in the scene, "it's just till June."

Dramatic function. Mrs. Muller is the only character who lives outside the walls of St. Nicholas. She brings in a set of beliefs that is foreign to Aloysius and that challenges her rigid worldview in a way no other character can. Regardless of Flynn's actions, Mrs. Muller believes he has been good to her son by giving him attention and time. Because of her pragmatism and rejection of moral absolutes ("Sometimes things aren't black and white"), she is a key contributor to the breakdown of Aloysius's certainty about how things should be.

■ TOPDOG/UNDERDOG

Parks's play explores the dynamics of a dysfunctional family in a dysfunctional society, but presents only two onstage characters: Lincoln (a.k.a. Link), described in the front matter as "the topdog," and Booth (a.k.a. 3-Card), described as "the underdog." They are brothers who were named by their father "as a joke" after Abraham Lincoln and his assassin, John Wilkes Booth. Their last name is not revealed, an omission that underscores their alienation from their parents.

Booth (a.k.a. 3-Card)

Personal description. A black man in his early thirties, Booth is a schemer and dreamer who is averse to holding a steady job and relies mostly on petty theft, or "boosting," to acquire what he needs, whether it's a "diamond-esque" ring for his ex-girlfriend Grace or fancy new suits for his brother and himself. Because of the potential danger of his trade, Booth always keeps a gun within reach.

His dream is to become a card hustler hauling in big bucks from suckers on the street. This dream is motivated by his desire to reconnect with Grace, who, he believes, would like him more if his pockets bulged with cash. In the meantime, he is relegated to fantasies provided by the girlie magazines hidden under his bed. Booth's view of himself and the world is greatly influenced by the fact that his parents abandoned his brother and him when they were teenagers. Booth now lives in a seedy furnished room that he shares with his brother.

Burning desire. What Booth wants most is to be a topdog who is richer, more powerful, and more successful in love than his brother. For Booth to become the topdog, therefore, his brother must become the underdog. It is a competition that only one can win.

Dramatic function. Booth has a dual function in the play: he is the protagonist of his own dramatic journey and the antagonist of his brother's. As protagonist, he sets the play in motion by trying to enlist his brother in a card hustling scheme. This proposition triggers the dramatic journey of both brothers and fuels their interactions throughout the play. Meanwhile Booth's inept approach to realizing his dream creates multiple opportunities to demonstrate why he is an underdog who will never rise above his loser status.

In the role of antagonist, Booth acts as the chief obstacle to his brother's quest to live an honest life. As he tries to convince Lincoln to join his scheme, Booth poses an ongoing threat to their brotherly relationship—he twice tries to evict Lincoln from the room they share—and is an ongoing source of temptation for Lincoln to return to criminal life. It is Booth's function as antagonist that brings his brother's dramatic journey—and the play—to an end, with the shooting of Lincoln over a twenty-year-old money-roll in a nylon stocking.

The play explores the lure of the American dream and why the brothers and their parents fail to realize it. Booth embodies the belief that success is measured by money and material goods and cannot be achieved by working within the system. He thus enters the play as a thief with a penchant for the finer things in life and the ambition to become a master con artist. This set of values and desires pits him against his brother and creates the story's central conflict.

Lincoln (a.k.a. Link)

Personal description. A black man in his late thirties, Lincoln was once a master dealer of three-card monte, earning up to a thousand dollars a day by playing the shell game on street corners with gullible passersby. When his partner was murdered, Link decided to give up the cards and seek honest employment. This led him to the unusual job of impersonating Abraham Lincoln in an arcade, where for the past eight months customers with toy guns have been shooting at him in reenactments of Lincoln's assassination.

As with Booth, loss has been a dominant theme in Lincoln's life. He has lost not only his parents and his business partner but also his wife, who threw him out of the house. This may explain why Lincoln now stays with his brother in a seedy room that is too small for two men, lacks running water and a bathroom, and requires him to sleep at night in an old recliner. It may additionally explain why he not only accepts this miserable living situation but also fronts the rent for it. Booth is the only family he has left, and Link doesn't want to lose him.

Burning desire. What Lincoln wants most is to be a topdog who has overcome his past and become an honest man with a family. This goal requires him to keep his brother under control so that Booth does not either draw him back to a life of crime or desert him. For Lincoln to succeed, therefore, Booth must remain in an underdog position.

Dramatic function. Like Booth, Lincoln is the protagonist of his own dramatic journey and the antagonist of his brother's. As protagonist, he pursues a vision of the American dream that has evolved from his past struggles as a son abandoned by his parents and as a three-card monte dealer whose partner was murdered. As antagonist, Lincoln acts as the chief obstacle to his brother's pursuit of a different American dream.

Thematically, Lincoln embodies the belief that success is measured by earned wealth and that one must work within the system to get ahead. He enters the play as an arcade employee who is willing to subject himself to daily humiliations in order to earn a legitimate paycheck. His desire for social conformity is so strong that he is willing to settle for less pay than his white predecessor and to live with the knowledge that he could be replaced at any time by a wax dummy. All of this puts Lincoln on a collision course with his scheming brother and generates the conflict of the play.

Lincoln also provides the play's most striking image: a black man in whiteface dressed as Abraham Lincoln. An ironic reconstruction of the Great Emancipator and an inversion of a white minstrel in blackface, the image suggests a man who is disconnected from himself and his past and is playing a role that could lead either to emancipation or to destruction.

■ **THE CLEAN HOUSE**

Act one of Ruhl's play introduces three women from different walks of life: Lane, a doctor; Matilde, her maid; and Virginia, a housewife who is Lane's sister. Act two adds Charles, a doctor married to Lane, and Ana, his cancer patient and lover. In a realm where characters share private thoughts directly with the audience, the lack of surnames contributes to the feeling of intimacy the story fosters: we are literally on a first-name basis with each character.

Four of the five characters are women, a choice that reflects the author's focus on women's relationships and roles in society. Though two of the women are currently married and one was previously married, none has children, a fact that separates them from their traditional roles as mothers and heightens their presence as individuals who must redefine who they are.

Lane

Personal description. Lane, in her early fifties, is a successful doctor at an important hospital somewhere in Connecticut. She has been married for three decades to a doctor named Charles whom she met in medical school over a dead body. Though they live in the same house and work at the same hospital, they rarely see each other due to their demanding work schedules. Lane's house—like her wardrobe—is white, and she expects it to be immaculate but feels it is beneath her station in life to clean it herself. She has recently hired a live-in housekeeper named Matilde.

Lane has an older sister named Virginia whom she rarely sees, even though she lives nearby. The emotional distance between them may be explained by Virginia's assessment that Lane has been "a bitch" since the day she was born. Lane sees herself in a more favorable light, as a smart, athletic, independent woman who has aged well and likes to be in control.

Burning desire. Lane disdains messiness of any kind, whether physical or emotional. What she wants most is a clean house and a perfect life with no complications. She sums up this desire in act one, scene 5, when she tells Matilde, "I just want my house—cleaned."

Dramatic function. Lane is one of the three women who share the role of protagonist and together drive the play. Of the three, she ranks highest socially and earns the most money. Though she is absent from half of the play's scenes and neither begins nor ends the play, Lane is the most active character and often the focal point of the action. The story takes place primarily in her living room and centers on the cleanliness of her house and the messiness of her relationships with her husband, her sister, her maid, and her husband's lover. Lane is thus a central link to all of the other characters, each of whom plays a role in her dramatic journey.

In a story that presents different perspectives on cleaning, Lane represents the classist view that cleaning is a task for other people, namely those beneath her. Thematically, she embodies the idea that the quest for cleanliness alienates us emotionally from the rest of the world and that it is by accepting life's messes that we develop meaningful relationships with others.

By making Lane a physician with a high income, Ruhl not only differentiates her from the other characters but also creates an organic way to bring Matilde and Ana into her life. Lane's financial status is what allows her to hire an immigrant Brazilian woman, whom she would otherwise not have met. Her physician's oath is what takes her to the home of her husband's dying soul mate, whom she would otherwise have shunned.

Matilde

Personal description. Matilde, in her early twenties, is a Brazilian cleaning woman who hates to clean and would rather be a comedian. Her parents were the funniest people in Brazil until her mother literally died laughing at one of her father's jokes and her father then shot himself. The tragedy prompted Matilde to move to the United States, where she landed a job as Lane's housekeeper. Matilde continues to wear black as an expression of mourning for her parents.

Her job as a cleaning woman not only depresses her but also keeps her in a low income bracket. As a result, she cannot afford to buy the things she wants or to move to New York to pursue her dream of becoming a comedian. In the meantime, she enjoys telling jokes in Portuguese and using humor to get along in life and help others do the same.

Burning desire. What Matilde wants most is to heal from the loss of her parents. This need is implied by her black wardrobe, her persistent efforts to keep her parents alive in her imagination, and her desire to emulate them by thinking up jokes.

Dramatic function. Matilde is one of the three women who share the role of protagonist. In contrast to the other two, she represents the lower working class, who often must defer their dreams and do jobs they dislike in order to survive. Matilde opens and closes the play, appears in more scenes than anyone else, and has the most inner-life monologues. She thus maintains a strong presence throughout the story even though she is often alone onstage or a passive observer of story events. At times, she functions as a *raisonneur* who states the play's themes related to cleanliness, dirtiness, and humor. At the end of act one, for example, she warns Lane that love does not always make people happy. "Love isn't clean like that," she says. "It's dirty. Like a good joke."

Matilde incites the play's conflict by refusing to clean Lane's house and triggers the climax by killing Ana with the perfect joke. Matilde also contributes to the main event by helping Lane and her sister Virginia overcome their differences and find a common bond as they care for the dying Ana.

By making Matilde a housekeeper, the playwright gives her a way to enter and affect the lives of four strangers in a new country. Her desire to be a comedian creates opportunities for humor and is integral to a story in which people die laughing. By giving Matilde a Brazilian background, the playwright also creates the opportunity to weave untranslated Portuguese into the dialogue, a dramatic element that embodies the thematic idea that life is full of mysteries that must be accepted for what they are.

Virginia

Personal description. Lane's older sister, Virginia, is a housewife in her late fifties with not enough to do. A Bryn Mawr graduate who specialized in Greek literature, she was once headed for the life of a scholar but now finds herself in a dull marriage with a barren husband. "I wanted something—big. I didn't know how to ask for it," she confesses to Lane in act one, scene 13. Virginia envies her sister, who seems to get the best of everything: a more important life, more interesting career, and more handsome husband. Virginia wishes she were closer to Lane, who is usually too busy to make time for her.

Unlike Lane and Matilde, Virginia loves to clean. She considers it a privilege and a way to find meaning in life. "I love dust," she tells the audience in one act, scene 3. "The dust always makes progress. Then I remove the dust. That is progress." Virginia's problem is that by approximately 3:12 every afternoon, her cleaning is done and she has nothing else to keep her busy. She has considered doing volunteer work but doesn't know whom to volunteer for.

Burning desire. What Virginia wants most is a meaningful task. This begins as a secret desire to clean Lane's house but evolves into a need to help her sister recover from a failed marriage.

Dramatic function. Virginia is another of the women who share the role of protagonist. Of the three, she is the one who feels most lost, a housewife whose life has been going downhill since the age of twenty-two. She is an eccentric character who appears in nearly half of the play's scenes and generates much of the humor.

By making her an unhappily married woman with no career or children, the playwright creates a character who has little to do but think morbid thoughts and attempt to repress them. Since graduating from Bryn Mawr, Virginia has come to see the world as an ugly place full of dirt, and she now retreats from this vision by cleaning compulsively. Because she views housework as a good thing, she brings to the play a perspective on cleaning that differs significantly from that of everyone else.

It is Virginia's cleaning addiction that draws her back into Lane's life, frees Matilde to think up jokes, and leads to her getting fired and working part-time for Ana and Charles. By concocting a scheme to secretly clean Lane's house, Virginia sets into motion a chain of events that affects all of the characters. She is thus a key architect of the story's throughline.

From a thematic perspective, Virginia is the character who undergoes the greatest shift in her perception of cleaning when, after years of obsessive housework, she learns to embrace the joy of messiness. This transformation culminates in act two, scene 9, when she wreaks havoc in Lane's living room and adopts a new mindset that empowers her to start getting her sister's attention.

Ana

Personal description. Originally from Argentina, Ana is an "impossibly charismatic" older woman who has been diagnosed with breast cancer and finds herself in love with her surgeon, Charles. This is a startling development, since Ana has always hated doctors. "I don't like how they smell," she tells us in act two, scene 2. "I don't like how they walk. I don't admire their emotional lives."

Ana has not been in love since her marriage decades ago to an alcoholic geologist who peed on lawns and died of cancer when he was thirty-one. She is a passionate woman who relishes life's pleasures, throws things when she gets mad, and once went to Brazil just to study rocks. To Charles, her free spirit is embodied by the magic of her name: "Ana, Ana, Ana, Ana," he tells her, "your name goes backwards and forwards."

One example of Ana's fierce nature is her response to the news of her breast cancer. Rather than discuss treatment options with Charles, she demands: "I want you to cut it off." She is a woman who knows what she wants and isn't afraid to ask for it.

Burning desire. Ana's primary goal is to enjoy the highest quality of life possible for one in the late stages of a terminal disease. For her, this means no hospitals, debilitating medical treatments, or toxic medications that would rob her of her final pleasures.

Dramatic function. Ana is the oldest, most beautiful, and most passionate character in the play and the one least bound by traditional roles and expectations. Such factors contribute to the exotic impression she makes on both Charles and the audience. As a free spirit, Ana is the opposite of Lane and brings into the play a different worldview, one that celebrates the joy of living and advises us to be brave in the face of adversity.

By falling in love with Charles, Ana functions dramatically as an antagonist to Lane and a catalyst for the changes that take place among Lane, Virginia, and Matilde in act two. Though Ana does not physically appear in the play until the start of act two, her cancer is a core plot element that explains how she and Charles met and that eventually motivates the other women to rise above their differences and care for her as she nears death.

By giving Ana an Argentine background, the playwright emphasizes the cultural contrast between her and Lane and thus widens the divide that must be crossed for them to connect. At the same time, Ana's roots help create a bond between her and Matilde, who is also from South America and, like her, speaks Spanish and Portuguese. Ana contributes to the untranslated language of the play as she and Matilde engage in friendly chats about life, death, jokes, and apples. Their friendship is important dramatically because it spurs Matilde to seek medical help for Ana and thus bring Lane into Ana's final days.

Charles

Personal description. Lane's husband, Charles, in his fifties, is a busy but compassionate doctor who performs nine surgeries a day. Faithful to his wife since they were married decades ago, he has recently fallen in love with Ana, one of his cancer patients. Though he is not Jewish, he comes to embrace the Jewish concept of *bashert*, or soul mate, and uses it to justify his need to be with Ana. "There are things—big invisible things—that come unannounced—they walk in, and we have to give way," he tells Lane in act two, scene 5, as he tries to explain why he must leave her for Ana.

When not being professional, Charles is a childlike man whose newfound love has filled him with a passion for life. He is a devoted lover who would learn to swim just to accompany Ana into the sea or would go to the ends of the earth just to find a yew tree to treat her cancer. Charles means well, but does not always understand what others really need.

Burning desire. What Charles wants most is to be with Ana, who has ignited in him a new appreciation of life. He explains this rebirth to Lane in act two, scene 5: "I want to live life to the fullest." For him, this means sharing with Ana what the world has to offer, whether it's apple picking in the country, a trip to the Incan ruins of Machu Picchu, or a day in bed making love while the responsibilities of his medical career go neglected.

Dramatic function. The only male in the cast, Charles is oblivious to cleaning, since the women in his life do it for him. He functions primarily as an antagonist who generates conflict by falling in love with Ana. Though he is often relegated to the offstage world, Charles plays a pivotal role in the chain of events that bring Lane, Virginia, and Matilde together. If Charles had not fallen for Ana, for example, Lane might have remained estranged from her sister and never grown beyond her strained relationship with her maid.

Charles's good looks have not escaped the attention of his sister-in-law, Virginia. Her attraction to him is useful dramatically because it adds to the conflict between her and Lane. His decision to go to Alaska is a key plot point because it leaves Ana alone while she's ill and challenges Lane to attend to her medical needs. Dealing with this messy situation is what weakens Lane's need for perfection and enables her finally to connect with her sister by asking for help.

As with Lane, the playwright chose to make Charles a doctor, a profession that establishes his upper-class status, helps explain the history he shares with his physician wife, and provides the opportunity for him to meet and fall in love with a beautiful stranger with cancer.

ANALYZING YOUR STORY

You can learn a lot about characters by simply describing them. Warm up by answering the following questions. Then write a telling description of each character in your play. This description does not need to be lengthy if it focuses on what matters most.

FOR EACH CHARACTER . . .

- What is the character's name? Does this name have a significance that is relevant to the story? If so, how is it significant?
- What are the character's key physical traits? Psychological traits? Social traits?
- What single trait, positive or negative, most strongly defines this character?
- What makes the character unique?
- What is the character's most universal trait, that is, what makes him or her similar to most other people, including yourself?
- Are any other characters similar to this one? If so, could they be combined?
- What is this character's greatest strength? Greatest weakness?
- What do you personally like best about this character? Dislike the most?
- What was the most significant turning point in his or her life before the play begins?
- How has that past turning point affected the character in a good way? In a bad way?

- Who matters most in this character's life when the play begins? When the play ends?
- What does the character want most in the story? Identify his or her burning desire.
- What is the character's dramatic function? Identify the main role that he or she plays in the dramatic journey.
- Why is the character essential to the story? Identify at least one reason that he or she cannot be removed.

In addition to the characters we meet onstage, a dramatic story often features characters whom we don't meet. This offstage population exists beyond the walls and vistas of the settings we enter. In some cases, characters are relegated to the offstage world because they are not important enough to be onstage. In other cases, they are kept offstage because their absence is more dramatically powerful than their presence, as in Samuel Beckett's *Waiting for Godot* where the title character's unknown whereabouts is a central problem of the play.

Offstage characters may be deceased (the antiwar activist Henry in *Other Desert Cities* by Jon Robin Baitz), missing (the Donnelly twins in *Faith Healer* by Brian Friel), fictitious (the unidentified person whom Gus and Ben are waiting to kill in *The Dumb Waiter* by Harold Pinter), or simply elsewhere (Grace and Ruthie in *American Buffalo* by David Mamet). Whether the influence they exert is positive or negative, the importance of such characters is measured by how much they affect the dramatic action of the story. Sometimes an absent character can be so significant that the play is named after him (*Hughie* by Eugene O'Neill).

■ DOUBT: A PARABLE

The offstage characters of *Doubt* are primarily the students and staff of St. Nicholas church and school. In scene 2, for example, as Aloysius and James confer about classroom issues, student names are sprinkled throughout the dialogue: William London, Donald Muller, Linda Conte, Stephen Inzio, Noreen Horan, and Brenda McNulty. Something is said about each one so that he or she feels distinct. Other offstage characters include Mrs. Bell, the art teacher; Mrs. Shields, the dance teacher; and Mrs. Carolyn, a strange woman with a goiter who plays the portable piano. Most of these invisible characters are of minor importance. Their purpose is to create the ambience of a busy school. Some, however, have vital functions:

Donald Muller

The first and only black student in a school full of warring Irish and Italians, twelve-year-old Donald Muller is a pivotal character in the play. He is the boy who returned to James's class with the smell of wine on his breath after a visit with Father Flynn and thus serves as the catalyst for Aloysius's campaign to bring the priest down. As the story unfolds, we learn that

Donald is gay and that this has led to beatings from his father at home and threats on his life from students at the public school he previously attended.

The fact that Donald remains offstage is essential to our experience of story events: it forces us to evaluate the reactions of the adults around him. Donald's absence also adds to the uncertainty of Aloysius's allegations against Flynn since we are not able to observe the boy's behavior or hear his version of what happened, such as how he acquired the altar wine.

William London

Eight grader William London triggers the play's second scene. He was sent to the principal's office earlier by Sister James because he had a nosebleed in her classroom during the Pledge of Allegiance. When she comes to the office now to find out how he is, we see the contrast between James, who is worried about the boy's well-being, and Aloysius, who believes he induced the nosebleed to escape school. It is thus a problem that introduces Aloysius's suspicious nature. The focus on William here is also important because it helps us remember him later, in scene 8, when Aloysius reveals to Flynn her initial reason for mistrusting him: "On the first day of the school year, I saw you touch William London's wrist. And I saw him pull away." William is thus a key figure in the backstory.

Mr. McGinn

The Irish caretaker is introduced at the beginning of scene 5, when Aloysius speaks to him on the phone about removing a fallen tree limb from the church courtyard. His primary role in the story emerges later in the scene, when Flynn claims it was McGinn who found Donald in the sacristy drinking altar wine. After the meeting with Flynn, James suggests to Aloysius that they corroborate Flynn's story with McGinn, but Aloysius resists, suspecting deception of some kind. Since McGinn is an offstage character, we are unable to hear his account of what happened and draw our own conclusions. This adds to the uncertainty surrounding Flynn's innocence or guilt.

Monsignor Benedict

Aloysius first refers to the monsignor in scene 2 as she lectures James about the chain of command in the Church. Aloysius introduces him by name in scene 4 when she expresses fear of running into him unexpectedly in the garden and thus violating the rule that forbids priests and nuns to cross paths unattended. She describes the senile seventy-nine-year-old Benedict as one who is "otherworldly in the extreme" and probably couldn't name the current president of the United States.

This incapacity proves to be of vital importance later, since Benedict is the only one in the Church to whom Aloysius can report problems. Because she has no one reliable to help her deal with Flynn, she will have to take matters into her own hands. The absence of help that Benedict represents is thus underscored by his literal absence from the play.

Sister Veronica

The only offstage nun who is mentioned by name, Sister Veronica is secretly going blind. This problem is introduced by Aloysius in scene 2, when she implores James to keep an eye on the old nun "so that she doesn't destroy herself." It is reiterated in scene 5, when Aloysius informs McGinn on the phone that Veronica has tripped over a tree limb in the courtyard and fallen on her face. When the accident attracts Flynn's attention, Aloysius attempts to minimize the problem ("Nuns fall, you know"), fearing that Veronica will be taken away if the priests view her as infirm. While Veronica is not important enough to be an onstage character, she provides an opportunity for the playwright to show Aloysius as one who comes to the rescue of others.

■ TOPDOG/UNDERDOG

Lincoln and Booth live in an isolated room physically removed from everyone else in their lives. The offstage population is dominated by their parents in the past and by Booth's ex-girlfriend Grace in the present. Though absent, these characters play vital roles in the onstage action.

Moms and Pops

The two most important offstage characters in *Topdog/Underdog* are the brothers' parents, who pursued but failed to achieve the dream of having a family and owning their own house. Moms ended up with a "Thursday man," with whom she ran off so quickly one day that she stuffed her things into plastic bags rather than take the time to pack a suitcase. Pops became a boozer, womanizer, and abuser who liked fine clothes and shined shoes, but vanished just as quickly two years later, leaving behind a closetful of clothes that Lincoln subsequently burned.

Before Moms took off, she gave Booth $500 and told him not to tell Lincoln about the money. Before Pops took off, he gave Lincoln $500 and told him not to tell Booth about the money. These secret displays of parental favoritism and mistrust help explain the competition between the brothers, who otherwise grew up dependent on each other.

Grace

Grace (a.k.a. "Amazing Grace") dominates Booth's thoughts and motivates his desire to be a topdog. She broke off a two-year relationship with him and now goes to cosmetology school. Still enamored with her beauty and charm ("She's so sweet she makes my teeth hurt"), Booth is determined to win her back.

Grace's physical absence is important to the story because it elevates her to near-mythical status and fuels her power as an impossible dream. This absence gains its greatest impact dramatically in scene 5, when we discover that Booth has been waiting for Grace for over six hours with champagne ready to pour, and it becomes obvious that she will never appear at his door. It is a key turning point in Booth's dramatic journey and a major step toward the tragic outcome of the play.

Others

Other offstage characters include Cookie, Lincoln's wife, who threw him out of the house after he lost sexual interest in her; Lonny, Lincoln's three-card monte partner, whose murder on the street inspired Lincoln's desire to reform himself; and Lincoln's Best Customer at the arcade, who "shoots on the left and whispers on the right." Whispered into Lincoln's ear are such profundities as "Does the show stop when no one watches or does the show go on?" and "Yr only yrself when no one's watching."

■ THE CLEAN HOUSE

As *The Clean House* unfolds, little is revealed about the offstage world, a writing economy that helps focus the story on the here and now. To diminish the impact of offstage characters, none are referred to by name. The two most important ones, Matilde's deceased parents, are included here as "offstage" characters because, even though they are occasionally visible to the audience, they have no dialogue and are presented only as figments of Matilde's imagination.

Matilde's parents

Existing somewhere between the worlds of the dead and the living, the real and the imagined, the offstage and the onstage, Matilde's unnamed parents appear only in her mind, where we can see them but never hear what they tell each other. The funniest people in Brazil, they met late in life through humor, lived in laughter, and both died as a result of a joke: her mother from laughing too hard at it and her father from shooting himself after having caused his wife's death.

The parents are dramatically important because their deaths represent the greatest loss in Matilde's life and remain the greatest obstacle to her peace of mind. Matilde continues to mourn them, still wearing black a year after their funerals. By showing her parents as stylized memories of happiness rather than multidimensional characters, Ruhl makes them larger than life, thus adding to the emotional impact of their absence.

Virginia's husband

Compared to Lane, Virginia feels that she always gets second best, and her husband—whom she never refers to by name—is no exception. While Virginia views Lane's husband as handsome and charismatic, she sees her own spouse as a functional part of her life, comparing him to "a well-placed couch." Because he is not too handsome and not too good in bed, she doesn't worry about losing him to another woman. In a twist on a gendered expression, Virginia attributes her lack of children to the fact that her husband is "barren." It is the dullness of her marriage to this man that fuels her need to make more meaningful connections with others.

Ana's husband

In act two, scene 5, Ana seeks to convince Lane that it has been decades since she was in love with anyone. Ana describes her husband as an alcoholic geologist who was great fun but too wild and crazy to be a father. He died of cancer at the age of thirty-one, shortly after he gave up drinking at her request. This brief but memorable reference to Ana's past helps both Lane and the audience understand that her attraction to Charles is serious and that she is not accustomed to carrying on with married men.

ANALYZING YOUR STORY

Offstage characters can be incidental to the onstage story or a critical part of it.

OFFSTAGE POPULATION

- Who are the offstage characters—past and present—in your play?
- In order of importance, who are the two or three most important offstage characters? What makes them stand out from the rest?
- It can be difficult for the audience to track names of characters they will never meet. Which offstage characters, if any, do not need to be referenced by name?
- Think about the world of your play. Have any important offstage

characters been overlooked? If so, how would references to them affect the story?

- Are any offstage characters so important that they should be brought onstage? If so, who, and how would that change the story?

- Think about the offstage character's dramatic function in the story. Why is it important to reference him or her in dialogue?
- What information about this character is revealed?
- Does the amount of information match his or her importance? If we need to remember the character, for example, have you included enough detail to make him or her memorable? If the character is of minor importance, have you included too much detail?
- Look at how and when the character is described in the story. Who refers to him or her? What is the onstage character's "here and now" reason for doing so?

While the terms "story" and "plot" are often used interchangeably, they have different meanings from a technical perspective.

"Story" is something that happens in the life of a character. In David Mamet's *Edmond*, for example, a man walks out on his wife. "Plot" is a selection of events from the story organized in a certain order to reveal how they connect. In Mamet's play, a man visits a fortune-teller who reads his palm and warns him that he is not where he belongs. Haunted by the fortune-teller's words, the man returns home to his wife. When she begins to complain about the maid, he suddenly tells her that he is leaving and not coming back. Startled, she asks why. He confesses that he has not loved her for years, that she does not interest him spiritually or sexually, and that he can't live this life anymore. He then walks out the door and into the night to search through the underworld of New York City for his true place.

In short, story is what happens. Plot is how and why it happens.

Both story and plot are made up of events—important happenings—that affect the world of the characters in a good or bad way. Some events are caused by characters who try to accomplish something and either succeed or fail. Some are triggered by outside forces, such as society, nature, or chance. Most dramatic events center on a beginning, ending, or change of some kind. Such events are usually arranged in chronological order, but there are exceptions, as in Tom Stoppard's *Arcadia*, where scenes from the past are interwoven with scenes in the present, or Harold Pinter's *Betrayal*, where the sequence of events unfolds in reverse order.

Since story structure may be linear or nonlinear, simple or complex, fast-paced or slow-moving, there is no formula to determine how many events a plot should include or how these events should be distributed over a framework of acts and scenes. Each scene in a play usually adds up to one main event, but it may include other, smaller events as well. What matters most is that each event is essential and occurs not in isolation but in relation to the rest of the plot, or throughline.

In a strong throughline, each event is a result of something that happened earlier and/or a trigger for something that will happen later. This dynamic produces a cause-and-effect chain of events that keeps moving the story forward and enables a transition to occur. Ideally, no event can be removed from this chain because the story would not make sense without it.

Sentence synopsis
The principal of a Catholic elementary school launches a campaign to drive away a priest whom she suspects of being a child predator.

Paragraph synopsis
1964. The Bronx. Sister Aloysius, the principal of a Catholic elementary school, begins to suspect that the parish priest, Father Flynn, may be hiding an inappropriate relationship with an eighth-grade boy. Though she has no factual evidence to support this belief, she becomes increasingly certain of the priest's guilt. Should she make her concerns public or not? Her decision to expose him leads to unexpected consequences, including questions about herself and the certainties that have ruled her life.

Chain of events
The plot is constructed so that almost every scene ties to at least one other scene as cause or effect. The exception is scene 3, which is described below the table.

CHAIN OF EVENTS: *DOUBT: A PARABLE*

Because of this	This happens
Unknown circumstances (offstage)	Father Flynn delivers a sermon on the subject of doubt (1)
The dark nature of Flynn's sermon (1)	Sister Aloysius worries about the priest's influence on her students and orders Sister James to be on the lookout for trouble in her classroom (2)
Aloysius's order to be on the lookout for trouble (2)	James reports to Aloysius a problem involving Flynn: he may have given wine to a student named Donald Muller during a visit to the rectory (4)
Unrelated circumstances (offstage)	Flynn gives the basketball team a pep talk (3)
James's report about Flynn and Donald Muller (4)	The two nuns meet with Flynn under a false pretext so that Aloysius can grill him about the alcohol on Donald's breath (5)
Aloysius's interrogation of Flynn (5)	Flynn denies wrongdoing, claiming that Donald got caught stealing the wine from the sacristy and that Flynn remained silent to keep him out of trouble (5)

Because of this	This happens
The insinuations underlying Aloysius's questions (5)	Flynn delivers a sermon on the subject of gossip (6)
Flynn's sermon on gossip (6)	James renounces her accusations against Flynn and sides with him against Aloysius (7)
The stress that James feels due to recent events (2–7)	James takes a leave of absence from the school, leaving Aloysius without an ally (offstage)
Aloysius's phone call to Donald's mother to request a meeting (5)	Mrs. Muller meets with Aloysius and, after hearing the charges against Flynn, unexpectedly sides with him (8)
Mrs. Muller's presence in the school (8)	Flynn storms into Aloysius's office to demand that she stop trying to ruin him (8)
Flynn forcing Aloysius into a showdown (8)	Aloysius demands that he confess and falsely claims to have proof of past child abuse (8)
Aloysius's demands and threats (8)	Flynn relents and calls the bishop's office to request a transfer (8)
Flynn's transfer request (8)	The bishop sends Flynn to St. Jerome's parish and promotes him to pastor (offstage)
Flynn's promotion (offstage)	Aloysius finally brings her concerns about Flynn to Monsignor Benedict, who doesn't believe her (offstage)
Aloysius's failure to defeat Flynn (offstage)	Aloysius is overwhelmed by doubts that leave her bent with emotion as James tries to comfort her (9)

The dramatic function of scene 3. Flynn's pep talk to the boys basketball team lies outside the chain of events because it is not caused by previous onstage action, nor does it result directly in future onstage action. The scene is nevertheless important to the story because it introduces character information that affects our perception of events. By seeing Flynn in casual clothing, we are reminded that he is not only a priest but also a man. If he is a child predator, the scene shows how he lures boys to the rectory. If he is not a predator, the scene provides an innocent explanation for why a child might recoil from his touch: the long fingernails Flynn brags about.

■ TOPDOG/UNDERDOG

Sentence synopsis

Sibling rivalry erupts when a petty thief tries to convince his brother, a reformed card hustler, to join him in a three-card monte scam and the brother turns him down.

Paragraph synopsis

Booth and Lincoln are African-American brothers whose names were given to them by their father as a joke. One is a petty thief who wants to be a three-card monte dealer even though he doesn't have the skill to do it well. The other is a reformed card hustler who wants to earn an honest living even if the work is underpaid and demeaning. Having been abandoned by everyone else they know, the brothers now share a seedy rooming-house room where they must try to overcome a troubled family past, economic hardship, and social inequalities so that each can achieve his distinct vision of the American dream.

Chain of events

The plot includes significant offstage as well as onstage events as the dramatic journeys of the two protagonists unfold and intersect. The role of offstage events is described below the table.

CHAIN OF EVENTS: *TOPDOG/UNDERDOG*

Because of this	This happens
Booth scoring a date with his ex-girlfriend Grace (offstage)	Booth decides to win Grace back for good by becoming a rich three-card monte dealer (offstage)
Booth's attempts to learn the art of three-card monte (1)	Booth sees how difficult it is to throw the cards and asks Lincoln to partner with him (1)
Booth's business proposition (1)	Lincoln, a reformed card hustler, rejects Booth's offer and the brothers get into a fight (1)
The brothers' fight (1)	Booth tells Lincoln he will have to move out and Lincoln sings a song about the bad luck in his life (1)
Lincoln's sad song (1)	The brothers reconnect (1)
The brothers' reconnection (1)	• Booth the next night offers his brother expensive stolen clothing so they can both improve their image (2) • Lincoln shares his weekly paycheck with Booth to cover their mutual living expenses (2) • As the brothers celebrate, Lincoln opens up and reveals a fear of losing his job at the arcade (2)

Because of this	This happens
Lincoln's fear of losing his job (2)	Lincoln asks Booth to help him practice his assassination routine, but Booth has other plans: his date with Grace (2)
Booth's date with Grace (offstage)	Booth returns home late that night and wakes up Lincoln to brag about his sexual exploits (3)
Booth's bragging (3)	Lincoln capitalizes on Booth's good mood by asking for help again with his assassination routine, but Booth is too tired and they get into another fight (3)
The brothers' fight (3)	Lincoln makes up to Booth by offering to introduce him to his old three-card monte crew (3)
Lincoln's offer of assistance (3)	Booth is too proud to accept the offer, but the brothers reconnect (3)
The brothers' reconnection (3)	• Booth helps Lincoln practice his work routine (3) • Booth tries to entice his brother back to card hustling, but Lincoln still says no (3)
Booth's efforts to tempt Lincoln back to card hustling (1, 3)	Lincoln finally succumbs to his addiction to the cards and begins to practice the patter and moves of a dealer (4)
ACT BREAK*	
Booth landing a second date with Grace (offstage)	Booth transforms the room into a romantic setting and tells Lincoln to spend the night elsewhere (offstage)
Lincoln losing his job at the arcade (offstage)	• Lincoln blows his severance pay in bars (offstage) • Lincoln returns home in need of Booth's company and discovers that Grace has stood up his brother (5)
Lincoln losing his job (offstage) and Booth getting stood up (5)	The brothers bond over memories of their childhood when they had to fend for themselves (5)
Lincoln's return to the cards (4) and the brothers renewed bond (5)	Lincoln tries to teach Booth how to throw the cards, but Booth is still no good at it (5)
Booth's frustration with failing to master the cards (5)	Booth finally acknowledges his larger failure—the loss of Grace—and storms away in a rage (5)
Booth's loss of Grace (5)	Booth finds Grace and kills her (offstage)
Lincoln's return to card hustling (4)	• Lincoln plays three-card monte on the street and wins $500 and a lot of admiration (offstage) • Feeling like a topdog, Lincoln relishes his success (6)

Because of this	This happens
Booth's murder of Grace (offstage)	Booth returns home and covers up his crime by claiming that Lincoln will have to move out because Grace is marrying Booth and moving in (6)
Booth telling Lincoln to move out (6)	Full of confidence and flush with money, Lincoln agrees to go, but covers up his return to card hustling by claiming to have a new job as a security guard (6)
Lincoln's quick agreement to move out (6)	Booth feels betrayed and taunts Lincoln about his failure to keep his job and to make his marriage work (6)
Growing tension between the brothers (6)	They face off over a game of three-card monte (6)
First round of three-card monte (6)	Lincoln lets Booth win (6)
Booth's win (6)	Booth wants to play the second round "for real." He bets the $500 his mother gave him years ago in a tied-up stocking and Lincoln bets the $500 he won tonight (6)
Second round of three-card monte (6)	Lincoln outfoxes Booth and wins (6)
Lincoln's win (6)	Lincoln takes Booth's money-filled stocking and threatens to cut it open to see what's really inside (6)
Lincoln's threat to cut open the stocking (6)	Booth stops him by confessing that he killed Grace (6)
Booth's murder confession (6)	Lincoln offers to return the money stocking, but Booth dares him to follow through on his threat to open it and Lincoln starts to do so (6)
Lincoln's attempt to cut open the stocking (6)	Booth stops Lincoln by shooting and killing him (6)
Booth's murder of Lincoln (6)	Booth lashes out at Lincoln, but ends up wailing in grief over the loss of his brother (6)

*While the term "act" is not used in the script, the story divides into two major units of action.

The role of offstage events. Because the play has only one setting, the throughline relies more than usual on offstage events to drive the dramatic journeys of both brothers. Booth's journey is significantly affected by what happens offstage between him and Grace, his ex-girlfriend. Lincoln's journey is significantly affected by what happens at the arcade where he works. This approach enables the playwright to present full portraits of both brothers' lives while maintaining the claustrophobic feeling of their single furnished room, which pits them against each other like two fighting dogs trapped in the same cage.

■ **THE CLEAN HOUSE**
Sentence synopsis
Three women—a doctor, a maid, and a housewife—struggle to overcome their differences as they care for a dying cancer patient who is in love with the doctor's husband.

Paragraph synopsis
Lane is a successful married doctor who hires a Brazilian housekeeper named Matilde to clean her house. But Matilde gets depressed and stops cleaning because she would rather think up the perfect joke. Lane's compulsive sister, Virginia, secretly comes to the rescue by doing Matilde's job for her while Lane is at work. Life gets messy for all three women when they discover that Lane's husband is in love with one of his cancer patients. As the women learn to deal with betrayal, loss, and class differences, they band together to care for the cancer patient in her final days, bringing new meaning to the words "I almost died laughing."

Chain of events
Most events unfold in linear fashion through cause and effect. In keeping with the nonrealistic style of the play, however, there are also random events and timeframe manipulations. These exceptions are described below the table.

CHAIN OF EVENTS: *THE CLEAN HOUSE*

Because of this	This happens
Matilde moving from Brazil to the US after her parents die (offstage)	• Matilde gets hired by Lane as a live-in maid (offstage) • Matilde tells us a joke in Portuguese (I, 1)
Matilde's job as a maid (offstage)	Matilde grows sad and stops cleaning (offstage)

Because of this	This happens
Matilde's refusal to clean (offstage)	• Lane tries unsuccessfully to order Matilde back to work and has her medicated at the hospital (I, 2) • Virginia disapproves of her sister Lane for giving up the privilege of cleaning her own house (I, 3) • Matilde gains time to tell us that her mother died laughing and her father shot himself (I, 4) • Lane tries again to order Matilde back to work, but succeeds only in getting her to polish the silver (I, 5) • Matilde gains time to imagine her parents dancing (I, 6) • Virginia comes to Matilde's rescue by offering to clean the house for her while Lane is at work (I, 7)
Virginia secretly cleaning Lane's house for Matilde (I, 7)	• Lane is impressed with her clean house (I, 8) • Matilde gains time to contemplate humor and imagines her parents laughing at an unknown joke (I, 9) • Virginia and Matilde find women's underwear in the laundry that is not Lane's (I, 10 and I, 13) • Lane and Virginia clash over their different views of having a maid (I, 11) • Matilde begins to think up the perfect joke (I, 12)
Charles falling in love with his patient Ana (depicted later in II, 4)	• Lane returns home late at night from work and discovers that her husband has not come home or called (I, 12) • Lane the next day discovers Charles's infidelity (offstage) • Lane returns home from work upset, "accidentally" cuts her wrist, and reveals to her sister and maid that Charles has gone off with a cancer patient (I, 13)
Lane's emotional reaction to her husband's infidelity (I, 13)	Virginia gets upset and compulsively rearranges the objects on Lane's coffee table (I, 13)
Virginia's rearrangement of Lane's coffee table (I, 13)	Lane figures out that Virginia has been cleaning her house for the past two weeks and fires Matilde (I, 13)
Lane's estrangement from everyone around her (I, 13)	Lane imagines Charles making love to his new wife, and Matilde, suitcase packed, tries to console her (I, 14)

Because of this	This happens
Charles and Anna falling in love (depicted later in II, 4)	Charles arrives at the front door with a woman whom Virginia describes as beautiful (I, 14)

ACT BREAK

Because of this	This happens
Charles and Ana falling in love (depicted later in II, 4)	• Charles lovingly performs surgery on Ana (II, 1) • Ana tells us how much she loves Charles (II, 2) • Charles tell us how much he loves Ana (II, 3) • Charles brings Ana over to meet Lane (I, 14 and II, 5)
Charles introducing Ana to Lane, Virginia, and Matilde (II, 5)	• Matilde and Ana strike up a friendship (II, 5) • Charles and Ana both try unsuccessfully to convince Lane that they are soul mates, or *basherts* (II, 5) • Ana offers to hire Matilde as her housekeeper, but Lane, not wanting to lose everything to Ana, fights to retain her, and Matilde decides to split her time between them (II, 5)
The failure of Charles and Ana to win Lane's support (II, 5)	• Lane angrily sends Charles and Ana away (II, 5) • Virginia offers her a hot-water bottle to relax and Lane reluctantly accepts her sister's help (II, 5)
Matilde's decision to split her time between Ana and Lane (II, 5)	• Matilde and Ana deepen their friendship and taste apples on Ana's seaside balcony (II, 6) • Matilde begins to develop a friendship with Lane and reveals that Ana's cancer has returned (II, 7)
The return of Ana's cancer (offstage)	Charles tries to convince Ana to go to the hospital for cancer treatment, but fails (II, 8)
The freedom Matilde has gained from living at Ana's (II, 6)	Matilde thinks up the perfect joke (II, 8)
The emotional stress caused by recent events (multiple scenes)	Lane screams at Virginia for vacuuming her floor and interfering with her life. Virginia fights back and makes an operatic mess in Lane's living room (II, 9)
Ana's refusal to go to the hospital for treatment (II, 8)	Charles leaves for Alaska to find a yew tree that might help treat Ana's cancer (offstage)
Charles's trip to Alaska (offstage)	Matilde informs Lane and Virginia that Ana is alone and in need of a doctor. Virginia convinces Lane to help Ana (II, 9)

Because of this	This happens
Lane's house call to Ana (II, 10)	• Lane has an emotional breakdown and acknowledges Charles's true love for Ana (II, 10) • Lane forgives Ana and they become friends (II, 10) • Lane invites Ana to move into her house (offstage)
Lane's decision to care for Ana in her final days (II, 10)	• Lane calls Virginia and asks for her help (II, 11) • Ana moves into Lane's house (offstage) • Virginia joins Lane and Matilde in caring for Ana and makes ice cream for the group (II, 12)
The sharing of ice cream (II, 12)	Lane, Matilde, Virginia, and Ana bond (II, 12)
The bond between Matilde and Ana (multiple scenes)	• Ana asks Matilde to kill her with a joke and Matilde agrees (II, 12) • Matilde tells Ana "the funniest joke in the world" and she dies laughing (II, 13)
Ana's death (II, 13)	Lane washes Ana's body while the others pray (II, 13)
Charles's discovery of the yew tree in Alaska (offstage)	Charles returns with the yew tree and discovers that he is too late to help Ana (II, 13)
Charles's request to Lane to hold the tree (I, 13)	Lane forgives Charles and takes his tree so he can be with his soul mate (II, 13)
Matilde's participation in Ana's life and death (multiple scenes)	Matilde imagines Ana as her mother giving birth to her under a tree. Matilde reaches a moment of completion with her parents (II, 14)

Breaking the linear chain of events. The play begins with Matilde telling a joke in Portuguese to the audience. This event has no direct cause or effect in the story and thus functions as a preface that introduces Matilde and sets the stage for comedy. Her other monologues—imaginings of her deceased parents joking and laughing—tie to the story's throughline only as random effects of the free time she gains from not having to clean Lane's house. While these imaginings contribute to Matilde's quest to recover from grief, they have no direct impact on the other onstage characters and thus exist outside the chain of events. The dramatic function of these flashbacks is to show Matilde's need to cling to an idyllic past that exists only in her mind and to help us understand her need to emulate her parents by telling jokes.

The linear sequence of events is broken again at the beginning of act two when the story reverses to depict past events: Charles and Ana falling in love, the cancer surgery he performs on her, and each one's reaction to these developments. Even within this flashback sequence, events are not chrono-logical. The surgery, which occurs after they fall in love, appears onstage first so the act can begin with the magic realism of an operatic operation. The linear sequence of events is resumed in act two, scene 5, which begins as act one ended with Charles entering the house offstage and calling: "Lane?" The repetition of this line helps us understand how the timeframe has been manipulated.

The nonlinear approach to Charles and Ana's love story adds to its emo-tional impact, helps us understand the transcendent nature of this love, and may make it easier for us to maintain empathy with an impossibly romantic couple whose actions have destroyed a marriage. The approach might be compared to that of a poem that reconfigures ideas and experiences to focus on what matters most and harness its visceral power.

In breaking the linear chain of events, the play occasionally employs si-multaneous action, as in act two, scene 7, when Matilde, in the living room with Lane and Virginia, describes a recent fight between Charles and Ana on the balcony. We see both events happening at the same time. The missing boundary between past and present is highlighted when a spice jar tossed by Ana in the past results in a cloud of yellow spice in Lane's living room in the present.

ANALYZING YOUR STORY

You can learn a lot about your plot by summing up what matters most and by exploring the chain of events that moves the story from beginning to end.

SHORT SYNOPSES

- In one sentence, what happens in the story? Sum up the main event with a focus on the main character and what he or she wants.
- In one paragraph, what happens in the story? Add details to the summary so that it reveals more about the situation and conflict.
- Review your two synopses as descriptions you can use when communicating with potential producers of your play. How well does each summary capture what matters most about the play? How interesting will it be to someone who doesn't know the story?

CHAIN OF EVENTS

- What are the key events of your story?
- Analyze each key event:
  - What previous onstage or offstage event is the primary cause of this event?

- What other events, if any, have contributed directly or indirectly to this event?
- What is the most important future event that will occur as a result of this event?
- What other events, if any, will also occur later as a result of what's happening now?
- Do all of the important turning points in the dramatic journey happen onstage? If not, which ones happen offstage?
- For any key offstage turning point, is there is a compelling reason for not showing this event onstage? How would the story be affected if this event moved from offstage to on?
- For each key onstage event, why is it important to show this happening here and now? How would the story be affected if this event moved from onstage to off?
- Analyze the throughline:
  - How is each onstage event different from the other onstage events in the story?
  - If two or more events feel redundant, which might you eliminate? How would this affect the story?
  - Think about how the events of the story connect from beginning to end. Are there any gaps, or missing events, in the chain? If so, where, and what is needed to fill them?
  - If new events need to be added, what should they be and how would this affect the story?
  - If you have an onstage event that does not tie to another onstage event as either cause or effect, how necessary is this unconnected event to the rest of the story?
  - If an unconnected event were removed, how would the story be different?

Two critical points in a character's life are the moment he or she enters the play for the first time and the moment he or she exits for the last time. The character's opening action and words create a first impression that can influence our perception of the character as the story goes on. The character's final action and words create a final impression that often stays with us after we leave the theatre.

In Tennessee Williams's *A Streetcar Named Desire*, for example, Blanche Dubois enters carrying a valise and dressed daintily in white "as if she were arriving at a summer tea." However, she has just stepped into a poor section of the French Quarter at twilight, where locals sit on the rickety steps of an old building. Blanche looks shocked and out of place as she tries to explain how she ended up here: "They told me to take a street-car named Desire, and then transfer to one called Cemeteries and ride six blocks and get off at—Elysian Fields!" She is thus introduced as one who is lost and looking for a desirable destination.

Her dramatic journey ends eleven scenes later with a very different image. A disoriented Blanche is now being led away to a mental institution by a gentle doctor, whose arm she grips tightly. "Whoever you are," she tells him, "I have always depended on the kindness of strangers." This exit from the play suggests that Blanche has finally found a refuge, though it is clearly not the Elysian Fields she had expected.

For most characters, the before-and-after points of the dramatic journey imply the arc of action, or transition, that he or she undergoes as a result of story events—for example, from lost to found. As we experience the final impression of the character in comparison to the first impression, we may gain a better understanding of what the story has been about and how the character has been affected.

■ **DOUBT: A PARABLE**
Sister Aloysius Beauvier
First impression. Our first view of Sister Aloysius is a serious one. As scene 2 begins, she is at her desk wearing rimless glasses and writing in a ledger with a fountain pen. Shanley describes her as "watchful, reserved, unsentimental." Her first line in the play is a response to a knock at her office door: "Come in." It's a simple enough opening, but it shows us that Aloysius is ready for business.

Final impression. When we last see Aloysius, life has changed dramatically. She is now outside in the garden, a "no man's land" in the shadow of the rectory, where she has no power. As the lights fade, she is bent with emotion and, instead of browbeating the nervous young Sister James, is being comforted by her. Aloysius's last words express her inner turmoil: "I have doubts! I have such doubts!"

Character arc. Regardless of how Aloysius's final line is interpreted, her words suggest a woman whose dramatic journey has taken her from a place of absolute certainty to a place of devastating uncertainty. Something big has happened, and, seeing how such a strong figure has been undone, we may go out of the theatre questioning our own certainties.

Father Brendan Flynn

First impression. Father Flynn first appears in scene 1, where he presents the classic image of a priest in his traditional place of authority: the pulpit. Dressed in green and gold vestments, he is delivering a sermon to his congregation. We see him here in isolation. He is the only onstage character, and the only words we hear are his monologue, though we will later learn that Sisters Aloysius and James are among those listening in the congregation offstage. Flynn's opening line is the question the play will tackle: "What do you do when you're not sure?"

Final impression. Flynn's last image in the play is quite different from the opening one. Dressed now in a black cassock, he is alone again, but this time in someone else's place of authority—the office of Sister Aloysius—and he is on her phone calling for help with his final line: "I need to make an appointment to see the bishop."

Character arc. Flynn begins his dramatic journey as a powerful man imparting words of wisdom and ends onstage as one who has lost power and is now in flight. We will learn in the final scene, however, that his loss of power is only temporary. In the offstage world, he will soon receive a promotion from the bishop and become the pastor of St. Jerome, another church and school. His overall arc, therefore, is circular: he begins and ends in a position of authority.

Sister James

First impression. Sister James enters the play as "a knock at the door." In effect, we hear her before we see her. This begins to establish her low status in this world. When the door opens, the impression is reinforced by the image we see. It is not the sight of a confident teacher walking in to discuss a problem with the principal. It is instead only part of a person—a head poking in cautiously. Her first line is a question that establishes her deference to the principal: "Have you a moment, Sister Aloysius?" James is so timid that she must be told twice to come in.

Final impression. We last see James in the garden with the emotionally wrought Aloysius. James is now asking another question: "What is it, Sister?" It's the question that prompts the play's final line, and it shows us James in a new role: comforting the woman she once feared.

Character arc. James begins her dramatic journey as an insecure and inexperienced teacher terrified of her superior. By the play's end, James has gained enough confidence to become her superior's caretaker and to feel a bond with her through the doubts they share.

Mrs. Muller

First impression. Like James, Mrs. Muller enters the play as "a knock at the door." However, she must knock twice, and more loudly the second time, because Aloysius is listening to music on a transistor radio. Mrs. Muller is the kind of person who will keep knocking until someone lets her in. Unlike James, Mrs. Muller does not poke her head in. She waits for the door to be opened for her, then enters confidently in her Sunday best. When asked if she is Mrs. Muller, she utters her first word in the play: "Yes." She has come here at the request of Aloysius in scene 5 and is ready for a showdown. Shanley says of her at this moment: "She's on red alert."

Final impression. As Mrs. Muller exits the office, her final words are "Nice talking to you, Sister. Good morning." This farewell has a crumbling impact on Aloysius, because nothing could be further from the truth. It has not been a "nice" talk, and Mrs. Muller does not wish her well. To complete her final image, Mrs. Muller leaves the door open behind her. This puts Aloysius in a vulnerable position, both literally and figuratively. Literally, the open door will allow an enraged Flynn to storm in for their climactic duel. Figuratively, the open door suggests that Aloysius has suffered a loss of defense, a setback that will be important to the final scene of the play.

Character arc. Mrs. Muller's dramatic journey has been short-lived—one scene—but powerful, taking her from concerned parent responding to a call from the school principal to formidable defender of her son's well-being.

■ TOPDOG/UNDERDOG
Booth (a.k.a. 3 Card)

First impression. We meet Booth in scene 1 as he sits alone in his room practicing to be a three-card monte dealer. The stage directions tell us, "His moves and accompanying patter are, for the most part, studied and awkward." This is the image of a man who has a grand plan but lacks the skill to make it work. The first words out of his mouth are the lines he hopes will one day enable him to con gullible players out of their money: "Watch me close, watch me close now: who-see-thuh-red-card-who-see-thuh-red-card? I-see-the-red-card. The-red-card-is-thuh-winner." These opening words are hyphenated to suggest the wooden quality of their delivery and sometimes spelled phonetically to indicate the dialect being spoken. As Booth struggles to get it right, we witness a key character need that will explain much of his behavior throughout the play: how badly he wants to win and how ill equipped he is to do so.

Final impression. The image of Booth that ends the play is a stark contrast to the one that began it. Having just killed his brother, Booth goes to retrieve the money-filled stocking that he lost to Lincoln in three-card monte but crumples to the floor instead. This is a man who has lost everything: his last remaining family member, his only friend, and his means of achieving his dreams. The stage directions describe him sobbing and hugging his brother's body as the money stocking, no longer important, lies beside him. He has no words to express his grief. His final line is only "AAAAAAAAAAAAAAAAAAAAH!" Ironically, this echoes a moment in scene 2, when the same line is used to express not grief but laughter as the brothers drink whiskey and happily count out the cash that Lincoln has brought home.

Character arc. As a result of the dramatic journey, Booth moves from success that is imaginary to failure that is deadly real.

Lincoln (a.k.a. Link)

First impression. As the stage directions indicate, Lincoln makes a striking entrance in scene 1. In addition to wearing whiteface, carrying Styrofoam containers of Chinese takeout food, and being inebriated, "He is dressed in an antique frock coat and wears a top hat and fake beard, that is, he is dressed to look like Abraham Lincoln." When we first meet him, therefore, he not only bears the president's name but also resembles him. As the play unfolds, we will discover that he is an Abraham Lincoln impersonator at an arcade, an "Honest Abe" who has given up his criminal past to seek legitimate work with a regular paycheck. When his startled brother pulls a gun on him, Link's opening line is a defense of why he wore his costume home: "I only had a minute to make the bus." He will later acknowledge that this excuse is not entirely true, suggesting that he secretly enjoys looking like Abraham Lincoln.

Final impression. The final image of Lincoln is a tragic one. His body is being held and hugged by his weeping brother, who has just murdered him.

Prior to this, the last line out of Link's mouth was simply "Don't." It is the final protest in his long-standing battle with Booth for topdog position. With Lincoln dead and Booth left alone with nothing, not even his dreams, both have ended up as underdogs.

Character arc. Link's dramatic journey takes him from the artificial life of impersonating Abraham Lincoln to the actual loss of life at his brother's hands.

■ THE CLEAN HOUSE

Lane

First impression. Dressed in white and facing the audience, Lane launches her role in the play with a complaint: "It has been such a hard month." We soon discover that her problem is not a life-or-death issue but, rather, a cleaning woman who has stopped cleaning. Lane's attitude is summed up by her conclusion: "I'm sorry, but I did not go to medical school to clean my own house." She is thus introduced as one who has an elitist view of the world and a need to control those around her.

Final impression. Lane last appears in her living room, holding an enormous yew tree. She has just kissed her husband, Charles, on the forehead and relieved him of the tree so that he can be near his deceased lover, Ana. Lane's final line in the play is a response to Charles's question, "Will you hold my tree?" She says, "Yes." This final affirmation, combined with her forehead kiss, signals her willingness to forgive Charles for betraying their marriage vows. It also suggests her determination to go on with her life.

Character arc. Lane evolves from a controlling elitist with petty problems to a woman who can accept the messiness of life, forgive others for their shortcomings, and begin to develop meaningful relationships.

Matilde

First impression. Dressed in black, Matilde begins the play by telling the audience a dirty joke in Portuguese. The playwright leaves the choice of jokes open but suggests one that would give these opening words to Matilde: *"Um homem tava a ponto de casar e ele tava muito nervosa ao preparar-se pra noite de núpcias porque ele nunca tuvo sexo en la vida de ele ..."* ("A man is getting married. He's never had sex, and he's very nervous about his wedding night ..."). Matilde is thus introduced not as a poor cleaning woman who hates her job but as a comedian who has mastered her craft. This is soon followed by another direct address to the audience, in which Matilde reveals in English why she wears black: she is in mourning for her parents who loved humor and who died last year in Brazil.

Final impression. As the play ends, Matilde is again directly addressing the audience. This time she is accompanied in her mind by her parents, who act out Matilde's imagining of her birth. It centers around an unheard joke that is whispered by her father into her mother's ear and causes her to laugh so hard that Matilde pops out. This magical moment is deepened by the fact that, in Matilde's imagination, her mother, who has just given birth, is portrayed by Ana, who has just died. The stage direction states that there is "A moment of completion between Matilde and her parents." Then she tells the audience, "I think maybe heaven is a sea of untranslatable jokes, / Only everyone is laughing." This final image and line are reminiscent of the play's opening, when Matilde tells us an untranslated joke.

Character arc. Matilde's dramatic journey begins with her attempt to use humor to numb the pain of losing her parents and ends with her acceptance of her parents' deaths and her acknowledgement of life as a mystery that produces both laughter and tears.

Virginia

First impression. Like Lane and Matilde, Virginia enters the play by facing the audience, but her opening line makes it clear that she has a unique perspective on cleaning: "People who give up the *privilege* of cleaning their own houses—they're insane people." She is thus introduced as the opposite of Lane, who has just complained about having to clean her own house since her maid won't. We later learn that Virginia and Lane are sisters and that they have little in common. Virginia here appears to be one who has nothing to do but clean. She later explains, "I know when there is dust on the mirror. Don't misunderstand me—I'm an educated woman. But if I were to die at any moment during the day, no one would have to clean my kitchen."

Final impression. When we last see Virginia, she is praying with Matilde over Ana, who has just died. Lane is about to enter with a bowl of water to wash Ana's body. Virginia's last words refer back to her apple-picking expedition with Ana, Charles, and Matilde on a happier day: "Ana. I hope you are apple picking."

Character arc. Virginia starts out as one who substitutes cleaning for a life not lived and ends up as one who has found meaningful tasks that enable her to connect with others, particularly her sister Lane.

Charles

First impression. We first see Charles at the end of act one as a silent figment of Lane's imagination, kissing and worshipping Ana. We next see him at the start of act two in a surreal hospital setting performing surgery on Ana and optionally singing "an ethereal love song in Latin / about being medically cured by love." In act two, scene 3, we finally meet the "real" Charles as he begins to address the audience: "There are jokes about breast surgeons . . ." This lighthearted introduction leads him to confess his love for the cancer patient on whom he has just performed surgery: "When I first met Ana, I knew: I loved her to the point of invention."

Final impression. We last see Charles in his former living room with the yew tree he has brought back from Alaska for Ana's cancer treatment. He has just learned that Ana died while he was transporting the tree. His final words reflect a recognition of his folly and are directed to Lane, who has kissed him on the forehead: "Thank you. Will you hold my tree?" When she does so, he moves in grief toward Ana's body.

Character arc. Charles enters the play as a great lover and ends up alone, as one who has lost his soul mate. This tragedy is heightened by the fact that he could have spent more time with Ana if he had accepted the messiness of her impending death and not gone to Alaska in vain.

Ana

First impression. Our first two images of Ana are passive. In act one, scene 14, she appears as a figment of Lane's imagination, being worshipped by Charles. In the surreal surgery scene that starts act two, she is being operated on by Charles. Ana has no dialogue here but may optionally sing "a contrapuntal melody." She emerges from the surgery in "a lovely dress."

It is not until act two, scene 2, that the real Ana appears in direct address to the audience. Her first words—"I have avoided doctors my whole life"—begin the revelation of her powerful but baffling love for Charles, her doctor. In reference to the surgery he performed on her, she touches her left breast and says, "I think Charles left his soul inside me, / Into the missing place."

Final impression. Our last image of Ana is also passive. Her dead body lies in the living room, with Matilde and Virginia praying over her and Lane washing her with water. Prior to this, Ana's last words were to Matilde in Portuguese: *"Matilde. / Deseo el chiste ahora"* ("I want the joke now"). It was a request for the perfect joke that she knew would kill her because of the choking laughter it would induce. In a play where characters can literally die laughing, it was a cancer patient's request for euthanasia.

Character arc. While Ana is a vibrant and uncompromising woman who changes everyone around her, she begins and ends the play as a character who is acted upon. She thus moves from being worshipped in life by Charles to being nursed through death by Lane, Matilde, and Virginia. On the physical plane, she journeys from life to death.

ANALYZING YOUR STORY

As basic tools of a dramatic storyteller, visual images and words can play a key role in defining character arcs of action. For each of your onstage characters, consider the following questions:

FIRST IMPRESSION

- What do we see when the character enters the story? Describe his or her opening image.
- What are the first words out of the character's mouth?
- Think about the character's first impression. What does it suggest about him or her? List two or three insights that we might gain as a result of this introduction.
- Given what you want to accomplish, how appropriate is the character's first impression? If it's not appropriate, how might you improve the opening image or words?

FINAL IMPRESSION

- What do we see when the character exits the story? Describe his or her final image.
- What are the last words out of the character's mouth?
- Think about your character's last impression. What does it suggest about him or her? List two or three insights that we might gain as a result of this conclusion.
- Given what you want to accomplish, how appropriate is the character's final impression? If it's not appropriate, how might you improve the final image or words?

CHARACTER ARC

- Think about the beginning and end points of the character's dramatic journey. How would you sum up his or her overall transition in the story?
- What are the most important ways in which the character has changed?
- In what important ways has the character stayed the same?
- Do you see the character's transition as a good or bad change, and why?
- If the quest is completed, what action or lesson most contributed to its success? If the quest is not completed, what are the chief reasons for its failure?
- What has the character gained from the dramatic journey? What has the character lost?

Just as each character in a dramatic story has an arc of action, the whole story has an arc that results in a main event and reflects the step-by-step transition that occurs in the world of the characters from the beginning of the story to the end.

The main event is the single most important thing that happens and is typically caused by someone pursuing an important goal and either succeeding or failing to achieve it. In Paula Vogel's *The Mineola Twins*, for example, twin sisters overcome thirty years of opposition to unite. In David Auburn's *Proof*, the daughter of a brilliant but mad mathematician proves that she is the author of an important mathematical proof attributed to her father. In Ayad Akhtar's *Disgraced*, an ambitious lawyer's attempts to conceal his Pakistani heritage and Muslim roots lead to the downfall of his career and marriage.

From a technical point of view, the main event is a structure to reveal and change character. As we watch the main event unfold, scene by scene, we learn who the characters are and see how each is affected by the dramatic journey. In stories with a single protagonist, the main character and main event are intrinsically bound: each defines the other. In stories with more than one protagonist, the principal characters may all experience the same main event but in different ways. Or each may encounter a separate main event in his or her own story line.

■ **DOUBT: A PARABLE**
Story arc: Certainty to doubt
Because *Doubt* is driven by a single protagonist, Sister Aloysius, the arc of action is closely tied to her individual character arc and quest.

First impression. As the play begins, we are introduced to a world governed by certainty. Though Flynn may be exploring the topic of doubt in his sermon, he wears liturgical vestments that reflect his high office and addresses the congregation from his place of authority: the church pulpit. When we first see Aloysius, she wears the commanding vestments of her religious order and sits in her place of authority: the principal's office. Her initial action is to write in a ledger with a fountain pen as she conducts school business. This is a rigid world in which the hierarchy of power is clearly delineated and the rules precisely defined.

Final impression. By the end of the play, Aloysius has succeeded in having Flynn removed but also paved the way for his promotion to pastor in another parish. She is left with unanswered questions that may be related to what she has done, Flynn's guilt or innocence, his future activities in the new parish, the integrity of the Catholic church and school system, her future within this system, and more. Such uncertainties are embodied by the final image: Aloysius on a garden bench, with James comforting her as she admits, "I have doubts! I have such doubts!"

Story arc. As Aloysius pursues her campaign to drive Flynn out of the parish, the world of the story shifts from certainty to doubt.

Main event: A woman's belief system is shattered

Aloysius's obsession with banishing a suspected child predator leads her to question her belief system. Doubt thus evolves from the theoretical subject of a priest's sermon to a robust force in the real world that can overwhelm even a strong-minded woman. It is a force that finally enables Aloysius to share her true feelings and for the first time in the play make a personal connection with someone else. The main event of the story, then, is not the ousting of Flynn but rather the result of that campaign: the undoing of the certainties that have defined Aloysius's rigid worldview and kept her emotionally insulated from those around her.

■ TOPDOG/UNDERDOG
Story arc: Hope to despair

In *Topdog/Underdog*, two protagonists drive the play by competing for the same goal: to be topdog. The overall arc of action equally encompasses the dramatic journeys of both characters.

First impression. As the play begins, we enter a lonely impoverished world made bearable by the hope that things will get better. The opening image is of Booth alone in his seedy room practicing to be a three-card monte dealer. His movements and patter indicate that he is not good at throwing the cards, but he has the hope that he can overcome this challenge and become a rich card hustler. Booth is soon joined by his brother, Lincoln, an Abraham Lincoln impersonator, who works at an arcade where customers with phony pistols pretend to assassinate him. He hopes to retain this job so that he can keep earning an honest living and avoid the dangers of swindling people out of their money.

Final impression. The play ends with Booth wailing as he hugs his brother's dead body on the floor of the same room. A nylon stocking containing a wad of money lies beside him. In his quest to be topdog, he has reenacted the crime that his father invited years ago by naming one son after Abraham Lincoln and the other after John Wilkes Booth. As a result, death has separated the brothers permanently and left Booth without family. Money—once a dominant force in their lives—has become irrelevant. There is no hope for the future.

Story arc. As the brothers go to increasing lengths to compete for topdog status, the world of the story shifts from hope to despair.

Main event: Sibling rivalry leads to murder

By focusing on the ups and downs of the duel between Lincoln and Booth, the play presents the complexities of a relationship that is both competitive and nurturing. At times, it appears that the rivalry between the brothers may doom them to failure because of their inability to resolve their differences. At other times, it appears that their brotherly love may enable them to build better lives by healing the psychological wounds inflicted on them by their parents and society. In the end, it is the rivalry between the brothers that wins out.

Booth's murder of Lincoln—and all it entails—is the main event of the play. It is the death not only of Lincoln but also of the American dream. Each brother pursued it in his own way, one as an underdog attempting to work outside the system and the other as a topdog attempting to work from within. In the end, the dream eludes them both. The tragedy of the play's outcome raises the question of whether the dream was ever really accessible to two men whose lives have been defined by a dysfunctional family, poverty, and low status in society.

■ THE CLEAN HOUSE
Story arc: Isolation to connection

In *The Clean House* three protagonists with individual quests eventually find themselves on the same journey.

First impression. The play introduces a trio of women—Lane, Matilde, and Virginia—who each live in isolation and have little in common. Lane is an important doctor who finds it inappropriate to socialize with her maid and feels estranged from her sister. Matilde, in mourning for her parents, feels sad among the living, especially in this new country where her only opportunity for work is to clean someone else's house. Virginia, a housewife in a childless marriage to a boring man, feels so alone and empty that she would rather spend the day cleaning house or asleep in bed. Each character's views reflect her social class, values, and approach to life.

Final impression. The play ends with the same three women working in harmony to nurse their new friend Ana through her cancer and death. In the final scene, Matilde imagines Ana as her mother giving birth to her in laughter. In contrast to the play's beginning, where each character stands alone, the ending shows the women supporting one another as they deal with the mystery of death and, in Matilde's imagination, the wonder of birth.

Story arc. As Lane, Matilde, and Virginia each emerge from their clean houses to accept life's messes, the world of the story evolves from isolation to connection.

Main event: Women from different walks of life connect

Lane, Matilde, and Virginia function together as a group protagonist whose need for meaningful human relationships drives the play. To fulfill this need, each must learn to accept the messiness of life, whether it's a failed marriage, the death of parents, or a dreary existence due to bad choices. As the women put their social and personal differences aside and join together to nurse a dying woman, they find a connection that will enable them to move on with their lives. It is this connection—embodied in the joyful act of eating ice cream together—that is the main event of the play.

ANALYZING YOUR STORY

Explore the story arc of your play and the main event it produces.

STORY ARC

- How does your story begin?
- What are the most telling details of this beginning?
- How would you describe the emotional environment at the beginning of the story?
- What information might this beginning suggest to an audience about your characters and the world they inhabit?
- How does your play end?
- What are the most telling details of this ending?
- How would you describe the emotional environment at the end of the story?
- What information might the ending suggest to an audience about your characters and the world of the story?
- Think about how the end of the story compares with the beginning. What is the story arc?

MAIN EVENT

- What is the most important thing that happens in your story? Define the main event.
- Do you see this main event as a positive or negative change, and why?
- What two or three story events most contribute to this outcome?

- How closely does the main event tie to the dramatic journey of your protagonist(s)?
- How does the main event affect your protagonist(s) in a good way? In a bad way?
- Who else, if anyone, is significantly affected by this event, and how?
- How is the world of the story affected by this event in the short term? In the long term?

No matter how long or complex a dramatic story may be, and regardless of the many topics and ideas it may present, it is ultimately about one thing. It has a subject, or main topic, such as love, and a theme, or premise, such as "love conquers all." The theme reflects who the story is about, what events the dramatic journey includes, and how the story ends. To understand the big picture of a dramatic story is to know its subject and theme and be able to state these global elements in simple terms. Ideally, a subject can be expressed in a word or phrase, but a theme requires a complete sentence.

Most dramatic stories also have a counter-theme that stands in contrast or opposition to the main theme and is embodied by the forces of antagonism. In a drama that aims to show how "love conquers all," for example, a counter-theme might purport that "love can be defeated by hate." These contradictory ideas could put a pair of young lovers on a collision course with others who are bent on keeping them apart.

The counter-theme is important because it fuels the central conflict of the story. If a play is weak on conflict, it is often a sign that the counter-theme has not been sufficiently developed. The counter-theme also helps define the main theme by providing a contrast to it. We come to understand the theme more clearly by seeing what it is not.

Though theme and counter-theme tend to be equally powerful through most of the story, the theme is the one that determines how the dramatic journey will end. If the theme is "love conquers all," for example, it will prove stronger and truer than its opposite, and the young lovers will ultimately triumph. In some cases, the counter-theme may maintain enough dramatic strength to compromise the ending. For example, the lovers may die but triumph over their adversaries by staying faithful to each other, as in Shakespeare's *Romeo and Juliet*.

■ DOUBT: A PARABLE
Subject: Doubt

Audiences may view *Doubt* from a number of different angles. Some may see it as a story about child abuse. Others may see it as an exposé about corruption in the Catholic Church. In both the title and preface of the script, however, Shanley tells us that the subject of the play is doubt. This subject is introduced in the opening line of the play when Father Flynn asks, from the pulpit: "What do you do when you're not sure?"

Webster's New World Dictionary defines doubt as "a wavering of opinion or belief, lack of conviction, uncertainty." This is a play that explores the human condition of feeling unsure. In scene 7, when Father Flynn meets secretly with Sister James to enlist her support, he implies the inevitability of experiencing doubt. "What actually happens in life is beyond interpretation," he says. "The truth makes for a bad sermon. It tends to be confusing and have no clear conclusion." In highlighting the difficulty of knowing the truth, Flynn has described the context for the play and its exploration of what happens when the forces of doubt clash with the forces of certainty.

Theme: Doubt can lead to wisdom and growth

Doubt centers on Aloysius's campaign to drive Flynn out of St. Nicholas parish because she believes he has abused an eighth grade student named Donald Muller, even though she has neither hard evidence to support her conclusion nor the support of the boy's mother in condemning the priest. By the time the play ends, Aloysius has succeeded in chasing Flynn away, but for the first time since the play began, she begins to experience doubts. Some of these doubts may be triggered by the events of her campaign, such as her deliberate use of deception to force Flynn into leaving. Some may be triggered by the aftermath: his departure has led not to exile and shame, but a promotion to pastor of another parish.

As she sits on a bench with Sister James, Aloysius's reflection on all that has happened prompts her to utter the final line of the play: "I have doubts! I have such doubts!" Shanley has described this breakthrough as the birth of a modern woman.[1] Having shattered her rigid belief system, Aloysius can now begin to think for herself and to evolve as an individual. It is notable that she refers here to "doubts" in the plural and that she repeats the word, as if a floodgate of questions has opened and begun to overtake her.

This ending suggests the theme that doubt is a necessary part of life, a complement to certainty that can contribute to wisdom and growth. The theme explains why the question of Flynn's innocence or guilt is never resolved. When all is said and done, the play is not about what Flynn did or didn't do. It's about Aloysius and the transformation that enables her to rise above her dogmatic approach to the world and, in acknowledging her vulnerability to Sister James, make a personal connection with someone else.

The emotional impact of this ending is heightened by the defeat of the

---

1. "The Making of Doubt" (discussion moderated by Roma Torre), *Dramatist* 8, no. 1 (September/October 2005).

play's counter-theme, which defines doubt as a sign of weakness that must be eliminated. During the dramatic journey leading to this final moment, we see that absolute certainty is a source of confidence, power, and peace of mind for Aloysius. Whether the topic is children writing with ballpoint pens, teachers managing their classrooms, or priests choosing topics for their sermons, she has no need to debate issues or compromise her views. She always knows how to proceed because she has a belief system that dictates the parameters of right and wrong, eliminates the complicated gray zone between them, and guides her through the demands of everyday life. Because this system has been handed down from the trusted authority of the Church, she sees it as a code of behavior that one embraces without question.

It is this belief system that fuels her campaign against Flynn from beginning to end. It is also this belief system that must be changed if Aloysius is to achieve her final transformation and see that, as Mrs. Muller earlier warned her, "Sometimes things aren't black and white."

■ TOPDOG/UNDERDOG
Subject: Family wounds
Parks's tragicomedy draws us into the claustrophobic world of Lincoln and Booth, brothers who vie for power within the confines of the rooming-house room that poverty and loneliness have forced them to share. Each comes to this room from failed relationships with women, a racially imbalanced society that offers little hope for advancement, and a history of parental abandonment that has left the older brother, Lincoln, the topdog and the younger brother, Booth, the underdog.

The dynamics of their competitive relationship dramatize such topics as sibling rivalry, brotherly love, family, identity, race, masculinity, inheritance, money, the power of the past, the con game three-card monte, and the American dream. In the introduction to the play, the playwright identifies the topic that matters most: "This is a play about family wounds and healing." It is through this lens that the other topics come into view.

Theme: Unhealed family wounds kill
Throughout *Topdog/Underdog*, we see the power of the past to affect the present, with a focus on the psychological and social wounds that family relationships can inflict. As the play unfolds, certain events illustrate the tragic theme that unhealed family wounds kill. Other events illustrate the counter-theme that unhealed family wounds bring the survivors closer together.

For Lincoln and Booth, such wounds were first inflicted at birth, when their father thought it would be funny to name them after Abraham Lincoln and his assassin John Wilkes Booth. Perhaps it was this cruel naming of the two infants that doomed them to a future where the original Booth's deadly act of violence would be reenacted over a wad of cash in a seedy furnished room.

During the story, we get glimpses of the early family life that shaped Lincoln and Booth into the men we meet in scene 1. We learn that they grew up in a two-room house with a cement backyard and a front yard full of trash, that their father was an abusive drunk, and that both parents had lovers on the side. We also learn that the parents had attempted to achieve the American dream by getting steady jobs and taking on a mortgage to buy a house, and that it was the strain of this effort that led to the breakup of the family.

When Lincoln and Booth were in their teens, both parents vanished, first the mother, then, two years later, the father, leaving the brothers to quit school and fend for themselves. "I don't think they liked us," Lincoln muses in a passing reflection of Moms and Pops. Their desertion has had both a positive and a negative impact on the brothers. In line with the hopeful counter-theme, parental abandonment has led them to join forces in a struggle against the world. We see their brotherly love in many moments throughout the play, such as Lincoln's efforts to soothe Booth's pain after he is stood up by Grace, his ex-girlfriend. Underlying the conflict of the play is the hope that this love will lead the brothers to a better life.

In line with the tragic main theme, however, the desertion of the parents has taught them that loved ones are not be trusted: they can be abusive and can disappear at any moment. Perhaps this is why the brothers have such a hard time managing relationships, not only with each other but also with the women in their lives.

Prior to running away, each parent gave one son a $500 cash inheritance. The mother secretly gave hers to Booth, and the father secretly gave his to Lincoln, each with the instruction not to tell the other brother about the money. This parental advice may explain why the brothers find it difficult to trust each other. The life example of the parents also taught them that steady employment is a source of misery and that they should pursue other lifestyles. For Lincoln, this meant card hustling. For Booth, it meant petty theft.

In their power struggles, we see that the brothers often use lies to impress each other and cruelty to exert control, behaviors that can be traced back to their parents. Because the brothers have not learned to overcome the wounds of their childhood, they find themselves on the path that leads to their final showdown. As the play ends with Booth hugging the body of the brother he has slain, we witness how unhealed family wounds can kill.

■ THE CLEAN HOUSE
Subject: Life's messes

While focusing on relationships among women from different walks of life, *The Clean House* explores a number of topics, such as housecleaning, humor, laughter, class differences, grief, apple picking, infidelity, soul mates, sibling rivalry, friendship, cancer, healing, death, forgiveness, and the nature of love. From a global perspective, the sum of story events suggests that the subject, or main topic, of the play is the messiness of human existence: not dirt and disarray in the physical realm so much as the failures, losses, accidents, and other disappointments that affect us emotionally and sometimes make life painful and complicated.

Theme: Accepting life's messes can lead to renewal

Each character in the play is faced with a mess: the end of a marriage (Lane), the loss of parents (Matilde), an everyday life that has become meaningless (Virginia), the potential loss of a soul mate to cancer (Charles), and the diagnosis of a fatal disease (Ana). Each of these messes threatens the character's "clean house" and challenges her or him to find a solution.

At first, most of the characters have difficulty accepting their messes and instead choose diversions that perpetuate their problems or make them worse. Lane clings to anger over her husband's betrayal. Matilde keeps her parents alive in an imaginary world where everything is perfect. Virginia tries to avoid the meaninglessness of her life by cleaning obsessively. Charles denies the inevitability of his soul mate's death and flees to Alaska in search of a cure. Only Ana immediately accepts the misfortune that has changed her life. Diagnosed with breast cancer, she demands a mastectomy, and later, when the cancer returns, she attempts to live the rest of her life on her own terms, even to the extent of choosing the time and manner of her death.

The other women eventually learn to accept their messes as well and begin to heal. Lane moves on with her life by letting go of her anger and forgiving Ana for taking Charles from her. Matilde learns to accept the loss of her parents by getting more involved in the real world and participating in the death of Ana. Virginia overcomes her cleaning compulsion by making an "operatic mess" in her sister's living room. Charles is the only character who fails to accept his mess in time; consequently, he loses the opportunity to be with Ana at the end of her life.

By showing how most of the characters grow, *The Clean House* asks us to understand that life is a mixed bag that includes both funny jokes and ruined marriages, apple-picking parties and lonely afternoons, chocolate ice cream and fatal disease. The underlying theme is that we cannot heal from our failures and losses until we come to accept them as parts of who we are. It is through the messiness of life's entanglements that we can become open enough to begin the process of reinventing ourselves.

This theme is opposed by the counter-theme that the key to true happiness is perfection and that life's messes must, therefore, be avoided or eliminated. The power of this contrasting idea explains why, at different times in the story, each character struggles to achieve his or her version of a "clean house," whether it takes the form of an immaculate dwelling, the world's funniest joke, the tastiest apple, the best way to treat cancer, or a soul mate.

ANALYZING YOUR STORY

The subject and theme are keys to understanding the "big picture" of a dramatic story.

SUBJECT

- What are the most important topics that your dramatic story addresses? List up to ten topics that are discussed by your characters or dramatized through story events.
- What is the main topic, or subject, of the story? Look for a subject that can encompass other topics you listed and sum it up in a word or phrase—for example, "truth."
- Words may have different meanings and connotations. How would you define your subject within the terms of your story?
- Why is this topic important to you? What is your emotional connection to it?

THEME

- Think about your subject in relation to your characters and story. What does your play demonstrate about this subject? List a few ideas, or themes, and express each one in a sentence that includes the subject word. If the subject is "truth," for example, a theme might be "The truth shall set you free."
- What is the main theme of your story? Sum it up in one sentence.
- Why is this theme important to you? What is your emotional connection to it?
- Who in your story most embodies the main theme, and how?
- Think about what happens in your story. What plot elements demonstrate the theme?
- What is the counter-theme of your story?
- Who most embodies the counter-theme, and how?
- What elements of the plot demonstrate the counter-theme?

- When the forces representing the counter-theme are equal to the forces representing the theme, conflict is intense and the end of the story unpredictable. What is the balance of power now between theme and counter-theme? Does either side need to be strengthened to make the balance of power more equal? If so, how might this be done?
- What message does the end of the story convey? Is this the right message for what you want to accomplish? If not, what changes will you make?
- What emotional response do you wish to elicit from the audience at the end of the play?
- Think about the other topics that your play addresses. What are some of the most important secondary themes that run through the script?
- Is there a connection between the main theme and any of these secondary themes? If so, how do these ideas relate?

DIALOGUE

Dialogue is what characters say as they interact with one another to satisfy their needs, address problems, or express ideas and emotions. In theatre today, the term "dialogue" is also loosely used to encompass any text spoken by a character, including monologues (long speeches to another character onstage), soliloquies (long speeches to oneself, the audience, or the universe), and asides (quick comments to the audience). Regardless of the form it takes, dialogue has a twofold purpose: to reveal character and to move the story forward.

Just as each character in a story has a unique manner of expression that arises out of his or her identity and life experience, the world of a story has a distinct voice that reflects the writer who created this world and the characters who inhabit it. This voice may be prosaic or poetic, delicate or coarse, reliable or unreliable. It may speed along in lean lines of dialogue that keep the characters interacting. Or it may move more slowly in monologues and soliloquies that isolate the characters in their words. In a realistic play, dialogue has the form and feel of everyday conversation. In a nonrealistic play, dialogue may be stylized. Either way, it is usually heightened speech driven by character objectives and shaped by conflict.

The language of the characters often includes terms that are indigenous to the culture of the story. In some cases, characters give special meanings to otherwise common terms. For most people, for example, Parnassus is a sacred mountain in ancient Greece. For George in Edward Albee's *Who's Afraid Of Virginia Woolf?*, it's the house where Martha's father lives. Characters may also use original terms to communicate with each other. In Warren Leight's *Side Man*, "Club 92" is how jazz musicians refer to the 92nd Street unemployment office.

■ DOUBT: A PARABLE
Dialogue

Most of the characters in *Doubt* are educators in a Catholic school, and their language throughout the play reflects this. Topics center on school business and issues related to specific students and occasionally to other staff. Personal issues are seldom discussed.

Sister Aloysius, Sister James, and Father Flynn all speak standard English and are articulate in doing so, though James's insecurity sometimes makes it difficult for her to find the right words to express herself. For Aloysius and

Flynn, dialogue tends to unfold in complete declarative sentences. Aloysius often speaks in paragraphs to wield her authority and impart her wisdom. James, as a sign of her low status and lack of confidence, is more likely to ask questions and utter single lines or sentence fragments.

The formality of the language is reflected in the way characters address and refer to one another. Each has a title—"Sister," "Father," or "Mrs."—that is always used in conjunction with his or her name. Even when Aloysius and James are discussing the possibility of Flynn committing vile and perverse acts, they still refer to him as "Father" Flynn.

In line with this formality, characters rarely interrupt each other and never use profanity or slang. During the heated confrontation between Aloysius and Flynn near the end, for example, no one interrupts, swears, or curses. This does not stop the characters from forcefully making their thoughts known, whether it's Aloysius condemning Flynn ("You're a disgrace to the collar") or Flynn condemning Aloysius ("You're insane").

Mrs. Muller is the only onstage character who does not work at St. Nicholas. Her voice is equally forceful but less formal ("I thought I might a had the wrong day . . .") and more colloquial ("My boy came to this school 'cause they were gonna kill him at the public school").

Language rhythms vary throughout the story. Six scenes unfold interactively in dialogue, while three short scenes consist only of monologues by Flynn: two sermons to a congregation and a pep talk to the basketball team.

The general tone of language throughout the story is realistic and down-to-earth. Aside from Aloysius's description of Flynn as a "wolf" and Flynn's description of Aloysius as "a block of ice," figurative speech is seldom used. The closest the dialogue gets to poetry is in Flynn's sermons—for example, when he tells the parable of a shipwrecked sailor to illustrate the challenge of doubt and when he uses the metaphor of feathers scattered in the wind to make a comment about gossip. Otherwise this is a world where characters speak simply and directly, and say what they have to say.

Indigenous terms

- **Altar wine.** Wine blessed and used by a priest during the celebration of Mass. This is the wine that James may have smelled on Donald Muller's breath after his visit to the rectory.
- **Mental reservation.** A principle of Catholic doctrine that allows one to make a misleading statement without technically telling a lie because the statement has another, unexpressed meaning that is true. In scene 8, when Flynn denies that he gave wine to Donald Muller, Aloysius accuses the priest of mental reservation, suggesting

that he interpreted the words to suit his needs. If he didn't physically place the bottle in Donald's hand, for example, he could mean that he didn't "give" it to him, even if he had made the alcohol available to the boy.

- **Monsignor.** A senior position in the Roman Catholic Church, usually conferred by a pope. In the chain of command, Monsignor Benedict is Aloysius's only recourse for reporting problems.
- **Rectory.** The residence of a parish priest. If Flynn's alleged abuse of Donald actually occurred, this is the scene of the crime.
- **Sacristy.** A room in a church where a priest prepares for Mass and where liturgical vestments and other items used in worship, such as altar wine, are kept. Flynn claims that the caretaker, Mr. McGinn, found Donald drinking altar wine here.
- **Second Ecumenical Council.** Established by Pope John XXIII in 1962 and known as the Second Vatican Council, or Vatican II, the council redefined the role of the Catholic Church in modern society, eliminating the Latin Mass and increasing lay participation in the Church. Flynn embraces the council's message, while Aloysius dismisses it.
- **Vows.** The solemn pledge to enter a religious order and live a life of poverty, chastity, and obedience in accordance with Church dictates.

■ TOPDOG/UNDERDOG
Dialogue

As a result of parental abandonment, Lincoln and Booth in their teens were exposed to life on the street and drawn into a world of crime. Their language reflects this history. Topics center on illegal exploits, worldly pleasures, and, most importantly, their parents and the past.

Both brothers speak in an African-American vernacular with vocabulary, grammar, and pronunciation that differs in many ways from standard English. Slang terms, double negatives, dropped initial and final consonants, and the use of nonstandard words such as "ain't" are common. Sentence construction and verb usage is systematically dissimilar to standard English. Parks often uses phonetic spelling to suggest the dialect being spoken: "the," for example, becomes "thuh," and "your" becomes "yr." Punctuation is streamlined, with commas and apostrophes omitted.

The speech of both brothers is robust, colorful, and laced with profanity, but each has his own voice. Booth's gritty language soars with poetry, as when he describes the power of Grace's allure: "She walks on by and the emergency room fills up cause all the guys get whiplash from lookin at her."

Another example of his lyricism can be found in his description of how much Grace loves him now: "She wants me back so bad she wiped her hand over the past where we wasnt together just so she could say we aint never been apart."

Lincoln's speech tends to be more matter of fact and analytical, as when he offers advice to Booth, who has decided to change his name: "You gonna call yrself something african? That be cool. Only pick something thats easy to spell and pronounce, man, cause you know, some of them african names, I mean, ok, Im down with the power to the people thing, but no ones gonna hire you if they cant say yr name."

Language rhythms suggest a stream-of-consciousness flow of ideas, a product perhaps of the playwright's fast writing of the script. Monologues and soliloquies occur regularly throughout the text—scene 4 is nothing but soliloquy—and often contain images of the past or offstage world. In scene 3, for example, as Lincoln describes his job at the arcade, he creates a vivid image of a metal fuse box on the wall where he sits in his Abraham Lincoln outfit and waits for customers with toy guns to enter from behind: "Its got uh dent in it like somebody hit it with they fist. Big old dent so everything reflected in it gets reflected upside down. Like yr looking in uh spoon. And thats where I can see em. The assassins."

A recurring element in the dialogue is the three-card monte patter that Booth tries to learn and Lincoln tries at first to resist. By scene 6, when the brothers face off over the cards, Lincoln has recaptured his mastery of the spiel: "Lean close and watch me now: who see thuh black card who see thuh black card I see thuh black card black cards the winner pick the black card thats thuh winner . . ." As the patter continues, its repetitive and hypnotic rhythm explains how the dealer can distract customers from tracking the money card among the three cards being shuffled before them. The lack of punctuation in the script adds to the hypnotic effect of the spiel.

The general tone of the dialogue throughout the play is emotional and intensely personal. These are characters who speak from their souls, even when they are trying to hide their true feelings from each other.

Indigenous terms

- **Boosting.** Stealing. This is Booth's primary means of acquiring merchandise.
- **Dealer.** The one in a three-card monte operation who controls the cards and plays the game directly with customers. Lincoln is a master dealer.
- **Lookout.** The member of a three-card monte crew who watches for the cops while the dealer plays the game on the street with passersby.

- **Mark.** A sucker who is easily cheated out of his or her money. Any customer in a three-card monte game is a mark.
- **Med-sin.** Whiskey. Like medicine, it is often a cure for what ails Lincoln and Booth.
- **Sideman.** A three-card monte shill who pretends to be winning the game in order to encourage passersby to play.
- **Skrimps.** A shrimp dish from the local Chinese takeout place.
- **Stickman.** A three-card monte dealer's partner who poses as a passerby and gets others to play the game. A stickman is similar to a sideman but knows the game inside out.
- **Three-card monte.** A shell game in which a player watches the dealer shuffle three cards face down and has to pick a certain card to win. Thanks to sleight of hand and a mesmerizing patter, the outcome of the game is always under the control of the dealer, who sometimes lets the customer win at first in order to encourage larger bets.
- **Three-card monte setup.** Three playing cards on a cardboard board atop two milk crates, one stacked on top of the other. The setup is designed so that it can appear quickly on the street and disappear even more quickly if the cops are approaching.
- **Throwing the cards.** Dealing three-card monte.

■ THE CLEAN HOUSE

Dialogue

The cast includes two doctors, a cleaning woman, a housewife, and a cancer patient. The diversity of their needs is reflected in the topics they discuss, from housecleaning to joke telling to death. With Ruhl coming to playwriting from a poetry background, it is not surprising that her approach to such subjects tends to be lyrical.

As in poetry, big ideas are often communicated with few words. In act one, scene 2, Lane's sense of self-importance and class privilege is established in a single line: "I'm sorry, but I did not go to medical school to clean my own house." In addition, the speech of the characters is frequently heightened by poetic comparisons, as in act two, scene 6, when Matilde uses a metaphor to describe humor: "The perfect joke is the perfect music. You want to hear it only once in your life, and then, never again."

While the play is contemporary, the language has at times a formality that echoes an earlier era. Modern slang is almost entirely absent, and profanity is rare. The dialogue in interactive scenes tends to be lean, but the play also includes a number of monologues, which account for more than a quarter of the play's scenes and isolate the characters in their words.

The dramatic journeys of the characters are often revealed by their speech. For example, Lane, in act one, approaches the world in a controlling and methodical manner that is reflected in terse language, such as "The house is very dirty." In act two, however, as life gets messy, her voice takes on a more emotional quality, as in act two, scene 9, when she attempts to acknowledge that she cannot compete with Ana for Charles's love: "You—glow—with some kind of—thing—I can't *acquire* that—this thing—sort of glows off you—like a veil—in reverse—you're like *anyone's* soul mate . . ."

Matilde and Ana, both from South America, speak English as a second language and occasionally address each other in Portuguese, which separates them from the others and fuels the intimacy between them. From a storytelling perspective, Matilde's name becomes a simple tool to advance the story. While Matilde uses the Brazilian pronunciation "Ma-chil-gee," for example, Lane uses the American pronunciation "Matilda," a distinction that highlights their cultural differences.

As a housewife, Virginia is most likely to use household references to express herself, as in act one, scene 10, when she describes married life to Matilde: "My husband is like a well-placed couch. He takes up the right amount of space." Charles, on the other hand, speaks with a voice that reflects his medical background, as in act two, scene 5, when he tries to convince Lane of his love for Ana: "It's as though I suddenly tested positive for a genetic disease that I've had all along, *Ana has been in my genetic code.*"

Indigenous terms

- **Bashert.** A traditional Yiddish term for a soul mate. Though Charles is not Jewish, he uses this term to describe Ana and to justify his decision to leave Lane.
- **Biopsy.** Removal of sample tissue from the body to test for disease.
- **Bone marrow.** The soft tissue inside large bones where new blood cells are produced.
- **Bryn Mawr.** An exclusive college for women in Philadelphia. This is where Virginia went to school, studied Greek literature, and dreamed of being a scholar.
- **Chemotherapy.** A treatment for cancer in which chemicals are used to kill cancer cells.
- **Lumpectomy.** Surgical procedure to remove a tumor in a breast.
- **Machu Picchu.** An ancient Incan fortress city in the Andes mountains in Peru. Charles imagines visiting exotic places like this in order to "live life to the fullest."

- **Mastectomy.** Surgical procedure to remove a breast as a treatment for breast cancer.
- **Microtubules.** Microscopic tube-shaped structures found in the cytoplasm of cells.
- **Radiation.** Anticancer treatment in which high-energy rays are used to destroy cancer cells.
- **Taxol.** Commercial brand name for an anticancer drug made from yew trees.
- **Yew tree.** A fir tree. The bark of the Pacific yew contains a chemical called *paclitaxel*, which stops the growth of certain cancer cells and can be used in chemotherapy to fight cancer. Matilde, who speaks English as a second language, at first interprets "yew tree" as "you tree" and thinks that Charles is planning to invent a "you medicine."

ANALYZING YOUR STORY

Besides evaluating dialogue line by line during revision, you may gain new insights by looking at the overall language of the script to see how it contributes to the experience of the story.

DIALOGUE

- How would you describe the style of dialogue in your script? Is it primarily prosaic? Poetic? Formal? Informal? Technical? Contemporary? Historical?
- How would you describe the overall rhythm of the language in your script? Does the dialogue tend to unfold at a fast pace? Slow pace? Mixed pace? How does that suit your story?
- How characters talk can reveal a lot about who they are, where they live, how they live, their educational backgrounds, what kind of work they do, what they value, and more. What does the dialogue reveal about the world of your characters?
- Compare and contrast the way your two most important characters express themselves throughout the story. How is their manner of expression alike? How is it different?
- Sometimes what is not said is more important than what is said. Do characters tend to say precisely what they think and feel or leave important thoughts unspoken? How does this affect character interactions and story events?
- Identify the ten most important topics your characters discuss at any time during the story.

- Identify the twenty most important words in the dialogue of your play.
- What do these key topics and words reveal about your characters? Your story?
- How truthful and reliable does the dialogue tend to be among your characters? What does this suggest about the world of your story?

INDIGENOUS TERMS

- What nicknames do your characters use, if any, to address or refer to one another?
- If your characters use slang terms, what are they, and how are they defined?
- Do your characters use technical or workplace jargon to express themselves, even when they aren't at work? If so, how are any such terms defined?
- If any common terms have unusual meanings among your characters, what are the terms and how are they defined?
- If your characters use any original terms, what are they and how are they defined?
- Some indigenous terms are more important than others. For those that matter most, how have you introduced each one so that the audience can understand or infer its meaning?
- Think about the balance between common and uncommon terminology in the dialogue of your play. How well does this balance support the story you want to tell? Do your characters use too many special terms? Not enough?

VISUAL IMAGERY

Just as a picture is worth a thousand words, visual imagery in drama can be a powerful way to reveal character and move the story forward. The images we see onstage are often more lasting than the words we hear—for example, a horribly deformed man in a hospital room building an elegant model of a church in Bernard Pomerance's *The Elephant Man*; a sea of stolen toasters in a suburban ranch house, each popping up toast, in Sam Shepard's *True West*; or a woman wrapped in a sheet in a bombed-out hotel room, feeding sausages and bread to a dying man whose head protrudes from a hole in the floor, in Sarah Kane's *Blasted*.

Imagery on stage draws its ingredients from the physical life of the story, such as the setting and what's in it, and the physicality of the characters, such as how they appear and what they are doing. To create the blueprint for such imagery, dramatic writers have two tools available:

Stage directions. These instructions from the playwright can generate visual imagery by describing key elements of the set, props, costumes, and lighting, as well as key actions of the characters. When the play goes into production, the director, designers, and actors will translate these directions into images that the audience sees and hears onstage as the story unfolds.

Dialogue. The words of the characters can also generate imagery but do so indirectly. Instead of instructing a set designer to make the set look a certain way or telling an actor to perform a certain action, for example, dialogue can command such images by making them a specific topic of discussion. For example, the line "Who locked this cabinet?" will not make sense unless the set includes a cabinet that cannot be opened. Robust dialogue often eliminates the need for stage directions and ensures that the writer's intentions are carried out in production.

■ DOUBT: A PARABLE

The visual images of *Doubt* portray the world of a Catholic church and school where routine activities are gradually overshadowed by unusual and troublesome events. Key images include:

Flynn delivering a sermon

In scene 1, the image of Father Flynn dressed in liturgical vestments and delivering a sermon immediately defines the world we have entered and establishes him as a man of authority to whom people listen. In scene 6, we see a similar image of Flynn sermonizing, but it is after his integrity has been questioned by Aloysius. The second image of Flynn at the pulpit reminds us of his position within the Church hierarchy and suggests how difficult it will be for Aloysius to unseat a man of his status. Both images are specified in stage directions—for example, "A priest . . . gives a sermon." The images are reinforced by Flynn's language, which is formal in tone, includes religious parables, and ends with the Catholic sign of the cross.

Aloysius wrapping a rose bush in burlap

In scene 4, the image of Aloysius wrapping a rose bush in burlap is a portrait of one who protects. We first witnessed this protective nature in scene 2 as she instructed James about being more aware of problems among her students. The wrapping of the rose bush translates that earlier character information into a concrete image specified in stage directions—"Sister Aloysius . . . is wrapping a pruned rosebush in burlap"—and suggested by her opening line, which also establishes that it is afternoon and that she is outside: "Good afternoon, Sister James. Mr. McGinn pruned this bush . . . but he neglected to protect it from the frost."

The image thus positions Aloysius not merely as one who protects, but as one who tackles trouble before it happens. When James questions whether there has been a frost, Aloysius explains, "When it comes, it's too late." This is the mindset with which she will launch her campaign against Flynn.

James shaking as she pours tea for Flynn

In scene 5, the growing tension of the meeting between Aloysius, Flynn, and James is manifest in the image of James trembling nervously as she pours a second cup of tea for Flynn. This moment is specified in a stage direction: "Sister James shakes as she pours tea." It occurs immediately after Aloysius brings up the name "Donald Muller" for the first time and begins to suggest that the real reason for the meeting is not Christmas music but child abuse. James's obvious anxiety is reinforced by Flynn's line: "Easy there, Sister, you don't spill."

■ TOPDOG/UNDERDOG

The visual images of *Topdog/Underdog* depict the claustrophobic world of a single rooming-house room inhabited by two brothers who live in poverty. During the story, we see many portraits of these men, both alone and with each other. Key images include:

Booth/Lincoln throwing the cards

Central to the play is the image of a man standing in front of a makeshift table—a cardboard board atop two mismatched milk crates—and shuffling three cards while reciting a hypnotic patter. This is the defining image of a three-card monte dealer and a demonstration of how the shell game works.

The first man we see in this role is Booth, who in scene 1 performs his task with difficulty. In scene 4, we see Lincoln perform the same task but with remarkable precision and skill. The latter image occurs just before dawn, with Lincoln in his underwear. Unbeknownst to him, Booth has just woken up and is watching him intently from his bed across the room. Both of these images are described in the stage directions and reinforced in dialogue by the dealer's patter, as in scene 1, when Booth begins, "Watch me close watch me close now: who-see-thuh-red-card-who-see-thuh-red-card?"

Booth pointing a gun at Lincoln in his Abraham Lincoln regalia

The opening scene introduces the memorable image of Lincoln, a black man in whiteface, dressed to look like Abraham Lincoln. He has just entered the room wearing an antique frock coat, top hat, and fake beard. Booth, who did not hear him enter, turns around, startled, while pulling a gun from his pants and pointing it at the unexpected presence behind him. This image is spelled out in the stage directions and suggests important information about both characters—for example, that Booth is armed and dangerous and that Lincoln is an Abraham Lincoln impersonator. The image also foreshadows the end of the play, when these same two men confront each other in a similar pose that will result in their mutual destruction.

The brothers styling and profiling

In scene 2, when the brothers try on the dressy outfits that Booth has stolen, we see them enjoying each other's company. Such images add complexity and warmth to the brothers' otherwise competitive relationship and fuel our desire to see them succeed. A stage direction spells out the image: "The men finish dressing. They style and profile." Their camaraderie is reinforced by dialogue. When Lincoln tells his brother that he looks sharp, Booth replies: "You look sharp too, man. You look like the real you."

■ THE CLEAN HOUSE

The visual images of *The Clean House* reveal a world of mundane and magical elements. The setting of the all-white living room is often dominant and adds a surreal quality to the action it frames. Key images include:

Matilde and Ana eating apples/Lane lying alone

In act two, scene 6, Matilda and Ana eat apples on a lofty balcony over-looking the sea while Lane lies below in her sterile living room. The image is created by stage directions that describe Matilde and Ana in sunglasses and sunhats with lots of apples, and Lane alone with a hot-water bottle. The dialogue between Matilde and Ana suggests that they have many apples of different colors. The directions then describe a tasting ritual: "They start taking bites of each apple / and if they don't think it's a perfect apple / they throw it into the sea. / The sea is Lane's living room. / Lane sees the apples fall into her living room. / She looks at them." The image thus adds magic to story events by merging two worlds while showing the contrast between them. The image also embodies the recurring theme of perfection versus imperfection.

Virginia making a mess/Ana listening to an aria

In act two, scene 9, after a screaming fight with Lane, Virginia retaliates by messing up Lane's living room. Most of this image is specified by stage directions: "Virginia dumps a plant on the ground and the dirt spills onto the floor. / She realizes with some surprise that she enjoys this. / Virginia makes an operatic mess in the living room." The grand nature of this mess is suggested by earlier stage directions that describe the simultaneous action of Ana sitting above on her seaside balcony and listening to opera music. The image thus depicts a key turning point in the story: Virginia freeing herself from her cleaning compulsion and her sister's oppressive reign.

Lane washing Ana's body

After Ana's death in act two, scene 13, Lane washes Ana's body while Matilde and Virginia pray. This image is created by stage directions that sug-gest the power and mood of the ritual: "Lane enters with a bowl of water. / She washes Ana's body. / Time slows down." The image is important because it depicts the fulfillment of Lane's dramatic journey from one who would not clean her own house to one who would clean the body of her husband's soul mate. The emotional impact of this transformation is heightened by the fact that it is shown visually.

ANALYZING YOUR STORY

Visual imagery on stage adds power to the story and reduces the need for words of explanation.

- Identify a few of the most interesting visual images that you have created at any time in the story through your stage directions and dialogue.
- Think about the rest of your script. Do you see opportunities to add new imagery that would increase the dramatic impact of a moment or reduce the need for dialogue?

FOR EACH IMAGE . . .

- As a focusing exercise, how would you title the image? (This is not a title that will appear in the script.)
- What story does the image tell?
- What is the most interesting visual detail?
- What does the image reveal about your character(s) physically, psychologically, or socially at this time in the story?
- How does the image move the story forward?
- Would the image be stronger if you added something or removed something from it? If so, what change would you make?

HOW IMAGES COMPARE

- How do your key visual images compare and contrast?
- If any images seem similar in content or tone, is there a dramatic reason for the repetition? If so, what does this repetition accomplish? If not, how can the images be changed to bring more visual variety to the story?
- What is the most important visual image in the story, and why?

World of the Characters

A dramatic story draws us into a world where we experience life through the characters. The writer creates this world by fleshing out its physical, psychological, and social dimensions and by understanding how the past can influence the present. To know the world of the characters is to know how it works on an everyday basis, what unprecedented events could arise here under certain circumstances, and how life could be affected as a result of these developments.

The physical realm of the story includes where and when the dramatic action occurs, as well as the objects, materials, and elements in this place at this time. This physical life grounds the characters in a certain reality and provides a concrete context for the action. Through physical life, we can literally see and hear the world that the characters inhabit and discover important truths about them and the dramatic journey under way.

Large or small, objects from this realm can become pivotal to the story, such as the automobile in Paula Vogel's *How I Learned to Drive* or the hat in Stephen Adly Guirgis's *The Motherfucker with the Hat*. Sound can also advance the story at a visceral level, such as the distant sound of an axe striking a tree at the end of Anton Chekhov's *The Cherry Orchard*.

Writers often make full use of sense experience to bring the world of the characters to life. In addition to the actual sights and sounds of this world, for example, the writer may use visual images, physical action, and dialogue to evoke vicarious smells, tastes, and physical sensations, such as the noxious smell of smoke from a smoldering urban wasteland in José Rivera's *Marisol*, the taste of coffee in Christopher Durang's *Vanya and Sonia and Masha and Spike*, or the sweltering heat of the Deep South in Tennessee Williams's *Cat on a Hot Tin Roof*.

■ **DOUBT: A PARABLE**
Setting: St. Nicholas church and school
The general setting is described as: "Saint Nicholas, a Catholic church and school in the Bronx, New York." Over nine scenes, this setting will break down into four playing areas:

- **Pulpit** of the church (scenes 1 and 6). No physical description is given.
- **Principal's office** of the school (scenes 2, 5, and 8). The setting is defined as a corner office. Except for references to a desk and a door, no further description is given.
- **School gym** (scene 3). No physical description is given.
- **Garden** between the convent and rectory (scenes 4, 7, and 9). The setting is described as "a bit of garden, a bench, brick walls."

A distinctive feature of this physical landscape is its isolation from the rest of the world. All of the dramatic action takes place in confined spaces. Even the outdoor garden has walls to separate it from the surrounding Bronx neighborhood. The effect is that of a self-contained arena subject to its own tenets and rules. The outside world is permitted into this arena only once, near the end of the play, when Mrs. Muller enters to meet with Aloysius.

Time: Fall, 1964

The story takes place in the fall of 1964. Shanley establishes the year in scene 1 when Father Flynn in his sermon makes a reference to the assassination of President Kennedy the year before. The first eight scenes span a period of about two weeks. The ninth scene occurs sometime later, after Flynn has had time to meet with the bishop and receive a transfer to St. Jerome parish. This gap in the sequence of events is also long enough for Sister James to visit her ailing brother in Maryland and return to the Bronx.

As the play begins, school has been in session for about two months, which means it is now early November. The time of year will provide Aloysius with an excuse to invite Flynn to her office for a meeting in scene 5. He believes he has come to discuss the school's Christmas pageant and will be caught off guard when he finds himself being interrogated about his relationship with an eighth-grade boy.

The timeframe also creates the opportunity for a power struggle between Aloysius and Flynn over what music will be performed in the pageant: "O Little Town of Bethlehem" versus "Frosty the Snowman." Underlying this debate are their opposing views of the Second Ecumenical Council, which urged religious members to become more integrated in the communities they serve.

Physical life examples

Clothing. As Sisters of Charity, Aloysius and James both wear black bonnets and floor-length black habits. This protective and confining attire is a manifestation of their vocation as well as a constant reminder of their submission to the Church. The liturgical vestments that Flynn wears in the pulpit in scene 1 tell us without words that he is a priest. In scene 6, when he returns to the pulpit after a confrontation with Aloysius, similar vestments remind us of his position within the hierarchy of the Church. It will not be easy for Aloysius to unseat him. In scene 3, he appears in a sweatshirt and pants as he addresses the basketball team. This sight of him in casual clothing lets us view him not just as a priest but also as a man with popular appeal and human foibles.

Character physicality. Aloysius's final words to Flynn in the play are "And cut your nails." This is a response to the fact that he wears his fingernails "a little long," an idiosyncrasy that may suggest to some the claws of a predator, but that also provides an innocent explanation for the incident Aloysius witnessed on the first day of school: a boy recoiling from Flynn's touch.

Objects and elements. From fountain pens and ledgers to ballpoint pens and notebooks, the physical life of the play is the everyday stuff of a school and church. Shanley occasionally uses this physical life to reveal his characters, as in scene 5, when the telephone on Aloysius's desk helps show that she is not afraid to tackle problems, whether she is calling the caretaker about a fallen tree limb or contacting a mother about possible abuse of her son.

When Flynn arrives for a meeting with Aloysius, the physical realm gives him an opportunity to establish the chain of command without uttering a word: he sits in her chair at her desk. It is a small power play but one that fuels her animosity toward him. The stage directions state, "She reacts, but says nothing." A bowl of sugar provides another opportunity to show the divide between them. When tea is served and Flynn displays his sweet tooth by asking for sugar, Aloysius rummages through her desk to find the sugar she stored there last year during Lent and then forgot. She reluctantly offers him one lump, but, to her dismay, he asks for three.

Natural environment. Scene 4 in the garden ends with the sound of a wind so cold that Aloysius must pull her shawl tightly around her. After James's disturbing report about Donald Muller and Flynn, this sudden change in weather suggests difficult times ahead. From a storytelling perspective, the wind also serves a practical purpose. It will cause a tree limb to fall overnight in the church courtyard. This, in turn, will cause James to be late for the meeting in scene 5, creating the first opportunity for Aloysius and Flynn to be alone.

Scene 7 begins and ends with the caw of a crow, an ominous sound suggesting danger. The first caw announces the arrival of Flynn, who comes upon James alone in the garden. The final caw seems to comment on Flynn's success in convincing her that he is innocent of wrongdoing. Flynn's response to the predatory bird: "Oh, be quiet."

■ **TOPDOG/UNDERDOG**
Setting: A rooming-house room
All of the dramatic action takes place in a single room in a rooming house somewhere in America. This is Booth's "humble abode," but Lincoln also has been living here since his wife, Cookie, threw him out. Although the location is not identified, we know from Lincoln that he lives in "the big city" and that, at the arcade where he works, one can smell the ocean. Such clues suggest that they live in a large urban area on the east or west coast. The lack of

specific identifying information adds to the sense of limbo that dominates the setting, described thus: "A seedily furnished rooming house room. A bed, a reclining chair, a small wooden chair, some other stuff but not much else."

As the play unfolds, we learn that the room has neither running water nor a private bathroom. There is a telephone, but it has been turned off due to nonpayment of the bill. Booth sleeps at night in the bed, while Lincoln sleeps in the recliner. For privacy, they can set up a folding screen to separate the two sleeping areas. At one point, Lincoln tells Booth, "You're living in thuh Third World, fool." It is this very world Booth wishes to rise above.

The rest of the rooming house remains unknown. The brothers never discuss other roomers and the only sign of a landlord is the fact that the rent is due on Fridays. The neighborhood is likewise not discussed, except for mentions of Lucky's, the local bar that Lincoln frequents, and the corner payphone that they use to make calls. Other notable offstage locations include the arcade where Lincoln works, the department store where Booth steals, and the place where Grace lives.

Time: Winter, circa 2000

The timeframe is identified only as "Now." If the play takes place around the time it was written, the year is about 2000. The wearing of coats and references to cold weather suggest that it is winter. The action spans a period of eight days, beginning and ending on a Thursday evening.

Physical life examples

Clothing. Featuring a frock coat, stovepipe hat, fake beard, and white pancake makeup, Lincoln's work outfit brings his job as an Abraham Lincoln impersonator onstage so we can see how he looks when arcade customers shoot at him with toy guns. The costume also suggests how little attention Lincoln pays to his appearance. He thinks nothing of wearing his costume home on the bus, even though it makes him look ridiculous. Booth, on the other hand, is obsessed with how he looks, especially when attempting to court his ex-girlfriend Grace. This is why he uses his shoplifting skills to acquire expensive clothing for himself and his brother. The nice new suits provide an opportunity for the brothers to bond as they "style and profile."

Character physicality. The complex personal dynamics between Lincoln and Booth trace back, in part, to their age difference combined with the physical fact that they are brothers. Lincoln, born first, has always been "big brother Link," a distinction that has put Booth in the position of being the "little brother" and fueled his desire to outshine Lincoln in every way. At the same time, their family connection is what keeps them together under the same roof in spite of their intense rivalry.

Dexterity with playing cards is another physical trait that contributes to the brothers' push-and-pull relationship. Lincoln has developed remarkable skill in manipulating cards and once used it to make big money on the street. Booth's lack of such dexterity has left him jealous of his brother, yet also dependent on him to launch a card hustling scheme. It is Lincoln's refusal to ply his trade for his brother's benefit that triggers the central conflict of the play.

Objects and elements. The gun that Booth keeps in his pants, the plastic cup that Lincoln uses to pee during the night, and other physical objects here reflect the brothers' criminal and impoverished lives. This physical realm is dominated by a three-card monte setup: three playing cards and a cardboard playing board atop two mismatched milk crates, one stacked on top of the other. The setup is a focal point of the dramatic action since it represents Booth's hope for a lucrative future and Lincoln's rejection of his shady past.

Other important objects include the girlie magazines under Booth's bed, which embody his delusional approach to women; $500 in a tied-up nylon stocking, which represents his final memory of his fleeing mother; and the family photo album, which brings the past into the present.

Much of the physical life consists of what the brothers bring to the room as the play unfolds, such as Chinese takeout food, wads of cash, whiskey, and a variety of stolen goods. For Lincoln and Booth, almost anything can spark sibling rivalry. They compete over such items as the takeout food (who gets the "skrimps"), a box of condoms (who needs the largest size), and a pair of neckties (who gets the better color). Their physical surroundings thus trigger and reflect their constant struggle for topdog position.

Natural environment. The only reference to the natural environment is to the cold weather outside, which adds to the harsh feel of the world beyond the brothers' room.

■ **THE CLEAN HOUSE**
Setting: A metaphysical Connecticut
The general setting is described as: "A metaphysical Connecticut. Or, a house that is not far from the city and not far from the sea." With Lane's living room at its center, the physical landscape is a fluid realm that includes both mundane and magical elements and enables settings occasionally to merge, as when snow falls in Lane's living room while Charles traipses through Alaska. It is a landscape that thus reflects the play's magic realism. Over twenty-eight scenes, the settings include:

- **Lane's living room.** The main setting is described as "A white living room. White couch, white vase, white lamp, white rug." This epitome of spotlessness suggests the manufacturing term "white room" or "clean room," an area kept virtually free of dust and other contaminants so that certain products, such as precision parts, can be assembled or repaired. The transformation of this clean room into a dirty room becomes a physical metaphor for the play's theme, as the characters learn to accept life's messes.
- **Ana's balcony.** In act two, a balcony appears above the living room. It is described as "a small perch, overlooking the sea" and has French doors that lead to the unseen room where Ana lives. The height and airiness of this setting provide a clear contrast to Lane's meticulously controlled living room below.
- **Other places.** Additional settings are minimally suggested. In the opening of act two, for example, Lane's living room becomes a hospital so we can witness how Charles and Ana fall in love. Some scenes take place in the realm of imagination, mostly Matilde's, as in act one, scene 9, when she pictures her parents at a Brazilian café laughing hysterically.

Time: Fall, present day

The script does not state when the story takes place. Character attitudes, dialogue, and medical references suggest a contemporary timeframe. Story events, such as apple picking and swimming in the sea, suggest that it is early fall.

Most scenes span a period of a few weeks. The latter half of act two suggests longer lapses of time between scenes to allow for the return of Ana's cancer and for Charles's trip to Alaska. Befitting the play's magic realism, time is skewed to fit the story. In act two, scene 12, for example, Charles notifies Ana by telegram that he has found a yew tree in Alaska for her, but that he can't take it aboard a commercial plane. Time speeds up offstage so he can learn to fly a private plane and return with the tree by the end of the next scene.

Physical life examples

Clothing. Lane wears white to match her living room and her relentless desire for cleanliness. Matilde wears black because she is in mourning for her parents. These wardrobe choices not only embody who these women are but also create a physical contrast between them. Other costume choices help tell the story as well and eliminate the need for words. In act two, scene 6, the sunglasses and sunhats worn by Matilde and Ana instantly create the atmosphere of a sunny day. A few scenes later, Charles begins to appear in a parka, apparel that reminds us that he is in Alaska, far removed physically and emotionally from the women in the living room.

Character physicality. Many story events center on the physical fact that Ana has cancer. It explains how Charles and Ana meet and later provides a catalyst for the other three women to band together. After Ana's surgery, references to her scarred torso have a lyrical quality and thus do not detract from her beauty and charisma. Another key physical fact in the world of this particular story is that one can literally die laughing. This phenomenon is established early in the play when we learn how Matilde's mother died, and leads ultimately to Ana's death from laughter after Matilde whispers a "cosmic joke" in her ear.

Lane's wounded wrist has two dramatic functions: it implies that she attempted suicide after learning about Charles's infidelity, and it demonstrates her need to cover up life's messes. Rather than admit the truth, she twice claims to have cut herself accidentally with a can opener.

Objects and elements. As one might expect in a play about cleaning that features two doctors, the physical life includes cleaning supplies and medical items. Less predictable is the underwear that Virginia finds as she folds her sister's household laundry. Virginia's reaction to Charles's underwear enables us to discover her secret crush on him: "It's a little weird to be touching my brother-in-law's underwear. / He's a very handsome man." The same laundry also yields women's underwear that is not Lane's—"Too sexy"—and thus foreshadows the revelation of Charles's infidelity.

In act one, scene 13, the objects on the coffee table gain dramatic potency when Virginia rearranges them to ease her stress. Besides showing her cleaning compulsion, the rearrangement advances the plot when Lane sees it and realizes that Matilde is not the one who has been cleaning her house. "These objects on the coffee table," she tells Virginia, "that is how you arrange objects." Other key physical items include the apples that manifest Matilde's and Ana's enjoyment of life; the houseplant that Virginia uses to make an operatic mess in Lane's living room; the chocolate ice cream that the four women savor as they find a common bond; and the enormous yew tree that looms in the living room as a physical reminder of Charles's folly.

Natural environment. Key elements of the environment include the dust that in act one, scene 7, helps create a telling portrait of Virginia. As soon as Matilde leaves the room, Virginia runs her finger over the tabletops to test for dust. Other environmental elements include the snow and wind in Lane's living room as Charles treks alone through Alaska.

ANALYZING YOUR STORY

Explore the physical realm of your story.

WHERE THE STORY HAPPENS

- What is the general setting for your story and how would you describe it?
- What parts of the general setting do we see onstage? Identify the specific scene settings and describe each with a focus on what matters most.
- What is the most interesting physical detail of each scene setting?
- Are there any specific settings that could be eliminated or combined? If so, which scenes would be affected and how would this change the story?
- Are there any new settings that need to be added? If so, what settings would they be, which scenes would be affected, and how would this change the story?
- Listen to the general setting. Loud or quiet, familiar or unfamiliar, what sounds do you hear? What opportunities have you missed, if any, to use sound to tell the story?
- Explore the setting through your other senses. What do you smell? Taste? Feel? What opportunities have you missed, if any, to ground the story in sensory experience?
- What objects or physical elements are most pivotal to the dramatic action?
- Have you missed any opportunities to use objects or elements to show, not tell, the story?
- What information does the physical realm suggest about the characters—for example, what does it reveal about their interests, values, and lifestyles?

WHEN THE STORY HAPPENS

- What is the general timeframe for your story? Identify the year, season of the year, and any other important details about when the dramatic action takes place.
- In what specific ways does this general timeframe affect the dramatic action? How would the story be different if it took place earlier or later in the characters' lives?
- From the beginning of the play to the end, how much time elapses?
- Would the play be better served by a time period that is either more compressed or more expanded? If so, how would this change the story?

Drama is an emotional experience for the characters, the actors, and ultimately the audience. The world of a dramatic story thus has an emotional environment that both reflects and influences life here.

While individual characters may experience a gamut of feelings as the dramatic journey unfolds, there is often a pervading emotion that sets a tone for the story and affects how characters behave. For example, the mood or atmosphere may be friendly (*Our Town* by Thornton Wilder), rebellious (*The Heidi Chronicles* by Wendy Wasserstein), or ominous (*Shining City* by Conor McPherson). Whether positive or negative, this emotional environment will later be translated into physical terms by the set, lighting, sound, and costume designers, but it begins in the script with the character and story choices made by the writer.

■ **DOUBT: A PARABLE**
Pervading emotion: Fear
Dominated by characters dressed in black and taking place mostly in a cheerless principal's office, the world of *Doubt* has an aura of austerity. Like the wind that blows through the bare branches of the garden, the mood here is cold and threatening, especially when concerns about penmanship and classroom performance are replaced by suspicions of child abuse. This is a world where music, art, and dance are dismissed and where danger can lurk anywhere, even in a church rectory. Underlying this mood is a pervasive sense of fear that fuels story events.

In scene 5, Sister James tells Sister Aloysius that the students of St. Nicholas are uniformly terrified of her, and Aloysius replies, "Yes. That's how it works." Fear is the fuel with which she runs her school and keeps it performing to her standards. This approach helps explain why James, in a brief outburst of courage and honesty, compares St. Nicholas to a prison.

Aloysius's philosophy of intimidation is introduced in scene 2, when she coaches James on how to be a moral guardian of her students: "Liars should be frightened to lie to you." This guiding principle will drive her attempts later to force Father Flynn to confess wrongdoing. While she never elicits that confession, she does scare him into courses of action that he had not anticipated. For example, Flynn ends his friendship with Donald Muller "for fear of it being misunderstood." He also retreats from his threats to have Aloysius sent away, "for fear of doing further harm" to the school. In the end, he agrees to request a transfer from St. Nicholas because he fears either that Aloysius has acquired incriminating evidence against him or that her relentless campaign will damage his reputation beyond repair.

It is fear of danger that colors Aloysius's perception of Flynn from the start and leads to her increasing concerns about him. At one point, she describes the priest as a wolf in search of little stray sheep. It is with this wolf in mind that she urges James, in scene 2, to be on the lookout for signs of trouble among the students.

Fear haunts James, who under the pressure of her superior's reign of intimidation begins to suffer a nervous breakdown that rattles her love of teaching, upsets her sleep, and finally forces her to take a temporary leave of absence under the pretext of caring for an ailing brother. Her distress is expressed in the nightmare image she shares with Flynn in scene 7: "I looked in a mirror and there was a darkness where my face should be."

■ TOPDOG/UNDERDOG
Pervading emotion: Loneliness

Topdog/Underdog brings us into a single room populated by two brothers who have lost everyone in their lives except each other. They have no parents, wives, children, lovers, or close friends, and their own relationship is so tenuous that at one point Lincoln asks, "You think we're really brothers?" The poverty of their emotional lives is reflected in the starkness of their furnished room and addressed by Lincoln's song in scene 1, in which he laments the loss of his parents and wife. "My luck was bad but now it turned to worse," he sings. "Don't call me up no doctor, just call me up a hearse."

Loneliness has been a hallmark of the brothers' lives since their teenage years, when their parents abandoned them and the boys were left to fend for themselves. With no healthy model of a family to guide them, they have failed not only to establish families of their own but also to build careers that might foster social relationships. Lincoln works in an arcade where he sits alone under a lightbulb being shot at by "miscellaneous strangers." Booth works alone as a thief.

Lincoln sometimes makes references to the crowd at a local bar, Lucky's, where he enjoys buying drinks for the house, but there is no sense of genuine friendship in the tales of his exploits there. Other than his ex-wife, Cookie, his closest relationship was with Lonny, one of his three-card monte crew, who years ago was murdered. Lincoln's history as a card hustler may have contributed to his feelings of isolation by forcing him to disconnect emotionally from his prey, such as the father who fell for Lincoln's scam, lost the money he had been saving for his kid's bike, and ended up in tears as Lincoln ran off with his cash.

Booth makes no reference to friends, implying that he has no one else in his life other than Grace, his ex-girlfriend. His longing for human warmth is perhaps most apparent in the care with which he has prepared the room for her arrival in scene 5 and in the rage he experiences later when he realizes she will never show up. As with Lincoln, Booth's career as a thief may have contributed to his isolation by keeping him emotionally detached from his victims.

While loneliness is a pervasive emotion in the brothers' world, they embody it in different ways. Lincoln's isolation has led to pessimism, melancholy, and selfishness, while Booth's has become a springboard for optimism, rage, and delusions of grandeur. For both brothers, the inability to maintain romantic relationships has resulted in sexual dysfunction. According to Booth, Lincoln's marriage failed due to his impotence. According to Lincoln, Booth's sex life consists only of fantasies fueled by his secret stash of girlie magazines.

Most importantly, though they rely on each other for companionship and survival, the brothers find it difficult to communicate in an honest way. In their constant vying for topdog position, they tell lies, deny their true feelings, and retreat into themselves when trouble gets the best of them. As a result, their most meaningful connection to each other lies not in the events of their lives today but in shared memories of the past that they cannot overcome.

■ THE CLEAN HOUSE
Pervading emotion: Unhappiness

While *The Clean House* is a comedy full of humor and wit, the world of the story is permeated by a gloom that hangs over the white landscape like a storm cloud and affects the characters who come and go here.

Lane's first words in the play are an expression of unhappiness: a complaint about her new cleaning woman. For Lane, revealing true feelings is so difficult that she nearly bursts into tears later as she attempts to give Matilde cleaning instructions. Most of the time, Lane successfully keeps her emotions in check while trying methodically to control the world around her.

This approach has produced many favorable results, such as a thriving medical career and a handsome husband, but the other details of her life tell a different story. She has trouble developing a personal relationship with the maid who lives in her house, rarely sees her husband and doesn't realize he loves someone else, and hasn't socialized with her sister or brother-in-law for several months, even though they live nearby. The discovery of Charles's infidelity is what exposes the truth about Lane's inner turmoil and results in an aborted suicide attempt, which leaves her with a bandaged wrist that she won't discuss.

Matilde's unhappiness is more overt from the beginning. Hired by Lane as a live-in maid, she stops working because of how the job makes her feel. "I don't like to clean houses," she tells Virginia in act one, scene 7. "I think it makes me sad." Matilde's problem stems from the realization that her job prevents her from fulfilling her desire to think up jokes and become a comedian in New York. This ambition ties back to her parents, who were the funniest people in Brazil until their deaths the previous year. Matilde's mourning for them fuels the melancholy she feels when, instead of thinking up jokes, she has to clean someone else's house.

Virginia attempts to present a facade of cheerfulness to the world, but she is also defined by a nagging sorrow that she longs to escape. Trapped in an unexciting marriage with no career or children, she believes that her life has been in a downward spiral for the past three decades and uses housecleaning to distract herself from dwelling on her failures. In her first monologue to the audience, she says, "If there were no dust to clean then there would be so much leisure time and so much thinking time and I would have to do something besides thinking and that thing might be to slit my wrists." She passes this off as a joke—"just kidding"—but the sentiment explains why, when she wakes up each morning, she wishes she could sleep through the day and avoid facing the truth of whom she has become.

For most of the play, Charles lives in a world shaped by his passionate love for Ana. Except for concerns about her medical condition and fights about her treatment options, he does not succumb to unhappiness until the final scene, when he returns from Alaska and realizes that he has missed his opportunity to see Ana in her final days.

Of all the characters in the play, Ana is the one who most consistently transcends gloom and lives life fully and happily on her own terms. In spite of her cancer diagnosis, mastectomy, and deteriorating health, she stands bravely against adversity like her twelve-year-old fighting fish that refuses to die.

ANALYZING YOUR STORY

Explore the emotional environment of your story.

MOOD

- What is the general mood in the world of the story when the play begins?
- What physical factors contribute to this mood? Psychological factors? Social factors?
- Who among the onstage or offstage characters is most responsible for the emotional environment when the story begins?
- What does the emotional environment suggest about the lives of your characters?
- What single feeling dominates this emotional environment?
- What character values, beliefs, and lifestyles are suggested by the pervading emotion?
- How does the pervading emotion affect each character?
- As the story unfolds, what is the biggest change that takes place in the emotional environment? When does this change happen and what triggers it?

SOCIAL CONTEXT

In any dramatic story, characters live within a social context that influences who they are, what they can and cannot do, and how they get along with others individually and in groups. This set of circumstances often explains not only why a story unfolds the way it does but also why it happens at all.

The broad social context may be related to a particular area of the world, as in Martin McDonagh's *The Cripple of Inishmaan*, set on a remote Aran island off the coast of Ireland, or a particular time in history, as in August Wilson's *Joe Turner's Come and Gone*, set in the 1910s, when freed slaves from the South began migrating to northern cities.

The immediate social context may be a family (*4000 Miles* by Amy Herzog), school (*The History Boys* by Alan Bennett), workplace (*The Flick* by Annie Baker), or other smaller community nestled within a broader one. Its makeup may be highly structured (*A Few Good Men* by Aaron Sorkin) or anarchistic (*Beirut* by Alan Bowne). Its basic nature may be nurturing (*A Thousand Clowns* by Herb Gardner) or oppressive (*My Sister in This House* by Wendy Kesselman).

Key elements of any social milieu are the values and beliefs that prevail among the characters and motivate behavior. In David Mamet's *Glengarry Glen Ross*, for example, most characters are driven by greed and a belief that material wealth is the true measure of one's worth. In Rebecca Gillman's *Luna Gale*, it is a child's welfare that drives story events.

■ DOUBT: A PARABLE
Broad social context

The year 1964 is a time of social unrest and change, when power in society has begun to shift in new directions. It is the year after a major civil rights march on Washington led by Dr. Martin Luther King Jr., the death of the popular Pope John XXIII, and the assassination of the first Catholic president, John F. Kennedy. Paul VI is now pope, and Lyndon B. Johnson is president. Meanwhile the Vietnam war is about to erupt. The Civil Rights Act has been passed, as has the Equal Pay Act. People are discussing black power, women's liberation, and gay liberation.

This environment of change contributes to the story of *Doubt* in different ways. It has resulted in the enrollment of St. Nicholas's first black student, Donald Muller, and it will lead his mother, during her meeting with Sister Aloysius, to speak frankly and without judgment about her son's sexual orientation. In addition, the empowerment of women may to some degree fuel Aloysius's decision to buck the patriarchal system of the Church and go after a man who has the power to have her removed from her position.

Immediate social context

St. Nicholas is a Catholic parish in the Bronx that serves two types of families: Irish and Italian. These populations are represented by a statue of St. Patrick on one side of the church altar and a statue of St. Anthony on the other. The demographics contribute to the social isolation that Donald Muller feels as the school's first and only black student. Because he is without friends, Aloysius believes he is a prime target for a predator. "The little sheep lagging behind," she tells Sister James, "is the one the wolf goes for." In effect, the social context contributes directly to her suspicions about Father Flynn when she learns that he has taken a special interest in the boy. At the same time, Donald's isolation may provide an innocent explanation for why Flynn spends extra time with him.

As with other parishes, St. Nicholas has been shaken up by the Second Vatican Council, or Vatican II, which asked the religious community to act less like emissaries from Rome and more like everyday members of the communities they serve. Some, like Flynn, have embraced this call to action. Others, like Aloysius, have resisted it and become more entrenched in traditional beliefs and practices that have served the Church for centuries. These dynamics contribute to the conflict between Flynn and Aloysius and their inability to find common ground, a difference that is heightened by the generation gap between them. Aloysius's steely resistance to change also helps explain her unwillingness to permit doubt in her belief system once she has reached a conclusion.

Prevailing values and beliefs

Education of children. For Sister Aloysius, education is a duty that demands vigilance, self-sacrifice, and hard work. This belief leads her to rule the school with an iron fist, to be on the lookout for trouble, and to issue such proclamations as "Good teachers are never content" and "Satisfaction is a vice." She is a school principal who views her domain with suspicion and disapproval. Her implied conclusion is that the world is full of lazy, restless children who need to be disciplined and evildoers who need to be punished. This view explains such statements as "Don't be charmed by cleverness" and "Innocence is a form of laziness."

Integral to Aloysius's view of her job is a strict sense of duty that embodies the letter of the law rather than its spirit. Her calling, she believes, is to provide "educational, spiritual, and human guidance" to her students, and she will do everything in her power to do so. This duty does, however, have a limit, extending only to students while they attend her school. Once they graduate, they are no longer her concern, as in the case of eighth grader William London, who, she believes, will never graduate high school. "But that's beyond our jurisdiction," she tells James. "We simply have to get him through, out the door, and then he's somebody else's problem."

While the other characters also revere education, they have significantly different views of it, and this leads to much of the conflict in the story. Flynn sees education as an opportunity to play a meaningful role in the lives of students. His humanistic approach is summed up in his belief: "Children need warmth, kindness, and understanding!" This view puts him at odds with Aloysius and enables him ultimately to form an alliance with James, who is of like mind. For her, education is a source of joy, especially when she's teaching history. For the more practical-minded Mrs. Muller, education is the path to a better future for her son.

Service to God. As members of a religious community, Aloysius, Flynn, and James all espouse service to God through the Catholic Church, though again they have different views of what this involves. For Aloysius, it means giving up worldly pleasures, such as sugar, the arts, and married life. "When one takes the habit," she explains, "one must close the door on secular things." Service to God for her also entails a selfless commitment to combatting evil, regardless of the cost. "When you take a step to address wrongdoing, you are taking a step away from God, but in his service," she says. This belief explains her campaign against Flynn and her decision to use deception in order to scare him out of the parish.

Flynn's view of his role as a priest is influenced by the Second Ecumenical Council, which asked the religious community to take a more inclusive approach to modern life. He distinguishes himself from Aloysius when he reminds James of the importance of love in administering their vocations: "Have you forgotten that was the message of the Savior to us all. Love. Not suspicion, disapproval, and judgment. Love of people." Flynn's belief may explain why he pays special attention to Donald Muller, the only black student in the school and a boy without friends.

For James, service to God translates into obeying rules and respecting her superiors. This faithfulness to the system leads her to report her suspicion about Flynn to her superior and then to suffer an emotional breakdown when she finds herself questioning what she has done.

■ TOPDOG/UNDERDOG
Broad social context

Assuming that the play takes place circa 2000, it is nearly 140 years since the Emancipation Proclamation abolished slavery and more than three decades since the civil rights movement legally ended segregation. African-Americans account for 12 percent of the US population and have made significant progress in most sectors of society, yet blacks still face many socioeconomic disparities as they reach for the American dream in the capitalist society of the new millennium.

Nearly a quarter of all blacks still live below the poverty level, compared to one-tenth of all whites. One in four black children who enter high school do not graduate, a dropout rate double that for white children. Adult blacks are twice as likely to be unemployed as their white counterparts, and those who are employed, on average, earn less. Due to a variety of factors, including a criminal justice system often weighted against them, black males are far more likely to be arrested: one in four will likely be incarcerated during their lifetime. Violence is a key contributor to the death rate among African-Americans, with homicide the leading cause of death among black males, usually from gunshot wounds.[1]

Such socioeconomic inequalities are embedded in the characters of *Topdog/Underdog* and woven throughout the story, but only occasionally do they surface as topics in the play's dialogue. In other words, the characters live these realities rather than discuss them. One exception is when Booth, in scene 2, tries to get Lincoln to admit that racial prejudice was the reason the arcade offered him less pay than his predecessor for doing the same job: "Go on, say it. 'White.' Theyd pay you less than theyd pay a white guy."

It is within this broad social context that the brothers' parents once attempted to achieve the American dream: a stable family, a house of their own, and work that would enable them to be upwardly mobile and enjoy a comfortable standard of living. It is the social context itself that raises the question of how attainable that dream really was for them and how attainable it will be now for their sons, who struggle to pursue new dreams they believe will make them happy.

---

1. "United States of America Overview/Country Data/Minorities/African Americans," in *World Directory of Minorities and Indigenous Peoples* (London: Minority Rights Group International, 2009).

Immediate social context

The immediate social context for the play is the family of Lincoln and Booth. This is a family once run by parents with good intentions. The mother put food on the table every night, kept her sons in clean clothes, and had a knack for sewing on buttons. The father prided himself on his wardrobe, kept his shoes shined, and drove off in his car each day to work. Though the professions of the parents are not revealed, we know that they once held steady jobs and earned enough money to buy a house. It had only two rooms, a cement backyard, and a front yard full of trash, but this was for them the beginning of a dream come true: their own property, where they could be "just regular people living in a house."

According to Lincoln, however, both parents were haunted by something they liked more than each other and more than their sons. For years, they resisted this longing, but eventually both mother and father surrendered to it. They stopped sleeping with each other, stopped talking to each other, took on other sexual partners, and fled separately for parts unknown, leaving their teenage boys to fend for themselves.

As the play begins, it has been more than twenty years since the parents disappeared. The brothers now live as social outcasts in a furnished room, where mother's homemade meals have been replaced by takeout food in Styrofoam containers. The parents' presence is nonetheless still felt in the brothers' everyday lives and is physically manifest in a family photo album. George C. Wolfe, who directed the play's world premiere, has talked about the pervasive effect on the brothers of becoming orphans at a young age: "One deals with one's history, one's personal history, and one's cultural history, every single time one walks out the door. The ramifications of the scars that these two brothers have because they were abandoned live with them moment to moment to moment."[2]

Prevailing values and beliefs

Family ties. In spite of being abandoned by their parents, or perhaps because of it, Lincoln and Booth both hold family in high esteem. Memories of their parents intrude throughout the play and demonstrate the power of the past to affect the present. In scene 5, for example, when Booth finds himself in a heartbroken rage after being stood up by his ex-girlfriend Grace, it is

---

2. *The Topdog Diaries*, a documentary film produced and directed by Oren Jacoby (Storyville Films, 2002).

tales from childhood—the rare "good times"—that Lincoln uses to distract him from his pain.

One of the most potent examples of reverence for family is Booth's treatment of the inheritance he received from his mother on the day she left: $500 in cash tied up in the toe of a stocking. Though decades have passed, the stocking has never been opened and is hidden in Booth's room like a precious jewel. It is Lincoln's threat to cut open this stocking that triggers Booth's impulsive decision to shoot him at the end of the play.

Prior to that tragic end, Booth and Lincoln each value their brotherly connection more than either would care to admit. Each is the only family the other has left and the only source of support. Lincoln needs Booth for companionship in a world that has rejected him. Booth needs Lincoln for rent money and business assistance that he hopes will make him rich.

In their competing quests to be topdog, the brothers often try to deny the importance of their relationship but never succeed at doing so for long. In scene 1, for example, when Lincoln rejects his business proposition, Booth evicts him and Lincoln readily agrees to go. Despite this decisive termination of their living arrangement, however, neither brother broaches the subject again and life goes on as usual, with each relying on the other for continued support.

Social status. As the title implies, much of *Topdog/Underdog* centers on the social position one can achieve in life. For Lincoln, a reformed card hustler, the road to topdog status in society is an honest job. This value is so important that he is even willing to be a human target in a shooting gallery. That Lincoln has not retreated to a high moral ground, however, is first made evident in scene 1, when he brags about conning a rich kid out of twenty bucks for an Abraham Lincoln autograph. Perhaps the greatest motivation for Lincoln's decision to go straight is concern for his personal safety after his stickman was murdered years ago.

For Booth, a topdog is measured by the amount of money he has and by the style with which he presents himself to the world, and especially to women. His dream of accumulating wealth is what inspires his idea to set up a three-card monte operation with his brother's help. His concern about style is manageable on his own thanks to his thieving skills, which enable him in scene 2 to return home with expensive clothing and in scene 5 to redo his room to impress his expected ex-girlfriend Grace. Like his father, who was also preoccupied with his appearance, Booth is obsessed with what others think about him and wants to look successful even when he's not.

■ THE CLEAN HOUSE
Broad social context

Set in contemporary American society and using housecleaning as a metaphor for life, *The Clean House* is deeply rooted in issues of gender. Housecleaning, for example, is a task traditionally associated with women. It has sometimes been called "invisible labor" because it produces not a product that can be sold for profit but a temporary absence of dust and dirt. When viewed in this light, housework tends to have low social and economic value, especially when it is performed by housewives for their families. In 1970, such attitudes prompted feminist Germaine Greer to describe women as "the most oppressed class of life-contracted unpaid worker, for whom slaves is not too melodramatic a description."[3]

Gender roles have changed as women have increasingly entered the labor market, yet housework still remains primarily the domain of women. According to the Bureau of Labor Statistics, 49 percent of women do some type of daily housework, such as cleaning and laundry, compared to 19 percent of men. When men do participate in household chores, they are more likely to do gendered tasks, such as yard work and repairs, rather than interior cleaning.[4]

When housekeeping is hired out to domestic workers, gender, ethnicity, and class combine to define a labor force that is virtually hidden from public view and unprotected by the Fair Labor Standards Act, which governs pay practices and other work conditions. In the United States, the members of this invisible labor force are overwhelmingly women (88 percent) and primarily women of color (66 percent).[5] In keeping with the traditional devaluation of women's labor in the home, professional housekeepers tend to earn low incomes with no benefits such as paid sick days or health insurance. Most live-in housekeepers (67 percent) earn less than their state's minimum wage.[6]

These general social circumstances help explain why each of the women

3. Germaine Greer, *The Female Eunuch* (London: MacGibbon and Key, 1970).

4. "American Time Use Survey—2013 Results," Bureau of Labor Statistics, US Department of Labor, Washington, DC, June 18, 2014.

5. "Labor Force Statistics from the Current Population Survey," Bureau of Labor Statistics, US Department of Labor, Washington, DC, February 26, 2014.

6. Linda Burnham and Nik Theodore, "Home Economics: The Invisible and Unregulated World of Domestic Work," National Domestic Workers Alliance, 2012, http://www.domesticworkers.org/homeeconomics/.

in the play has such strong feelings about cleaning. By putting a dramatic focus on cleaning, the playwright has paved the way for a story about women and their relationships across ethnic and class lines.

Immediate social context

The immediate social context for the play is a two-class household: the upper middle class of Lane and Charles, the married doctors who own the house, and the lower class of Matilde, the Brazilian immigrant housekeeper who was hired to keep the house clean.

As successful doctors at an important hospital, Lane and Charles earn enough to live in the kind of house they want and to hire help to free them from laborious household chores. By giving the characters the social status of doctors, Ruhl creates a stark contrast to Matilde's status as a cleaning woman and sets up a story in which class difference will matter. The professions of Lane and Charles also put them in a position to deal with cancer patients and thus bring Ana into their lives. Lane's need to forgive Ana near the end of the play is specifically triggered by the fact that Lane is a doctor who can provide medical help for her.

The boundary between the classes is clearly shown in act one, scene 5, when Lane attempts to order Matilde back to work after she has grown sad and stopped cleaning. Lane makes it clear that she is not interested in Matilde's personal problems and that their relationship is to be nothing more than employer and employee: "I just want my house—cleaned."

When Matilde first stops cleaning, it is Lane, not Charles, who must pick up the slack and clean the house herself. Charles is the only male character in the play and the only one with no perspective on housecleaning. He simply knows that he likes things to be clean, and the women in his life accommodate him. When Lane discovers that Charles has been unfaithful, she blames it on her poor domestic skills: "He didn't want a doctor," she tells Virginia in act one, scene 13. "He wanted a housewife."

Prior to its breakup, the marriage of Lane and Charles is a distant one. Because of their work schedules they rarely see each other, and they have shrugged off any expectation of changing that. Their emotional separation is underscored by the fact that they do not appear together physically in the same room for the first 18 scenes of the play.

As the character with the lowest rank and pay, Matilde has the fewest resources to live the life she wants. She left Brazil to become a comedian in New York but now finds herself doing housework in Connecticut because it's the only work she can get. Since her parents are dead and she has no friends in this new country, Matilde lives a life of solitude, retreating often into her imagination to conjure up idyllic memories of her parents or to think up jokes.

Virginia enters Matilde's world from the middle class. Unlike Lane, however, Virginia has no career and no delusion that her life is working the way she wants. A compulsive cleaner with nothing better to do, she needs desperately to reinvent herself, and this inspires her to reach across the class boundary to become friends with her sister's maid.

Prevailing values and beliefs

Perfection. The characters in the play all value perfection and believe it will make them happy. As a result, they spend most of their time trying to achieve it, whether it comes in the form of an immaculate house, a model family, a perfect joke, or a soul mate. This hunger for the ideal is what leads Lane to hire Matilde as a live-in housekeeper. It is also what inspires Matilde to abandon the duties of her job so that she can have more time to think up jokes. For Virginia, perfection translates into an absence of dirt that will enable her to believe that she is making progress in her life. For Charles and Ana, it is the justification for a love affair that will ruin a marriage.

Desire for perfection is thus a motivating factor behind each character's actions, a vital source of conflict in the play since it often pits one character against another, and a key element of the plot and theme. It is by overcoming their yearnings for perfection and accepting life's messes that the characters begin to make true progress in their lives.

Love. The characters all value love and believe it will make them happy. Ranging from true romance to familial affection to friendship, love often explains why the story unfolds as it does.

Lane loves Charles even after he reveals that Ana is his soul mate. This spousal love prevents her from accepting that her marriage is over. Matilde loves her mother and father, who died last year in Brazil. This filial love draws her inward to keep them alive in her mind and propels her to emulate them by thinking up jokes. Virginia loves Lane, even though their relationship is competitive. This sisterly affection motivates her recurring efforts to help Lane and become more involved in her life. Charles and Ana love each other as soul mates, and this creates unprecedented turmoil in Lane's life, shifting the focus of the dramatic action from physical cleaning in act one to spiritual cleaning in act two.

Though powerful and revered, love is complicated by the expectations it inspires. "People imagine that people who are in love are happy," Matilde cautions Lane in act one, scene 14. "That is why, in your country, people kill themselves on Valentine's day." Love thus ties directly to the play's theme of relinquishing impossible standards and embracing life's messes. "Love isn't clean like that," explains Matilde. "It's dirty. Like a good joke."

ANALYZING YOUR STORY

Explore the social context of your story.

BROAD SOCIAL CONTEXT

- How would you describe the broad social context of your story?
- What historical or current events influence how your story unfolds?
- What major social trends influence what happens?
- What common social practices affect character relationships and story events?
- Why is this broad social context important to the story you want to tell? How would the story be affected if it took place at a different time in history or in a different part of the world?

IMMEDIATE SOCIAL CONTEXT

- How would you describe the immediate social context of your story?
- How does this smaller social context affect the way your characters usually feel?
- How does this context affect the way your characters interact?
- For most characters, what are the most positive aspects of this social milieu? The most negative aspects?
- Why is this immediate social context important to the story you want to tell? How would the story be affected if the specific nature, makeup, or structure of this world were different?

VALUES AND BELIEFS

- What common values dominate the world of your story? List a few examples of what matters most among your characters.
- Onstage or off, who is most responsible for these values?
- Who in your story is most influenced by these dominant values, and how?
- What values may be important elsewhere but dismissed by most of your characters? For example, truth is held in high regard by many people but is of little use to the ruthless real estate agents of *Glengarry Glen Ross*.
- Right or wrong, what two or three beliefs dominate your characters' lives and most explain why the story unfolds the way it does?
- What do these beliefs reveal about your characters?
- How is each of these beliefs shown in the story?

In any dramatic story, characters are governed by laws and customs that affect how they behave with others. These social rules can be as varied as the disparate societies that have existed around the world and throughout history. In nineteenth-century Norway, if a woman needs a bank loan, she is legally required to get her husband's written permission (*A Doll's House* by Henrik Ibsen). In 1930s Berlin, if a man is openly gay, he can be sent to a Nazi concentration camp (*Bent* by Martin Sherman). In seventeenth-century Salem, Massachusetts, if someone is accused of witchcraft by a court official, he or she can be put to death (*The Crucible* by Arthur Miller).

Sometimes the laws and customs that influence characters stem from a subset of society, such as a family, business, club, or other organization. In *Circle Mirror Transformation* by Annie Baker, for example, a group of strangers enrolled in an adult acting class find themselves subject to the rules of theatre games devised by their instructor.

Individual characters may regard the rules that govern them as good or bad, important or unimportant, protective or threatening. A character's decision to obey social mandates or to rebel against them often explains how and why dramatic events occur.

■ DOUBT: A PARABLE

The world of St. Nicholas is subject to the rules and tenets of the Catholic Church as well as the policies and dictates of the school's principal, Sister Aloysius. Laws and customs here include:

Dress code. Nuns and priests are subject to a strict dress code, which adds to the formal atmosphere of the play. As Sisters of Charity, Aloysius and James must wear black bonnets and floor-length black habits. As a Roman Catholic priest, Father Flynn wears liturgical vestments when he's in church saying Mass and a black cassock when he is elsewhere in public. Informal dress is allowed, however, when he is teaching gym.

Chain of command. The Catholic church and school system has a chain of command that Aloysius has taken a solemn vow to obey. When issues arise at school that she cannot resolve on her own, her sole recourse within the system is to report the problems to the monsignor. This rule is introduced in scene 2, when Aloysius reminds James about how the system works. It becomes important in scene 4, when she learns that a student in James's class had alcohol on his breath after meeting with Flynn in the rectory. Aloysius fears that, if she were to report the incident to the senile Monsignor Benedict, he would not believe her, since he worships Flynn, and would instead brand her a heretic for besmirching a priest's reputation. Because Aloysius cannot trust the monsignor or go above his head to the bishop, she must deal with the problem of Flynn herself.

The Church's chain of command gains further weight in scene 8 during Aloysius's final confrontation with Flynn. He reminds her that she has no right to act on her own because she is a member of a religious order who has taken the vow of obedience. For a woman who has devoted her life to the Church, it is a powerful reminder that she has stepped outside of her traditional bounds. It is also a foreshadowing of the doubts she will experience at the end of the play.

Altar boy conduct. Any altar boy found drinking altar wine must be removed from his post. This rule is introduced in scene 5 when Flynn must explain why Donald Muller had wine on his breath after a visit to the rectory. According to Flynn, the caretaker, Mr. McGinn, caught Donald in the sacristy drinking the wine. When Donald begged to remain an altar boy, Flynn decided to give him another chance by keeping the incident secret. The rules governing altar boy conduct thus provide a relatively innocent explanation for an incriminating circumstance.

Meetings between nuns and priests. A nun and a priest may never be closeted alone or even cross paths in the garden without a third party present. This rule is introduced in scene 4, when Aloysius demands that James be present while she grills Flynn about Donald Muller. It is demonstrated in scene 5, when Flynn arrives for the meeting and cannot enter the office until James also arrives. As the meeting begins, we learn another part of the rule: when priests and nuns meet, the door of their room may not be closed completely. Accordingly, Aloysius "closes the door but for an inch."

The third-party rule becomes important in scene 7 when a distraught James, sitting in the garden, is visited unexpectedly by Flynn. They proceed to have a private meeting, which breaks the rule and adds a forbidden quality to their interaction. The rule is again important in scene 8, when Flynn storms into Aloysius's office without a third party present. To heighten the tension of the moment, he not only fails to leave the door ajar but also slams it shut. It is a signal that no holds will be barred during the showdown that is about to take place.

■ TOPDOG/UNDERDOG

The immediate world of *Topdog/Underdog* is governed by the rules of three-card monte and the dictates of Booth, who considers himself in charge of the premises. Social rules include:

Winning and losing. We learn how three-card monte works in scene 1, while Booth imagines himself as a dealer on the street conning a fool out of his money. The game challenges the player to guess the location of a particular card among three face-down playing cards shuffled by the dealer. The rule here is simple but binding: if you pick the right card, you win; if you pick the wrong card, you lose. The power of this rule is reinforced throughout the story and becomes paramount in scene 6, when winning and losing leads to murder.

Head of household. However small his "humble abode" may be, Booth is the head of household who decides not only how things work within these four walls but also how long Lincoln may remain as a paying guest. All other household rules flow from this basic assumption. Booth likes to wield his power so he can feel like a topdog, as in scene 1, when he threatens to evict Lincoln.

Money matters. As head of household, Booth has declared that, while Lincoln is responsible for most living expenses, Booth controls the budget. These dynamics are established in scene 2, which takes place on a Friday, when Lincoln gets paid and the weekly rent is due. Of the $314 that Lincoln brings home from the arcade, Booth must allot $100 for rent and then determine how the rest of the money will be divided to cover basic costs. When distributing funds for personal use, it is Booth's prerogative to give himself twice as much as he gives his brother.

Sleeping arrangements. There is only one bed in the room and it is for Booth. Lincoln must sleep in the old recliner, another demonstration of Booth's reign over the premises.

Boosting. While Lincoln's income covers certain expenses, it is not enough to meet all of the brothers' needs. "Boosting," or stealing, is thus an acceptable means of obtaining whatever else is needed. This rule is established in scene 1, when Booth brags about boosting a "diamond-esque" ring for his ex-girlfriend, Grace.

■ THE CLEAN HOUSE

In the world of *The Clean House*, Lane is a dominant force in deciding how things are supposed to work, though her authority weakens as the story unfolds. Laws and customs include:

Housecleaners. When a professional like Lane hires someone to clean her house, she expects this person to keep the premises clean without being told what to do, to be invisible, and to remain emotionally uninvolved in her life. "I want a stranger to clean my house," Lane says in act one, scene 13, after finding out that it is her sister, not her maid, who has been cleaning. Lane's view of housecleaners accentuates the class differences between Matilde and her and fuels Lane's resistance, in act one, to developing a personal relationship with Matilde even though they live under the same roof.

Marriage vows. When two people marry, they are supposed to love and honor each other for the rest of their lives. For Lane, fidelity is so integral to married life that until act one, scene 13, she could not conceive of Charles being with anyone but her: "How, I thought, could he even *look* at anyone else. It would be absurd." Reverence for marriage explains why Lane is so devastated by Charles's infidelity and also why Charles and Ana try so hard to justify their relationship. Though he is not Jewish, for example, Charles cites a Jewish law that he interprets as a mandate to be with Ana since she is his soul mate, or *bashert.* Bowing to the sanctity of marriage, Ana meanwhile feels compelled to stress that she is not a home wrecker and that, before Charles, she has loved no one since her late husband.

Helping others. As doctors, Lane and Charles have a professional obligation to care for the sick. This is why Charles heads to Alaska in search of a cancer treatment for Ana and why Lane visits her husband's dying soul mate while he is away. Lane does not believe, however, that anyone should take care of her. She makes this clear more than once to Virginia, whose desire to help others, especially Lane, drives much of her behavior. It is not until late in the play that Lane is able to accept the social rule that Virginia cites after Lane's marriage fails: "Everybody needs to be taken care of."

Mourning attire. Matilde's clothing reflects the social custom of wearing black to mourn the loss of a loved one and is an ongoing reminder of her deceased parents' influence on her life.

ANALYZING YOUR STORY

Think about laws and customs that govern your characters and affect story events.

KEY SOCIAL RULES

- Are there any federal, state, or local laws that affect story events because a character chooses to obey them or to break them? If so, what laws are most relevant?
- What moral codes most influence your characters during the story?
- At home, at work, or in social groups, what personal dictates or expectations govern character behavior and affect how the story unfolds?

- Who established this rule?
- How long has this rule been in effect in the world of the characters? How has it affected life here?
- What are the rewards for obeying this rule? The consequences for breaking it?
- How do your characters each view this rule, and why do they see it that way?
- How and when is this rule first introduced to the characters? To the audience? When does it become important to the plot?
- Who is most affected by this rule during the story, and in what way?

ECONOMICS

Money, or lack of it, often determines who characters know, where they live, how they live, what they can do, and what they cannot do. It contributes to their outlook on life and their ability to get what they want. It is a common source of conflict and a frequently recurring motivation for human behavior. This is why many dramatic stories—from Shakespeare's *King Lear* to Joe Orton's *Loot* to Caryl Churchill's *Serious Money*—center on characters and their relation to wealth, whether they are trying to acquire it, use it, protect it, or deal with its loss.

■ DOUBT: A PARABLE

Doubt is a story about certainty and doubt in the world of a Catholic elementary school. Money is of little relevance dramatically and never mentioned in the dialogue of the play.

■ TOPDOG/UNDERDOG

Economics is a driving force in the world of *Topdog/Underdog*. It contributed to the breakup of the family twenty years ago and underlies the hardships that the brothers face today.

The financial pressure of buying and maintaining a house was a key reason for the growing problems between the parents and their decisions eventually to abandon their teenage boys. In reliving this loss in scene 7, Booth remarks that, "She split then he split. Like thuh whole family mortgage bills going to work thing was just too much."

For both brothers, money is the last memento of their parents: their mother secretly left Booth $500 in a tied-up nylon stocking, and their father secretly left Lincoln $500 in a clean handkerchief. While this cash may have eased the parents' guilt about deserting their sons, it has become a defining factor in the brothers' relationship to each other and to money. Because each inheritance was bestowed in secret by only one parent on only one son, money has created a wall between the brothers, who were implicitly encouraged to mistrust each other.

Since money is so closely associated with both parental love and abandonment, the brothers have come to view it differently. For Booth, who survives by theft, money is not a means of acquiring goods so much as a magical power to earn respect and attract women. This attitude explains why money is such an integral part of his plan to win back Grace, his ex-girlfriend, and also why he has never spent the cash his mother left him. For Lincoln, money is a means to pursue life's pleasures and should be spent as soon as possible. When he receives a week's severance pay after losing his job, he blows it all the same day. It is no wonder that the inheritance from his father is long gone.

Booth's money decisions have led him to view honest employment as oppression and to work outside the system to get what he wants. Lincoln's money decisions have led him to become a pawn of the system, allowing himself to be humiliated and underpaid in order to earn a legitimate income. Though the brothers have arrived at their small room by different paths, they now find themselves in the same economic distress, a shared poverty that forces them at times to seek comfort in each other.

■ THE CLEAN HOUSE

In the world of *The Clean House*, economics translates into the class differences that shape the events of the story. As successful doctors, Lane and Charles have the money to do as they please, such as hire a live-in maid to keep their house clean. Thanks to the freedom and mobility that money brings, Charles, in act two, can shrug off the responsibilities of his job in order to be with Ana or to travel to Alaska at a moment's notice to find a yew tree for her. He is even able to take flying lessons and rent a plane when he learns that this is his only option for getting the tree home.

In contrast, Matilde has so little money that she must live in someone else's house and work as a cleaning woman, a job that saddens her. She can't afford even to buy the kind of underwear she likes. As a result, she must defer her dream of becoming a comedian in New York. It is her lack of money that traps her here and contributes to her unhappiness. For Virginia, a housewife married to a middle-class man, money is not an issue in her daily cleaning routine. She has the resources to live comfortably and to entertain thoughts of doing volunteer work, if only she could figure out who might need her. For Ana, money is of little interest. She appears to have what she needs and is more focused on the challenges of having cancer.

ANALYZING YOUR STORY

Review the financial dimensions of your characters' world.

ECONOMIC CONDITIONS

- Think about the world of your characters in relation to wealth and poverty. How would you describe the general economics of this world?

- In what specific ways are these economic conditions shown?
- How do economics affect the physical environment and what's in it?
- Do economics contribute to the emotional environment of this world, and, if so, how?
- How do economics influence character lifestyles?
- Think about the collective spending habits of your characters. For what purpose is money or material wealth most often used in this world?
- What do the spending habits of your characters suggest about their values and beliefs?
- Who in this world has the most money and spending power? Who has the least?
- At what points in the story is money—or lack of it—most important?

FOR EACH CHARACTER . . .

- What is the character's economic status when the story begins? When it ends?
- How does the character view material wealth or lack of it?
- How do economics affect the character physically? Psychologically? Socially?
- How much does the desire for wealth or the fear of poverty motivate the character's actions during the story? What are the most significant examples of this?
- How would the character be different if he or she had greater wealth? Less wealth?

POWER STRUCTURE

Politics is a key ingredient of any dramatic story. Politics in this case means power: the ability to influence the behavior of others or the course of events.

Drama often explores how power is structured and how it affects the world of the characters. A power structure may exist personally between individuals, as in David Ives's *Venus in Fur*, where a director and actor vie for dominance during an audition for a play. Or a power structure may exist formally within a group, organization, or society, as in Martin McDonagh's *The Pillowman*, where agents of a police state determine the fates of two brothers whom they hold prisoner.

Whether personal or institutional, the power structure affecting characters tends to be dynamic. It can change from scene to scene or within a scene. It is often a major power shift that leads to the main event of the story.

■ DOUBT: A PARABLE

The chain of command at St. Nicholas church and school is clearly defined by Sister Aloysius in scene 2 when she tells Sister James, "You are answerable to me, I to the monsignor, he to the bishop, and so on up to the Holy Father." Since James is at the bottom of this weighty pile, she must do whatever she is told. This power dynamic permeates her interactions with Aloysius and contributes to James's decision in scene 4 to report her concerns about Father Flynn.

The same power dynamics make Aloysius's campaign to get rid of Flynn extremely difficult. He holds a position of authority that she cannot easily question and that cannot easily be overcome. In fact, the patriarchal power structure of the Catholic Church is what makes the play necessary after Aloysius learns about Flynn's questionable relationship with an eighth-grade boy. Within this hierarchy of authority, she is allowed to report problems only to one person—Monsignor Benedict—who is not only senile but also a staunch ally of the popular priest. For the problem of Flynn to be resolved, Aloysius must take matters into her own hands.

■ TOPDOG/UNDERDOG

As the title implies, *Topdog/Underdog* is all about power: who has it and who doesn't. From a broad social perspective, both brothers are underdogs who live in poverty, with few opportunities for advancement and success. Whether they try to work within the system or outside it, neither seems able to rise above the broken family, social inequalities, and bad habits that led them here.

Within their brotherly relationship, Lincoln is the topdog and Booth the underdog. These roles are clearly defined by the playwright but not always obvious as the story unfolds. As a card hustler, Lincoln knows it can be advantageous to "lose" a game in order to give the player a false sense of confidence. What the player doesn't know is that the dealer is always in control and that the money on the board will be his when it is ample enough to be a worthy prize. Lincoln often uses this strategy with Booth, letting him win small battles so that Lincoln can win big ones later.

In scene 2, for example, when the brothers spar over stolen ties, Lincoln lets Booth have the one they both appear to want so that Lincoln can get the one he *really* wants. Lincoln uses the same strategy in scene 6 when he lets Booth win one round of three-card monte so that Lincoln can win the next one and con Booth out of his inheritance. This final power struggle is one that has no winner, however, as one brother ends up dead and the other a killer.

■ THE CLEAN HOUSE

In act one, when the action centers on physical cleaning, the well-to-do doctors Lane and Charles have the most power and the housekeeper Matilde the least. Though Lane at times feels uncomfortable with her household authority, she has no problem firing Matilde a few scenes later when the truth comes out about who has been cleaning her house. Virginia, as a middle-class housewife and sister to Lane, starts out somewhere in the middle of this chain of command. She is trapped, however, in a meaningless life and soon relinquishes her power to Matilde, becoming the cleaning woman's invisible labor force in an effort to keep herself busy.

In act two, when the action centers on spiritual cleaning, the power balance shifts, with Matilde gaining authority and Lane shrinking into an emotional weakling who must be told what to do. After thinking up the perfect joke, Matilde becomes the play's most powerful character, with the ability to grant Ana's wish to die laughing. Matilde presides over Ana's dying needs and guides Lane through the ordeal of being a doctor to her husband's soul mate. During this time, Virginia builds the confidence to stand up for herself, rebel against her sister's regime, and begin to define the terms of her own life. In act two, scene 11, for example, she refuses to support Lane until she first acknowledges that she needs Virginia's help.

Charles and Ana likewise experience a shift in power as the story unfolds. At first, Charles is the doctor with the knowledge and authority to oversee Ana's care. This authority is toppled when they fall in love, and he becomes increasingly childlike in her presence. When her cancer returns, Charles is unable to convince Ana to go to the hospital for further treatment and, in the end, finds himself standing helplessly over her dead body.

ANALYZING YOUR STORY

Explore who has power and who doesn't in the world of your characters.

POWER DYNAMICS

- What role do politics play in the world of the characters?
- How would you describe the political environment? Why is it like this?
- Onstage or off, who rules the world of the characters?
- How would you describe this ruling power?
- What are the usual rewards for obeying the ruling power? The usual consequences for rebelling against it?
- What is the pecking order of the characters when the story begins? When the story ends?
- If during the story there is a significant shift in the power structure, what causes it? Where and how does this occur?

FOR EACH CHARACTER . . .

- What are the character's political beliefs and how important are these to the story?
- What is the character's personal power status when the story begins?
- What people or events have most contributed to this power status?
- How does the character's power status affect his or her needs?
- Who are the character's greatest allies when the story begins? When it ends?
- Who are the character's greatest adversaries when the story begins? When it ends?
- Right or wrong, how does the character view the ruling power in this world?
- Does the character take any significant action in obedience to this power or in rebellion against it? If so, what does the character do? How does this affect the story?
- How would the story be different if the character had more power? Less power?

The spiritual realm can have a powerful influence on characters in a dramatic story. Spiritual factors include beliefs, activities, and events related to God, higher powers, faith, religion, the afterlife, the supernatural, the occult, reincarnation, ghosts, angels, miracles, psychic phenomena, and anything else above and beyond the natural plane.

In John Pielmeier's *Agnes of God*, for example, a novice nun gives birth and claims that her pregnancy was the result of a miracle—an immaculate conception. In José Rivera's *Marisol*, a woman's guardian angel leaves her to join the other angels in a revolution against God. In Rajiv Joseph's *Bengal Tiger at the Baghdad Zoo*, ghosts roam the streets of Baghdad in search of the meaning of life. Sometimes it is the lack of spirituality that most affects a character, as in Tennessee Williams's *The Night of the Iguana*, where a defrocked minister's crisis of faith drives him to self-destructive behavior.

■ DOUBT: A PARABLE

The world of *Doubt* is governed by the Catholic Church. The religious beliefs and operational principles of this age-old institution fuel the certainty with which Sister Aloysius approaches everyday life and the duties of her job as the principal of St. Nicholas school. Armed with a credo that is both comprehensive and ironclad, she has no room for doubt. This credo is what will be undone by story events and lead to the final scene, where she begins to question not only the authority she has trusted but also the actions she has taken under its rule.

For a story dominated by the clergy, there are few demonstrations of religious practice. Aside from the attire of the characters, the only observable evidence of religious ritual are Flynn's two sermons from the pulpit. We see no signs of other religious activity, such as praying or participating in sacraments. The role of the Church in modern life is debated briefly in scene 5, but spiritual topics are rarely discussed. Two exceptions occur in that same scene, when Sister James expresses her love of the Nativity and when Aloysius condemns the song "Frosty the Snowman" as pagan and heretical. The most direct biblical reference can be found in scene 7, when Flynn cites "the message of the Savior" to convince James of his innocence.

One spiritual idea that recurs in the play is the notion of being "close to God." It leads to one of Aloysius's final speeches: "In the pursuit of wrongdoing, one steps away from God. Of course there's a price." Aside from these brief references, spirituality is more implied than stated, residing between the lines in the subtext of the play.

■ TOPDOG/UNDERDOG

Topdog/Underdog brings us into a secular realm of two brothers who are barely surviving in an underfurnished single room and exhibit no interest in spiritual matters. If any element of this world has transcendent power, it is the playing cards that Booth tries so eagerly to master and Lincoln struggles so desperately to resist.

■ THE CLEAN HOUSE

In a *New York Times* interview, Ruhl described *The Clean House* as "a play about cleaning as transcendence, spiritual cleansing."[1] Her comment highlights the importance of spirituality in the lives of the characters. While the dramatic action begins with a focus on dusty tabletops and dirty floors, it rises to a metaphysical plane that includes the aching heart and damaged soul.

Through Matilde, humor is presented as a powerful tool for cleansing at this higher level. "A good joke cleans your inside out," she tells Virginia in act one, scene 10. This belief explains Matilde's relentless need to think up jokes and elevates it to a quest with spiritual dimensions. By thinking up the perfect joke, Matilde believes she can heal herself after the loss of her parents. Since her mother died from hearing a perfect joke, however, Matilde worries that she is endangering her own life by tapping into so potent a force. Laughter and death are thus paired in a cosmic relationship that keeps them closely bound throughout the play.

The love between Charles and Ana introduces another spiritual element: the concept of the *bashert*, or soul mate. According to traditional Jewish teachings, God pairs you with your soul mate while you are still in your mother's womb and you must spend your life trying to find him or her. Charles first learns about this *midrash* on public radio and uses it to justify his relationship with Ana, even though he is not Jewish.

During the story, the characters discover ways to clean spiritually for each other. For example, Lane forgives Ana and nurses her through her final days. Virginia helps Lane recover from her failed marriage. Matilde grants Ana's final wish to die laughing at a perfect joke. By the end of the play, as Lane

---

1. Dinitia Smith, "Playwright's Subjects: Greek Myth to Vibrators," *New York Times*, October 14, 2006.

bathes Ana's body with water, the three surviving women have learned how to share their lives, not unlike the women of old who, in Virginia's words, "would gather at the public fountains to wash their clothes and tell stories."

Though mentioned only once in the play, prayer is also presented as a tool for spiritual cleansing. After Ana dies, Matilde tells Virginia to pray: "A prayer cleans the air the way water cleans the dirt."

ANALYZING YOUR STORY

Explore the spiritual realm of your story.

KEY SPIRITUAL BELIEFS

- How dominant are supernatural beliefs in the world of your characters?
- What specific beliefs do most characters have about God, higher powers, or the afterlife?
- What beliefs and attitudes do most characters have about organized religion?
- What beliefs do most characters have about miracles, the occult, extrasensory perception, or other paranormal phenomena?
- What people, places, or things, if any, are considered sacred in this world, and why?
- How do spiritual beliefs, or the lack of them, influence everyday life here?
- Have spiritual matters ever played an important role in the history of this world? If so, what happened and how has that affected your characters?

IMPACT ON STORY EVENTS

- Who among your characters is most spiritual? Least spiritual?
- What significant actions, if any, do your characters take during the story as a result of their spiritual beliefs or religious practices?
- Do spiritual matters contribute in any way to the conflict of the story, and, if so, how?
- How would the story change if any of the characters had different spiritual beliefs? If certain characters were more spiritual? Less spiritual?

The secret of a great story is a great backstory that is always suggested but rarely explained. The backstory includes everything that happened in the lives of the characters before the play begins. The only parts of this history that matter, however, are those that affect how the play unfolds.

A basic challenge for any dramatic writer is figuring out how to reveal critical information about the past without intruding upon the present. Facts about the offstage world tend to work best when they support a character objective, as in Yasmina Reza's *Art*, where Marc informs Ivan that their friend Serge recently went to an exclusive art gallery and paid two hundred thousand francs for an oil painting of white stripes on a white background. Marc reveals this backstory fact because he has an objective: he wants to convince Yvan that Serge has become a snob.

An explanation about the past or anything else that cannot be observed here and now is called "exposition." How a dramatic writer handles it is a sign of professionalism. Exposition can be a vital and powerful part of a dramatic story when used judiciously to expose important facts about the offstage experiences of the characters.

■ **DOUBT: A PARABLE**

The past experiences of the characters remain unknown, with a few exceptions.

Sister Aloysius

Husband who battled evil. Before joining the Sisters of Charity, Aloysius was married to an American soldier who died in World War II, which she describes as "the war against Adolph [sic] Hitler." This is all we learn about her life outside the convent. It is first revealed in scene 4, when she and Sister James are discussing Mother Seton, the founder of the order, who was also married prior to taking religious vows. Aloysius's objective is to startle James, who seems to know little about life and its complexities. The Hitler reference is also a foreshadowing of the evil that Aloysius will perceive in Father Flynn and the war she will wage against him. Since this reference to her marriage is her only disclosure about her personal life, it stands out in the mix of who she is, even though it is barely mentioned.

Similar trouble at another school. Aloysius is worldly enough to know that, despite their halos, some priests may be far from saintly. Eight years ago, when she worked at St. Boniface school, she learned that one of the priests was a child abuser and succeeded in having him removed. The knowledge she gained from this incident will contribute to her campaign against Flynn. It is in scene 4 that Aloysius reveals the past encounter with a pedophile priest. The revelation is motivated by James's report that Flynn may have given wine to an eighth grader. Aloysius's objective is to convince James that her success at Boniface was due to a reliable monsignor and that they will have to take matters into their own hands now, because they have no such ally at St. Nicholas.

Disturbing sight on the first day of school. At the start of the school year, Aloysius saw a young boy named William London recoil from a touch on his wrist from Flynn. Though she witnessed nothing more, she has secretly suspected the priest of wrongdoing and has been eager to prove her intuition correct. This eagerness is stoked in scene 4, when James first reports her concerns about Flynn, but the London incident is not revealed until scene 8, when Flynn asks why she always treats him with mistrust. Her objective is to convince him that she has no doubts about his corrupt nature. She sums it up in three words: "I know people." This proclamation helps us understand that Aloysius operates more from instinct than from fact and that her conclusions make deep and lasting impressions.

Father Flynn

Childhood friend with unclean fingernails. One of the only facts we learn about Flynn's personal history is that a childhood friend supposedly died of spinal meningitis for reasons related to unclean fingernails. Flynn makes this claim in scene 3, when he is trying to convince the boys on the basketball team to take better care of their nails. The dramatic function of this exposition is to draw attention to Flynn's preoccupation with his fingernails, an idiosyncrasy that could help explain his innocence or guilt, depending on how it is viewed.

Three parishes in five years. We also learn that, since he became a priest five years ago, Flynn has been assigned to three different parishes. This transiency is brought up in scene 8 by Aloysius, who believes his transfer from parish to parish is a sign of misconduct. This backstory fact provides more circumstantial evidence in the case against Flynn and helps us understand why Aloysius is determined to bring him down.

Sister James

Sheltered life. Outside of her role as the new eighth-grade teacher at St. Nicholas, Sister James also remains an enigma. We learn little about her past except that she took her religious vows at an early age. She reveals this to Aloysius in scene 2 because she needs to make the point that she does not have enough life experience to talk to girls about how to be a woman. We also learn that James previously taught at an all-girls school named Mount St. Margaret's. These backstory facts help paint the picture of James as an innocent with little knowledge of the world.

Brother in Maryland. The only other fact we discover about James's personal life is that she has a sick brother in Maryland. She reveals this in scene 7 as she tries to get Flynn's sympathy. This backstory fact explains why she will request a leave of absence and not be present when Flynn's transfer to St. Jerome's occurs. As a result, she—and the audience—will need to be told about what happened to Flynn after he left St. Nicholas.

Mrs. Muller

Gay son. During Mrs. Muller's brief time in the play, we learn something important about her son's backstory but little about her own. Our key discovery is that Donald is gay and has been beaten up because of it by his father at home and by his public-school classmates the previous year. Mrs. Muller reveals these facts in response to Aloysius's allegation that Flynn is having an improper relationship with the boy. Her objective is to convince Aloysius that the priest is the only one who has been kind to her son and that she chooses not to think ill of him. Her backstory helps us understand her unexpected reaction to Aloysius's charges.

■ TOPDOG/UNDERDOG

To explore family wounds and healing, the play relies heavily on the past to inform the present.

Lincoln and Booth

Dysfunctional family. Lincoln and Booth share a history of being raised by parents who, in their pursuit of the American dream, moved from a substandard apartment to a modest house with a mortgage and soon found themselves under increasing financial pressure that led to their estrangement. Moms eventually ran away. Two years later, Pops did the same. As a result, the teenage boys were forced to rent a room downtown, do odd jobs to pay the bills, and rely on each other for survival and support. This background set the stage for their current symbiotic relationship and for the difficulty each has maintaining personal relationships.

Booth

Mother's infidelity. According to Booth, Moms had a "sideman" who came to the house on Thursdays, when no one else was around. Booth learned of this one Thursday when he cut school, returned home earlier than usual, and discovered his mother having sex with a strange man. It was an affair that led to a pregnancy, an abortion, and then one day the running motor of Mr. Thursday's car waiting outside to take her away. All of this is revealed by Booth in scene 6, as he and his brother bare their souls and rev up for their final duel. The mother's infidelity is one of many family experiences that have led Booth to mistrust everyone around him, especially those who are supposed to be closest.

The day mother left. The mother's flight from the family was for Booth a day that still haunts him and remains present in the form of a tied-up nylon stocking holding five $100 bills. This bundle—his "inheritance"—is what Moms gave him just before she left home, with the warning to keep the cash secret from Lincoln. The stocking endures as the last physical trace of her, a treasure that Booth not only keeps hidden but also has never opened. The history of the stocking becomes important in scene 6, when Booth loses it to Lincoln in a game of three-card monte and sees his brother about to cut it open. The backstory helps us understand the sacred nature of this inheritance and Booth's impulsive decision to protect it by killing Lincoln.

Life with Grace. For two years, Booth dated a woman named Grace, who broke up with him after he had a "little employment difficulty." Though not much about that period is revealed, we can infer from story events that it was for Booth a happy time that he longs to regain. His dream now is to win Grace back and live with her happily ever after. This is what fuels his desire to become a rich card hustler (scene 1) and triggers his heartbreak and rage when Grace fails to show up for their dinner date (scene 5).

Lincoln

Father's infidelity. According to Lincoln, Pops had not one but many women on the side. To bond with his eldest son, he would bring Lincoln along to introduce him to "the ladies" and would sometimes even allow him to watch their lovemaking. Lincoln claims that he was occasionally more than a passive observer. "One of his ladies liked me, so I would do her after he'd done her. On thuh sly, though," Lincoln tells Booth in scene 6, as they share untold secrets from their childhood. By showcasing his infidelities, Pops provided his teenage son with a model for how to ruin a marriage, a lesson that would contribute to the breakup of Lincoln's own marriage.

The day father left. Two years after Moms fled, Pops took off as well and secretly gave Lincoln ten $50 bills in a clean handkerchief with a warning not to tell his brother about the money. Pops took nothing with him when he fled, not even the fine suits hanging in his closet. Lincoln's response to the abandonment was to burn the suits and squander the money. This backstory fact sheds light on Lincoln's longing for companionship. It may also explain his attitude toward money. By spending it as fast as he can, he can continue to rebel against the father who thought that a parting gift of cash would excuse his running away.

Life as a dealer. One of Lincoln's most important backstory experiences was his life on the street as a three-card monte dealer. He claims that he used to earn a thousand dollars a day and enjoy the attention of many beautiful women. All of this glory ended when his partner Lonny was murdered. Fearing for his own life, Lincoln swore off the cards and vowed to earn an honest living. This backstory fact fuels a central conflict in the play: Lincoln's resistance to partnering with Booth in a new card hustling scheme.

A failed marriage. Unlike Booth, Lincoln managed to get married. It was not, however, a happy marriage, nor was it a long one. His wife, Cookie, threw him out after he lost interest in her and, like his father, began pursuing other women. Booth at times uses Lincoln's failure with Cookie to get the best of him. In scene 6, for example, in a heated moment that leads to their deadly showdown, Booth claims that Cookie seduced him. This emotional jab contributes to Lincoln's decision to get revenge by conning his brother out of his inheritance.

■ **THE CLEAN HOUSE**

Except for Matilde's idyllic imaginings of her parents, the past lives of the characters are rarely revealed. One fact the four women share is that none has had children, even though three of them have been married. Only Virginia and Ana address this fact. Virginia claims that her husband is "barren" and that she wouldn't want children anyway because the world isn't good enough for them. Ana says that her husband was too wild and crazy to be a father. The absence of sons and daughters may contribute to the women's need to rely on one another as they reach out under stress for the kind of support that a family might provide.

Lane

Good life. When we meet Lane, she has a successful medical career, attractive spouse, and clean house. All we learn about her past, however, are a few details about her relationship with Charles. In act one, seven 12, she tries to rationalize why he has not telephoned to say he will be home late. She recalls their lives as young doctors who often worked long days and used special pager signals to say goodnight. Though trifling, this is one of her most personal memories about her marriage. Another occurs with Ana in act two, scene 10, when we learn how Lane and Charles met: in an anatomy class over a dead body. It is an ironic image for Lane to conjure up in her now lifeless marriage.

In act two, scene 9, as Lane and Virginia fight, we gain an important insight from Virginia about her sister's approach to life's challenges: "Since the day you were born, you thought that anyone with a *problem* had a defect of the will." It is a succinct analysis of one who in her quest for success has failed to learn the value of compassion, a shortcoming that has contributed to the emptiness of Lane's relationships with her husband and sister.

Matilde
History of laughter. The funniest man in his Brazilian village, Matilde's father did not marry until he was sixty-three because he wanted a wife who was as funny as him. Her mother also waited to marry because she couldn't stand the thought of laughing at jokes that weren't funny.

Once they found each other, her parents lived a life filled with laughter. Then one day, on their wedding anniversary, after hearing a special joke that her husband had thought up for her, Matilde's mother literally died laughing, perhaps choking on her own spit. Her father subsequently shot himself. Matilde reveals this backstory because she wants us to know why she came to the United States in search of a new life and why she wants to be a comedian.

Virginia
Bad life. In act one, scene 7, while getting to know her sister's new housekeeper, Virginia confesses that her life has gone downhill since the age of twenty-two because she did not do what she wanted. For example, she did not follow her dream of becoming a scholar. She reveals this and other facts about her life as part of a strategy to convince Matilde to let her secretly clean Lane's house and divert herself from the void in which she now finds herself. She recalls a summer trip to Europe with her husband when she was still studying Greek literature: "We were going to see ruins and I was going to write about ruins but I found that I had nothing to say about them. I thought: why doesn't someone just sweep them up!"

Ana

Wild husband. One of the few facts we learn about Ana's past is that she was married many years ago to a wild, alcoholic geologist who died of cancer at the age of thirty-one after finally giving up drinking at her request (act two, scene 5). Her reason for revealing this is to show that she is not accustomed to falling in love with married men and that her relationship with Charles was both unexpected and exceptional.

Charles

Good life. Like Lane, Charles appears to have enjoyed a good life that yielded a successful medical career, attractive spouse, and clean house. We learn nothing about this past except that he fell in love with Lane when they were twenty-two and remained faithful to her until he met Ana. This abbreviated backstory is revealed in act two, scene 3, when he introduces himself to the audience in an effort to say that he is a good man who simply became overwhelmed by love.

ANALYZING YOUR STORY

Think about how the past affects the present.

FOR EACH PRINCIPAL CHARACTER . . .

- What key facts from the character's recent or distant past are revealed during the story?
- Is it necessary to reveal all of these backstory facts? If not, which can be cut?
- Do any important facts from the past need to be added, and, if so, what?
- Which facts from the character's past are most important, and why?

FOR EACH KEY FACT FROM THE PAST . . .

- Who reveals this fact to whom, and what is the character's reason for doing so?
- How has this experience affected the character physically? Psychologically? Socially?
- Are there any details about this fact that can be cut? Any that need to be added?
- Think about how the fact is revealed. Is there an opportunity to use a visual image, object, physical element, or action to reduce the need for words of explanation?
- Characters sometimes make mistakes, suffer delusions, or tell lies.

How accurate is the revelation of this fact? If it is inaccurate, why has the truth been obscured, either by the character or by you, the writer?

- What is the dramatic purpose for having this fact revealed?
- How would the story be different if this fact were not revealed?

Steps of the Journey

Story is the series of events that occurs when a character pursues an important goal that is difficult to achieve. The pursuit of this goal is a dramatic journey that begins at a turning point in the character's life and advances, step by step, through untried and often unexpected territory until a final destination is reached. With each new step, the character typically encounters greater obstacles and either succeeds or fails to overcome them. It is in the process of dealing with these obstacles that the character is revealed and, in most cases, changed.

POINT OF ATTACK

A play is the part of a dramatic story that the audience sees and hears on-stage. While the story can include any number of characters, settings, and events over any period of time, the play presents a limited selection of these elements so that it is feasible for a theatre company to stage it and for an audience to watch it in one sitting. The dramatic writer has the task, therefore, of deciding which story elements to include in the script.

During this process, the writer faces the question of when to start the play in relation to the story. For life to be in progress when the curtain goes up, the play cannot start until the story is already under way. For example, the story of *Rabbit Hole* by David Lindsay-Abaire begins when a four-year-old boy is killed in an automobile accident outside of his home. The play does not begin, however, until eight months later, when his mother has reached the point in her healing process that she can let go of her son's things and donate them to Goodwill. As the play begins, she is in the kitchen folding and sorting the boy's laundry while she visits with her sister. It is not until later that we will discover the significance of the neat piles of clothes on the kitchen table.

The moment the play begins is sometimes called the "point of attack." It may occur early in the story so that most important events take place on-stage, as in Shakespeare's *Macbeth*, which begins just before the title character's thirst for power is aroused by a trio of witches. Or the point of attack may occur late in the story, with certain critical events having already happened before scene 1, as in Tracy Letts's *August: Osage County*, which begins decades after a family's web of betrayal and secrecy was first spun.

Deciding when to set the point of attack is a critical step in the storytelling process. In plays with an early point of attack, little of the past, or backstory, needs to be explained, since it is not relevant to the dramatic journey. In plays with a late point of attack, the critical events of the past must be revealed so that we know what happened. A play with a late point of attack relies more on exposition, that is, information about the offstage world.

Regardless of when the point of attack occurs, it is surrounded by a set of given circumstances that influence how it happens. Ideally, the play begins when something important is going on in the world of the story. At least one character wants something, is dealing with a problem, and has something at stake. Yet the conflict is not so intense that it repels the audience before they have time to get to know the characters and become emotionally invested in them.

■ DOUBT: A PARABLE
Point of attack: A sermon

The point of attack is the moment Father Flynn begins to deliver a sermon in St. Nicholas church on the subject of doubt. We hear the sermon from beginning to end and imagine the congregation to whom it is being delivered. In the next scene, we will learn that the offstage listeners include Sister Aloysius, who is disturbed by Flynn's descriptions of feeling confused and lost. Why would a priest dwell on such dark subjects?

This point of attack occurs early in the story of Aloysius's campaign against Flynn. That story began two months before, on the first day of school, when she saw something that bothered her: the priest reaching out to touch a boy's wrist and the boy pulling away. Though there was nothing more to it, the incident aroused in Aloysius a mistrust of Flynn. The sermon now reminds her of what she saw that day and prompts her to take steps to learn more about the priest. Because it triggers Aloysius's campaign against Flynn, the sermon is not only the point of attack for the play but also the inciting event that launches her dramatic journey.

Immediate given circumstances

At the moment he begins his sermon on doubt, Flynn has been at St. Nicholas for about a year. The exact time period is not specified, but we later learn that this is his third parish in five years. In addition to his priestly duties, he is the school's gym instructor and a popular figure among the students. His relationship with the school principal, however, is tentative for reasons that he does not understand.

We will learn later that his ideas for sermons grow out of his daily life and are recorded in a little black book that he carries with him. The circumstances surrounding his idea for a sermon on doubt are never disclosed. Is this the advice of a compassionate priest with a troubled parishioner? Or is it an expression of guilt from a man who preys on children? Such unanswered questions foster the doubt that is central to the story.

■ TOPDOG/UNDERDOG
Point of attack: An imaginary shell game

The play begins with Booth practicing to be a three-card monte dealer. He is alone in his rooming-house room playing against an imaginary mark. Booth's moves and patter are "studied and awkward." He is clearly a novice.

This point of attack occurs late in the story of two brothers who were abandoned as teenagers by their parents and as adults by the women in their lives. The brothers now live together in a barely furnished room without running water, a private bathroom, or a working phone. Because so many relevant events have preceded this point of attack, the past will play a frequent and important role in the present tense of the story. The script will rely heavily on exposition to fill in the blanks.

Immediate given circumstances

Booth has scored a date for tomorrow night with his beautiful ex-girlfriend Grace. In celebration of his victory, he presented her today with a stolen ring that is slightly smaller than her actual ring size, so that she cannot easily remove it.

Believing that his earlier failure with Grace was due to a lack of funds, Booth has devised a scheme to get rich quick. He will become a three-card monte dealer like his brother once was and rake in so much money that Grace will come crawling back to him. As a first step, he has gathered the tools necessary for the shell game—three playing cards, a cardboard board, and two milk crates—and set them up in his room so he can practice.

Lincoln, his brother and roommate, is currently coming up the street in full Abraham Lincoln regalia, the outfit he wears for his job as a human target in a shooting gallery. Having conned a rich kid out of twenty dollars on the bus ride home from work, Lincoln stopped at a Chinese takeout place to pick up tonight's dinner. He also stopped at the local bar, Lucky's, to blow the rest of his loot on drinks with his buddies. Lincoln is now inebriated.

■ THE CLEAN HOUSE
Point of attack: An untranslated joke

The Clean House begins with a woman in black telling the audience a dirty joke in Portuguese. This point of attack introduces Matilde, one of the three protagonists, and sets the tone for comedy. Since the play is written for an English-speaking audience, the untranslated joke also lets us know that we are in store for unusual events, such as more jokes in Portuguese and characters who speak directly to the audience as if there were no "fourth wall" between them.

The point of attack occurs early in the story of Matilde's career as a cleaning woman who enters the lives of Lane and Virginia. Most of the key events of this story, therefore, take place during the here and now of the play with a minimal need to reveal events of the past. The main exception is Matilde's need to recall her parents in Brazil through dialogue and through living imagery that depicts what she envisions in her mind.

By introducing Matilde in the context of joke telling, the play establishes her not as a disgruntled cleaning woman but as a skillful comedian. This first impression will color our view of her struggle to escape her housekeeping duties and use the time instead to think up jokes. We are more likely to sympathize with her plight if we see her as a comedian trapped in the wrong job.

The untranslated joke that begins the play also ties to Matilde's vision at the end of the play of heaven as "a sea of untranslatable jokes. / Only everyone is laughing." The ending thus includes an echo of this beginning and the unexplained mystery it evokes.

Immediate given circumstances

The stage directions do not specify where or when Matilde tells the opening joke. The fact that she is dressed in black suggests only that it is after the death of her parents and that she is in mourning. Her use of Portuguese shows how closely she associates humor with her life in Brazil. We will find out later that Matilde once saw herself as the third funniest person in her family and that, when her parents died, she became "the first funniest," a burden that she could not bear and that motivated her move to the United States to start life anew.

ANALYZING YOUR STORY

Explore how the onstage action of your play begins.

POINT OF ATTACK

- Where and when in the story does the play start? Who is here now? If two or more characters are present, what is their relationship?
- Are there any important physical circumstances—environmental or personal—that affect the point of attack? If so, what are they?
- What psychological circumstances contribute to how the play begins?
- What social, economic, or political circumstances contribute to this beginning?
- What is the opening image of the play?
- Why is this point of attack the best moment to start the play?
- Think about what's happening in the opening scene. Who wants what from whom? What is the problem? What's at stake?

IMPACT ON AUDIENCE

- What emotional response might the point of attack produce in the audience?
- What questions or expectations might it trigger?
- Is enough happening at the point of attack to engage the audience? If

not, you may have raised the curtain too soon. Is there a later time in the story that would work better?

- Is so much happening at the point of attack that the audience may not want to get involved? If so, you may have raised the curtain too late. Is there an earlier time in the story that would give the audience a better chance to get to know the characters before their lives erupt into crisis?
- Ideally, the play will immediately grab the audience's attention. How interesting is the point of attack now? Do you see any way to increase its grabbing power?

Every story is a quest. It centers on a character who is after something important and faces obstacles that will make it difficult to attain. The quest is triggered by an experience that somehow upsets the balance of the character's life. It may be a turn for the better—an insecure writing student becomes the protégée of a famous author (*Collected Stories* by Donald Margulies)—or it may be a turn for the worse—a merchant in dire need of money discovers that a wealthy widow will not pay the debt her deceased husband owed him (*The Bear* by Anton Chekhov). Whether positive or negative, large or small, this turning point typically grows out of the backstory and stirs something new in the character: a burning desire to restore the balance that has been upset.

The experience that sets the quest in motion is sometimes called the "inciting event." It may be something that the character does or something that happens to the character. Whether it takes the form of a decision, discovery, action, or external development, the inciting event is often the first important thing that happens in the story. It tends to have the most power dramatically when it occurs onstage during the play rather than offstage before it begins.

The quest translates technically into an all-important overriding goal, or superobjective, that is triggered by the inciting event and drives the story. In *Collected Stories*, for example, as a result of her new relationship with an established author, an insecure writing student sets out to become a successful author herself. In *The Bear*, after his polite attempt to collect a debt fails, a desperate merchant decides to do everything possible to get his money from the debtor's widow.

Once the character's superobjective is aroused, it typically remains in place until one of two things happens: the character achieves the goal or fails to achieve it. Either way, the story is over.

■ DOUBT: A PARABLE
Inciting event: A sermon

When we meet Sister Aloysius, the principal of St. Nicholas school, she is predisposed to mistrust Father Flynn, the parish priest and gym instructor, because of something she saw in the backstory: a boy on the playground recoiling from his touch. The incident occurred weeks ago on the first day of school and aroused her concern, but not enough to do something about it. Because no action ensued, the play did not begin then.

What incites Aloysius to action now is the sermon Flynn gives in scene 1, a sermon on doubt that begins with the question "What do you do when you're not sure?" As we hear the sermon delivered, we see only Flynn at the pulpit. We do not yet know that Aloysius is in the church listening to the sermon and being affected by it. In scene 2, as she discusses school business with the new eighth-grade teacher, Sister James, we begin to see that Flynn's sermon has disturbed Aloysius and prompted her to grill James about the priest and his choice of topic. "Is Father Flynn in Doubt?" Aloysius wonders. "Is he concerned that someone else is in Doubt?"

As they continue, her concern leads her to take further action. She orders James to be more aware of her students and more vigilant in reporting their problems. Knowing that her suspicions, if made public, could cause scandal, Aloysius remains purposefully vague about the reason for this edict: "I can only say I am concerned, perhaps needlessly, about matters in St. Nicholas school." The scene goes on and the topic changes, but the story engine has been ignited.

Quest: To expose and expel a suspected child predator
Flynn's sermon on doubt has stirred in Aloysius a quest that begins with suspicion and leads to a deep and relentless need to expose the priest and force him out of the parish. This goal is what drives most of the dramatic action and holds the story together. The play cannot end until Flynn has been removed or Aloysius has been defeated. As the story unfolds, the nature of her quest will become increasingly transparent until it leads to an open confrontation with the priest and a final showdown to force his resignation.

■ TOPDOG/UNDERDOG
Inciting event: A business proposition
Parks's play has a dual-protagonist structure that centers on two brothers: Lincoln, a reformed card hustler, and Booth, a petty thief. Each functions dramatically as the protagonist of his own quest and the antagonist of his brother's. Both quests are incited by the same event.

When the play begins, Booth has already decided to change his life and become a rich man with the resources he believes are necessary to win back his ex-girlfriend Grace. "She's in love with me again," he tells Lincoln, "but she don't know it yet." Booth plans to accomplish this rise in status through the art of three-card monte, a shell game played on the street for money.

What incites the play is Booth's proposal, in scene 1, to bring Lincoln in on the scheme and Lincoln's rejection of his offer. It is a clash of wills that rekindles the brothers' sibling rivalry and drives the rest of the play to its deadly conclusion.

Booth cannot walk away from this clash for two reasons. First, the scam requires at least two partners working together in secret: a dealer who uses sleight of hand to trick players into losing their cash and a stickman who lures customers by pretending to win the game. Second, Booth has no talent for card hustling, while Lincoln is a master dealer who can throw the cards with legendary skill. For Booth's plan to succeed, he must get his brother's help. "Oh, come on, man, we could make money you and me," he tells Lincoln. "You would throw the cards and I'd be your Stickman."

Lincoln declines Booth's offer because of a commitment he made years ago to give up card hustling and seek only legitimate employment. His change of heart was inspired by the murder of his stickman Lonny. Fearing for his own safety, Lincoln reformed himself and has since resisted the cards, which he now views as an addiction. "You know I don't touch thuh cards, man," he tells Booth. "I don't touch thuh cards."

Booth's dream of a new life and Lincoln's pledge to avoid card hustling force the brothers onto a collision course that sets each brother's quest into motion.

Booth's quest: To become topdog

Lincoln's rejection of his business proposition rekindles in Booth the burning desire to be topdog. For Booth, this means proving to both Lincoln and himself that he is the better of the two. He plans to do this by outperforming his brother at three-card monte, filling his pockets with cash, and winning back Grace. In the end, it is the desire to rise above his older brother that most drives Booth. This is why the other onstage character is Lincoln and not Grace. It is also why all of the onstage dramatic action takes place in the room he shares with Lincoln and not in other areas of his life.

Lincoln's quest: To stay topdog

Booth's business proposition has stirred up in Lincoln the need to protect his topdog status. For Lincoln, this means being the head of the family—what's left of it—and keeping his volatile younger brother in tow. A key part of this quest is to maintain a legitimate job with a regular paycheck that can cover both brothers' living expenses. Booth's offer has threatened the status quo by creating an antagonistic home environment and arousing in Lincoln old demons he thought he had put to rest.

■ THE CLEAN HOUSE
Inciting event: A cleaning woman who won't clean

The role of protagonist is shared by three characters—Lane, Matilde, and Virginia—who have individual dramatic journeys as well as a collective one. The event that sets these journeys into motion is Matilde's decision to stop cleaning Lane's house, even though it is her new job as a live-in maid to do so. Rather than see this inciting event unfold onstage, we learn about it through Lane in her opening words of the play: "It has been such a hard month. / My cleaning lady—from Brazil—decided that she was depressed one day and stopped cleaning my house." This decision generates a chain of events that will change the lives of all three protagonists.

By reporting the inciting event in a monologue rather than revealing it through character interaction, the playwright compresses a month's worth of experience into a few lines that immediately establish the opening conflict. The monologue also creates the opportunity to reveal Lane. From her description of the event, we can see that she has a lofty opinion of herself and a condescending view of the woman she expects to clean up after her.

Lane's quest: To regain control of her universe

When her new live-in housekeeper stops cleaning, Lane begins to lose control of her house and the dust and dirt that is ever accumulating in it. When her efforts to order Matilde back to work fail, Lane has her professionally medicated. When that also fails, Lane ends up having to clean the house herself, a vexing development for one who sees herself above such menial labor.

Matilde's decision to stop cleaning thus presents a challenge to Lane's authority and arouses in her the need to reassert control of her universe. Initially, her eye is on the cleanliness of her house and the efficacy of her position as a housekeeper's employer. Over time, Lane's need for control will expand to include her interfering sister, her unfaithful husband, and the exotic older woman whom her husband introduces as his soul mate.

Matilde's quest: To heal from the loss of her parents

The daughter of parents who lived and died in laughter, Matilde wants to follow in their footsteps and become a comedian. Having to work as a cleaning woman makes her feel sad, not only because it's a job she dislikes but also because it removes her from this legacy of humor. Sadness is what motivates Matilde to stop cleaning and reclaim her time and her future. It is a decision that arouses in her the determination to think up the perfect joke and, in doing so, to recover from the loss of her parents, for whom she still mourns.

Virginia's quest: To have a meaningful task

With a life that has been in a downward spiral for three decades, Virginia is looking for ways to distract herself from her failures. When she learns that her sister's new maid is too sad to clean, Virginia concocts a scheme to rescue the maid by secretly cleaning the house for her. Underlying this scheme is a desire to have a meaningful task in her otherwise empty life and to reconnect with her estranged sister, Lane, whom she cannot help but envy.

ANALYZING YOUR STORY

Explore the event, positive or negative, that sets your main character's quest into motion.

INCITING EVENT

- What is the inciting event of your story? Where and when does it take place?
- Who is present when the inciting event occurs? If the main character is not present, how does he or she learn about it?
- What causes the inciting event to happen?
- Right or wrong, how does the main character perceive this event?
- What is his or her immediate emotional response to what happens?
- How does the inciting event affect the character physically? Psychologically? Socially?
- How has the balance of the character's life been upset in either a good way or bad way?
- Who else, if anyone, is affected by the inciting event, and how?
- What, if anything, happens onstage prior to the inciting event? If it does not occur early in the script, what is the reason for delaying it? How does this delay serve the story?

QUEST

- What goal, or superobjective, does the inciting event arouse in the main character?
- Why is this goal important to the character? Identify what's at stake.
- Is this goal positive (a desire to acquire or achieve something) or

negative (a desire to get away from something)? If the latter, how would you restate it as a positive goal?

- Why is this quest an appropriate choice for this character in this situation?
- What does this quest reveal about the character?
- At the time of the inciting event, what allies, skills, and resources does the character have available to complete the quest? What challenges does the character anticipate?
- Large or small, what is the first step the character will take to pursue the goal?

Drama is often called the art of conflict. Whether large or small, ordinary or unusual, there is always a problem to be solved from the beginning of the play to the end. Conflict tends to be associated with argument, but that is only one form of conflict. Anything that stands in the character's way and makes his or her objective difficult to achieve is a conflict.

Such obstacles may arise from the inner world of the character, as in Jenny Schwartz's *God's Ear*, where a mother tries to heal from the drowning of her child but suffers from inconsolable grief that makes healing seem impossible. Or conflict may arise from another character with opposing needs, as in August Wilson's *The Piano Lesson*, where a woman wants to preserve a valuable family heirloom—a hand-carved piano—but is confronted by her brother, who wants to sell it. Or conflict may arise from the current situation in the world of the story, as in Tony Kushner's *Angels in America*, where a young gay man with AIDS in the 1980s wants to survive but faces a society that rejects him because of his sexual identity and medical condition.

The central conflict of the story is the most difficult obstacle that the character must overcome. This big problem is typically introduced early on and not solved, if at all, until the end. It is by observing the character's efforts to deal with the central conflict that we come to understand the quest and its importance to the character. If the quest feels unclear or unimportant, it often means that the conflict is not strong enough.

■ DOUBT: A PARABLE
Since the play is structured around a single protagonist, the dramatic conflict arises primarily from the obstacles Sister Aloysius faces as she pursues her story goal.

Aloysius's main problem: Flynn
Aloysius wants to protect the students of St. Nicholas from Father Flynn, a priest whom she suspects of child abuse. Many problems make this quest difficult. For example, she has no proof of his wrongdoing, and the nature of her suspicion is so explosive that, if made public, it could backfire and harm not only herself and the child in question but also the whole school.

Of all the obstacles she faces, the most overwhelming is Flynn himself, who is, in classical story terms, the antagonist. As a priest in the 1960s, he is a trusted and respected religious figure who is virtually beyond reproach.

He is also a charismatic and popular leader in the parish, a factor that further protects him from insinuations about his moral character. Moreover, he ranks above Aloysius in the patriarchy of the Church and has friends, such as Monsignor Benedict, who are even higher. Most importantly, Flynn will deny wrongdoing and fight back to stop Aloysius from damaging his reputation. If her quest is to succeed, Aloysius must find a way to bring Flynn down.

This central conflict is introduced in scene 4, when Sister James first reports her concerns about Flynn and Aloysius acknowledges the difficulty of defeating him. "I don't know what to do," she says. "There are parameters which protect him and hinder me." The conflict rises to a boil in the showdown between Aloysius and Flynn in scene 8 and reaches its end point in scene 9, when Aloysius must finally acknowledge that Flynn has triumphed.

■ TOPDOG/UNDERDOG

As the dramatic journeys of Booth and Lincoln unfold and intertwine, each must deal with certain conflicts, the most formidable of which is a brother who wants to be better than him. The fundamental dilemma is similar to that in a fight to the death between two dogs: only one can end up the winner.

Booth's main problem: Lincoln

Booth wants to be topdog, with Grace at his side and pockets full of cash. His biggest problem is his older brother, Lincoln, who intentionally and unintentionally creates obstacles to Booth's success, whether by resisting his pleas to join him in a three-card monte scheme or by walking around in a strange outfit—an Abraham Lincoln costume—that could scare Grace away. Booth expresses this central conflict in scene 1 when Lincoln refuses to become his partner in throwing the cards: "Here I am trying to earn a living and you standing in my way, YOU STANDING IN MY WAY, LINK!"

Lincoln's main problem: Booth

Lincoln wants to stay a topdog who earns an honest living and holds the last shreds of his family together. His biggest problem is his brother Booth, who denigrates Lincoln's job at the arcade and keeps trying to tempt him back to life on the street as a three-card monte dealer. Booth knows that Lincoln has an addiction to the cards and uses this weakness throughout the play to wear him down. The conflict rises to the three-card monte game the brothers play in scene 6, when the demons that Booth has awakened turn against him.

Each of the three protagonists faces obstacles that will make her individual quest difficult to achieve.

Lane's main problem: A failed marriage

Lane wants to regain control of her personal universe. Her biggest problem is that life is far from perfect and not everything can be the way she wants. Just as a clean house is an impossible dream due to ever-accumulating dust and dirt, Lane's desire to create a perfect world is unattainable. Instead, she must deal with life's inevitable messes, whether it's a cleaning woman who refuses to clean her house, a sister who schemes behind her back, or a husband who falls in love with another woman.

Of these problems, the one that taxes Lane most is the unexpected and devastating loss of Charles, whom she still loves, even after he has left her. It is a conflict that tests her to the core and brings her to a crisis in which she must do the unthinkable: forgive the woman who ruined her marriage.

Matilde's main problem: The challenges of a perfect joke

Matilde wants to heal from the loss of her parents. She believes she can accomplish this by learning what they both knew but never shared with her: a perfect joke. Discovering this treasure is a difficult task, requiring time, inspiration, and comedic skills, all of which are hard to come by. Matilde's attempts to tackle such challenges account for much of her inward behavior during the play, as in act one, scene 12, when Lane returns home late and discovers her new maid sitting alone in the dark living room. "I was trying to think up a joke," she explains. "I almost had one. / Now it's gone."

In the world of *The Clean House*, the problems associated with conjuring up humor also include the threat of death, since a perfect joke has the power to make one die from laughter. This threat explains why Matilde, after thinking up the perfect joke in act two, scene 8, asks herself, "Am I dead?"

Virginia's main problem: Lane

Virginia wants to do something meaningful in her otherwise empty life. She starts out with a plan to rescue Lane's new maid and ends up with a plan to rescue Lane in the aftermath of her failed marriage. A key purpose of both plans is to get more involved in Lane's life and to become "real sisters who tell each other real things."

Virginia's biggest problem is that Lane is too busy for such a relationship, does not think she needs anyone's help, and resents Virginia's attempts to interfere in her life. This contrary position is supported by years of rivalry tracing back to their early childhood. Lane's resistance to Virginia's unwanted help reaches a peak in act two, scene 9, when Lane lets her have it for secretly cleaning her house: "I WILL NOT LET MY HOUSE BE A BREEDING GROUND FOR YOUR WEIRD OBSESSIVE DIRT FETISH. I WILL NOT PERMIT YOU TO FEEL LIKE A BETTER PERSON JUST BECAUSE YOU PUSH DIRT AROUND ALL DAY ON MY BEHALF."

ANALYZING YOUR STORY

Explore the central conflict that will make your main character's quest difficult to achieve.

WARM UP

- The conflict in your story is defined by what the main character wants and why he or she cannot easily achieve it. As a step toward exploring the central conflict of the story, define your main character's quest, or superobjective.

SOURCES OF CONFLICT

- Think about your main character's physical, psychological, and social limitations. What personal traits or conditions, if any, make it difficult for him or her to succeed? In other words, how might the character be his or her own worst enemy?
- Think about the other characters in the story: who they are and what they want. Which of them pose obstacles to the success of your main character's quest?
- Which character poses the greatest threat, and why?
- Think about the physical, emotional, social, economic, political, and spiritual dimensions of your character's world. What elements make it most difficult for him or her to succeed?

CENTRAL CONFLICT

- Of the problems you have identified, what is the biggest single obstacle that your character must overcome if the quest is to succeed?
- What makes this conflict so powerful?
- Does the central conflict have roots in the backstory? If so, how does the past add to the power of the conflict in the present?
- Where and how in the script is the central conflict introduced?
- Right or wrong, how does the character perceive this challenge?
- What is the character's emotional response?
- What do the character's reactions to the central conflict reveal about him or her?
- Do you see any opportunities to strengthen the central conflict, and, if so, how?

Objective is *what* the character wants. Motivation is *why* the character wants it. This motivation can be measured by what will be gained if the quest succeeds or what will be lost if it fails.

Motive is a key ingredient in everything that characters do, from visiting friends to conquering kingdoms. For behavior to make sense, there must be a reason to act—even if it is faulty or illogical. Motivation may be noble or base, healthy or unhealthy, profound or petty, as long as it makes sense to the character at the moment of action.

For the quest that drives the story, the character needs a compelling reason to keep pushing forward in spite of the obstacles that stand in the way. If the stakes are not high enough, the character's efforts to deal with big problems may seem unbelievable or melodramatic. Ideally, what's at risk is so significant that the character cannot give up or compromise the goal as long as it is still possible to pursue it.

In Rajiv Joseph's *Gruesome Playground Injuries*, for example, an accident-prone daredevil tries over a period of thirty years to protect his relationship with his soul mate, whom he first met in a school nurse's office when they were both eight years old. What's at stake for him is not only love but his only chance for love in a dangerous world.

■ DOUBT: A PARABLE

Sister Aloysius has compelling reasons to expose and expel Father Flynn.

What's at stake for Aloysius: Duty

Aloysius's campaign to drive Flynn out of St. Nicholas parish is motivated, in part, by her concern for the welfare of the students, especially Donald Muller, whom the priest may already have abused. Her work philosophy suggests, however, that there is something even more important at stake. Aloysius reveals this philosophy in scene 2 when coaching Sister James about how to handle an eighth grader named William London. Aloysius views him as a troublemaker who is unlikely to graduate high school, but shrugs that off since it is beyond her jurisdiction: "We simply have to get him through, out the door, and then he's somebody else's problem."

Aloysius's lack of concern for William's future implies that she is more preoccupied with her duties as principal than with the boy's well-being outside the walls of her elementary school. As one who embraces the Catholic church and school system, and has taken a religious vow of obedience, fulfillment of duty is key to Aloysius's identity. If she fails to protect her children from the perceived threat of Flynn, she will have failed to meet her responsibilities. It is perhaps this concern for duty that most motivates her campaign against him.

■ TOPDOG/UNDERDOG

The duel between Lincoln and Booth is fueled by high stakes that make it impossible for either brother to surrender.

What's at stake for Booth: Self-esteem

Booth's quest to be topdog is motivated by his need to improve his image. Abandoned by his parents at a young age, forced to live in the shadow of an older brother, and subjected to racial disparities in the world around him, Booth has grown up with a low sense of self-esteem. It is a disposition that he tries to cover up with braggadocio and threats of violence. Now in his thirties, he longs for the respect and power that a successful man would enjoy. Though he often declares his love for Grace—"Aint no man can love her the way I can"—he sees her beauty as a prize that will prove his worth to himself and to his brother, with whom he constantly competes.

What's at stake for Lincoln: Security

Lincoln has been abandoned by most of the important people in his life. His quest to stay topdog is thus motivated by a deep need for security. For Lincoln, this means having the support of family and avoiding dangerous pursuits like card hustling, which led to the death of his partner Lonny. This is why Lincoln now clings to his arcade job, which every Friday generates an honest paycheck that buys his brother's affection and keeps a roof over both of their heads.

■ THE CLEAN HOUSE

The three protagonists—Lane, Matilde, and Virginia—collectively provide the reason for the story because each has high stakes hanging in the balance as she pursues her individual goal.

What's at stake for Lane: The perfect life

Lane's quest to regain control of her universe is motivated by her dream of the perfect life in which everyone and everything meets her impossibly high standards. Flaws, failures, and disappointments are not permitted in this universe. Even a relatively small problem, such as a dusty house, must be addressed and eradicated. The stakes attached to Lane's vision of perfection are so high that when a large problem arises, such as a husband who falls in love with another woman, her first response is a suicide attempt.

What's at stake for Matilde: Peace of mind

Though her parents died last year, Matilde still wears black to express mourning and still retreats regularly from the real world to her storybook imaginings of them. She hopes that, through humor, she will be able to understand and accept her loss. Matilde's quest to heal from the death of her parents is thus motivated by her need to reclaim the peace of mind she had enjoyed when her family was intact.

What's at stake for Virginia: A reason to live

After three decades of bad decisions, Virginia is haunted by a feeling of uselessness. In act one, scene 13, she explains her failure this way: "I wanted something—big. I didn't know how to ask for it." Virginia's quest to find a meaningful task is motivated by her need to justify her existence. This motivation is implied in her opening monologue when she half-jokingly admits that she might slit her wrists if she had too much time to think about how her life has turned out.

ANALYZING YOUR STORY

Explore the motivation of the main character to complete the quest.

WARM UP

- Define your main character's quest, or superobjective.

POTENTIAL GAIN OR LOSS

- What will your character gain if the quest succeeds? What will be lost if it fails?
- Will another individual also be affected by the outcome of your character's quest? If so, who would be affected most? What would this other character gain or lose?
- Will any group—such as the character's family, friends, co-workers, or community—also be affected by the quest? If so, who? What would they gain or lose?
- Think about the greatest good that will be achieved if the quest succeeds or the greatest loss that will be suffered if it fails. What is the highest stake hanging in the balance?
- Are the stakes high enough to prevent your character from

compromising or giving up the quest when it becomes challenging? If not, can you raise the stakes by:
- Making the potential gain greater?
- Making the potential loss worse?
- Broadening the potential impact of the quest—for example, by increasing the number of people who will be affected by its outcome?

MOTIVATION
- Dramatic characters tend to be noble in some way. What is your character's noblest reason for wanting to complete the quest?
- When your character launches the quest, does he or she have any misperceptions about what is really at stake? If so, how does this affect the story?
- Does your character's motivation to complete the quest stem from any backstory experience, positive or negative, and, if so, what?
- Does your character have any selfish, base, or cowardly reason for wanting to complete the quest, and, if so, what?
- What does your character's motivation suggest about his or her values and beliefs?
- Sometimes characters are unaware of their true motivations for taking action. Does your character have any subconscious reason to pursue this goal, and, if so, what?

A strategy is a general action plan designed to achieve an overall goal. Tactics are the specific steps of the plan. If a character's overall goal is challenging, he or she usually has to try a number of different strategies and tactics, with some succeeding and some failing. Ideally, the actions undertaken by the characters become more difficult and risky as the story unfolds so that the conflict keeps rising.

In Lynn Nottage's *Ruined*, for example, a traveling salesman in the civil war–torn Democratic Republic of Congo wants to convince a brothel owner to buy two teenage girls from him and put them to work in her establishment. He employs different strategies and tactics to accomplish this goal. One strategy is to put the brothel owner in a good mood. His tactics are to give her gifts—a new tube of lipstick and a rare box of Belgian chocolates— and to recite a poem he has written for her. Another, more difficult strategy is to gain her sympathy. His tactics are to remind her of the personal danger he has risked by traveling here during the war and to convince her that, without a place to live and work, the abused homeless girls in his wagon may not survive.

By employing a variety of strategies and tactics, characters reveal different dimensions of who they are. They also move the story forward and keep it from growing stale. Their actions typically break down into two basic types of objectives:

Behavioral objectives. Most strategies and tactics are behavioral objectives, which focus on affecting another character in a specific way. There are four basic types of behavioral objectives:

- To make someone feel good—for example, to flatter, seduce, or cheer up.
- To make someone feel bad—for example, to threaten, scold, or frighten.
- To find out something important—for example, to ask questions, probe, or elicit confessions.
- To convince someone of something important—for example, to persuade or prove a point.

Physical objectives. Strategies and tactics may also be primarily physical—for example, to acquire an important object, complete a physical task, or effect a change in the environment. Physical objectives do not necessarily require a response from someone else and are thus less common in dramatic stories, which typically center on character interactions.

■ DOUBT: A PARABLE

Sister Aloysius tries a variety of strategies and tactics to protect her students from a suspected pedophile.

Aloysius's plan to expose and expel Flynn

Learn the truth. One of Aloysius's primary strategies is to uncover the truth about Father Flynn. Her first tactic in this plan is to put the staff on alert for signs of trouble among the students without identifying the nature of that trouble (scene 2). This is an easy step since she is not implicating Flynn directly. Result: *success*. Sister James reports disturbing news about Flynn and a boy in her class named Donald Muller.

Aloysius responds to the report from James by grilling her about the details of what she observed (scene 4). This tactic is more difficult than a general edict since it focuses on Flynn by name and lets another person know what she's thinking. Result: *success*. Though her only evidence is the possible smell of alcohol on a boy's breath, Aloysius becomes convinced that Flynn is guilty of child abuse.

Her next tactic is to get Flynn into her office on a false pretext so she can catch him off guard and get him to confess to wrongdoing with a witness present (scene 5). This is a far more demanding tactic that requires her to confront Flynn openly and put herself at risk by challenging someone above her in the Church hierarchy. Result: *failure*. Flynn claims that he is innocent and condemns her insinuations and unorthodox conduct.

Gather allies. Another of Aloysius's key strategies is to get help in bringing the priest down. Because of the potential scandal, as well as the limitations of the patriarchal system in which she and Flynn operate, Aloysius has few potential allies other than Sister James and Donald's parents. Aloysius consequently meets with Mrs. Muller to discuss Flynn's relationship with her son and get her support (scene 8). This tactic carries high risk since it takes Aloysius's concern about Flynn out of the school and into the community. Result: *failure*. Mrs. Muller chooses not to think ill of the priest and turns against Aloysius.

Attack. When Aloysius finds herself cornered by Flynn in her office, she employs her most dangerous strategy: to threaten his existence as a priest (scene 8). Her key tactic is to frighten him by falsely claiming to have incriminating evidence against him from a nun in his previous parish. Immediate result: *success*. Flynn requests a transfer from St. Nicholas. Delayed result: *failure*. Flynn is promoted to pastor of another parish.

■ TOPDOG/UNDERDOG

Booth and Lincoln try a variety of strategies and tactics as they compete in a duel that has room for only one winner.

Booth's plan to become topdog

Make money. In his quest for power, one of Booth's primary strategies is to get rich quick by becoming a card hustler. His first tactic is to gather the tools necessary for three-card monte and to practice being a dealer (scene 1). This is a simple step since the materials are easy to find and he is familiar with the routine. Result: *failure*. Throwing the cards is much harder than he thought.

His next tactic is to get Lincoln to partner with him in the scheme (scene 1). This is a logical step since Lincoln is not only his brother but also a master card hustler. Result: *failure*. In spite of Booth's promises of wealth and women, Lincoln is a reformed man who refuses to touch the cards. As the story unfolds, Booth repeats this tactic several times. Though he eventually weakens his brother's resistance to the cards, he never succeeds in acquiring him as a partner.

Have the best sex life. Another of Booth's strategies is to win back his beautiful ex-girlfriend Grace so he can prove his superiority over his brother as a sexual dynamo. Booth's initial tactics include asking her out on a date and giving her a special ring. This is a logical tactic since it used to work in the past. Result: *success*. Grace agrees to see him tomorrow night.

Attuned to the allure of personal image, Booth takes tactical steps to improve his own. After changing his name to 3-Card, a moniker more befitting a card hustler, he improves his wardrobe by stealing expensive clothing for his brother and himself (scene 2). This riskier strategy entails the chance of getting arrested. Result: *success*. Booth transforms himself into a sharp dresser with a new name.

Whether his triumphs in the bedroom are real or imagined, Booth makes sure his brother knows about them. Returning home from his date in scene 3, for example, Booth wakes Lincoln up so he can crow about his sexual exploits. This tactic is difficult since he has to make most of it up. Result: *failure*. Lincoln acts impressed but knows Booth is lying.

Another recurring tactic is to denigrate Lincoln's sexual prowess by bombarding him with insults and accusations of impotence. In scene 6, Booth taunts Lincoln about the failure of his marriage and his wife's coming to

Booth for sexual favors. This is a risky move since it could provoke a show-down. Result: *success*. The punch lands and leaves Lincoln vulnerable.

Beat Lincoln at his own game. Booth's most difficult and risky strategy is to challenge Lincoln to a game of three-card monte for money. Even though he is facing a master dealer, Booth puts his $500 inheritance at risk. Result: *failure*. Booth loses his pride and his most treasured possession.

Lincoln's plan to stay topdog

Hold down an honest job. One of Lincoln's key strategies for success is to keep his job as an Abraham Lincoln impersonator at a shooting arcade. However odd the job may be, it is honest employment that has saved him from the dangers of being a card hustler. This is why Lincoln, in scene 1, re-jects Booth's offer of a three-card monte partnership. His tactic is to respond repeatedly with the mantra "I don't touch thuh cards." The tactic is easy since he has no interest in partnering with his brother anyway. Result: *success*. Lincoln in the first few scenes resists the temptation to throw the cards.

Aware that there will be cutbacks at work and that he could be replaced by a wax dummy, Lincoln wants to ensure that his Abraham Lincoln rou-tine is in top form. His tactic is to convince Booth to help him practice being "assassinated." This is a difficult step since Lincoln must acknowledge that he needs Booth's help. Result: *failure*. Booth at first has other plans (scene 2) and then, when he does agree to help, gives bad advice that could get Lincoln fired (scene 3).

Save the family. Another of Lincoln's key strategies is to protect what's left of his family. A recurring tactic is to let Booth win certain power struggles, just as a card hustler might "lose" a small pot now in order to win a big one later. In scene 2, Lincoln not only surrenders his hard-earned money to cover both brothers' living expenses but also lets Booth keep the lion's share of the leftover cash. Result: *success*. Lincoln continues to have what matters to him most: companionship and a roof over his head.

Another of Lincoln's recurring tactics is to come to his brother's rescue. In scene 5, when Booth is devastated by Grace's rejection, Lincoln tries different tactics to take Booth's mind off his distress, such as reminding him of the "good times" they had as brothers. This is a difficult step since there weren't many good times and it forces Lincoln to relive painful memories. Result: *success*. The brothers make a friendly connection.

Show Booth who's boss. Though Lincoln wants to protect his last family relationship, he must sometimes use harsh tactics to keep his brother in tow. In scene 6, Lincoln shows Booth who's boss by beating him at three-card monte and taking away his life's savings. This is Lincoln's riskiest tactic since it most jeopardizes his family ties. Immediate result: *success*. Lincoln wins the pot. Delayed result: *failure*. He loses his life.

■ THE CLEAN HOUSE

Each of the play's three protagonists has an important goal. Lane wants to regain control of her universe. Matilde wants to heal from the loss of her parents. Virginia wants to find a meaningful task. Each woman uses a variety of strategies and tactics to deal with the obstacles standing in her way.

Lane's plan to regain control of her universe

Take charge. As a successful doctor at an important hospital, Lane is used to being in charge. In her quest for control, her most common strategy is to tackle problems head-on by asserting her authority and ordering everyone else to do what she wants. In act one, scene 2, when Matilde grows too sad to clean, Lane's first tactic is to take her to the hospital and have her medicated. Lane expects this to be an easy solution to the problem. Result: *failure*. Matilde only pretends to take her pills and still won't clean.

Deny the truth. When faced with a problem she can't control, one of Lane's recurring strategies is to deny that it exists. In act one, scene 13, after her marriage has failed, Virginia offers to help her through the difficult time. Lane responds by insisting that she does not need help. This is especially difficult since nothing could be further from the truth. Result: *false success*. Virginia leaves her alone and Lane continues to suffer.

Diagnose problems. Accustomed to evaluating medical conditions, Lane at times applies a diagnostic approach to other types of problems as well. In act two, scene 7, her probing skills come into play when Matilde returns from Charles's new home and Lane pumps her for information about his relationship with Ana. This is a difficult step since it exposes how much Lane still cares for Charles. Result: *success*. She learns that Ana's cancer has returned.

Matilde's plan to heal from the loss of her parents

Become a comedian. Matilde's parents were both comedians who loved to joke and laugh. One of Matilde's key strategies to cope with their deaths is to become a comedian like them. When she realizes that her job as Lane's maid makes her too sad to think up jokes, Matilde stops cleaning. This tactic is easy since it enables her to trade work she hates for work she loves. Result: *success*. Matilde manages to avoid most of her household duties and is soon rescued by Virginia, who secretly cleans the house for her (act one, scene 7).

Since her parents both died as the result of a perfect joke, Matilde believes she will be better able to understand and accept their deaths if she can think up a perfect joke herself. This is a challenging step, but it becomes her primary tactic to cope with her loss. Result: *success*. Matilde spends a lot of time alone and eventually thinks up the perfect joke (act two, scene 8).

Keep her parents present. Another coping strategy for Matilde is to keep her parents alive in her mind. She does this by talking about them with others and by imagining them in idyllic moments of great laughter. These tactics are difficult because no one else really understands the depth of her loss and because illusions of perfection are not easy to maintain. Result: *success*. Matilde's inward moments with her parents free her from sadness and help her maintain the frame of mind she needs to think up jokes.

Get more involved with others. As the story unfolds, Matilde begins to fill the void her parents left by becoming more involved in the lives of those around her. Her tactics include telling jokes, giving advice, orchestrating the bond that the women form, and, finally, granting Ana's wish to die laughing. These tactics are increasingly difficult because they require Matilde to spend less and less time in her inner world where everything is perfect. Result: *success*. Matilde eventually reaches a moment of completion with her parents (act two, scene 14).

Virginia's plan to find a meaningful task

Keep busy. In her quest to improve her life, Virginia's primary strategy is to keep so busy that she will not have time to think about her failures. When cleaning her own house isn't enough, Virginia offers to clean Lane's house secretly so that Matilde can have more time to think up jokes (act one, scene 7). This is an easy choice since Virginia loves to clean, but it involves the risk of getting caught. Immediate result: *success*. For two weeks, Virginia indulges her cleaning compulsion while getting an unprecedented look at her sister's things when she isn't home. Delayed result: *failure*. Lane figures out what's going on and puts a stop to Virginia's clandestine activities (act one, scene 13).

Lend a hand. To add meaning to her life, Virginia repeatedly tries to help others, especially her estranged sister. In act two, after learning that Lane's marriage has failed, Virginia launches into help mode. Her tactics include openly cleaning Lane's house, co-hosting a tense visit with Charles and Ana, bringing Lane a hot-water bottle to help her relax, and offering to make a new slip cover for her filthy couch. Result: *failure*. While Lane reluctantly accepts the hot-water bottle, she ends up screaming at Virginia for having a weird dirt fetish and meddling in her life (act two, scene 9).

Fight back. As one who usually takes a back seat to others, Virginia decides to try a new approach and stand up to Lane. This is Virginia's most difficult strategy since she has always been second best to her domineering sister. The strategy gathers strength in act two, scene 9, after Lane screams at her and Virginia fights back: "No wonder Charles left. You have no compassion." The rebellion reaches its tactical peak when Virginia creates an operatic mess in Lane's living room. Result: *success*. Virginia gains stature in her sister's eyes and forces her to admit that she needs Virginia's help.

ANALYZING YOUR STORY

Explore the strategies and tactics your characters use to reach for their goals.

FIRST STEP

- The character's first strategy to achieve his or her superobjective is usually the one that seems easiest, safest, or most logical. What is your character's first strategy?
- What are the key steps, or tactics, of this action plan?
- How successful is this action plan?
- What does this strategy reveal about your character?

LAST RESORT

- The character's last resort typically occurs late in the story and is the step that he or she perceives to be most difficult or risky. What is your character's most challenging strategy to achieve his or her superobjective?
- What are the key steps, or tactics, of this action plan?
- How successful is this action plan?
- What does this strategy reveal about your character?

KEY INTERMEDIATE STEPS

- What are one or two other strategies that your character tries between the first strategy and the last resort?
- What are the key steps, or tactics, of these action plans?
- How successful is each action plan?
- What do these intermediate strategies reveal about your character?

STRATEGIES IN SEQUENCE

- Look at the strategies in chronological order. Does this sequence feel logical and true for this character? If not, how might these steps be revised or rearranged?
- Are the character's strategies truly different or only variations of the same theme? If the strategic approach feels redundant, how can you make it less predictable?

POINTERS AND PLANTS

The effectiveness of a story depends on how actively the audience is engaged in the dramatic journey and how willing they are to believe the events that occur. To keep audience members leaning forward in their seats, dramatic writers use two types of preparation tools:

Pointer. A pointer is a character trait, speech, action, image, or object that overtly paves the way for a future story development by suggesting it might happen. The purpose of a pointer is to create suspense by making the audience anticipate an outcome. In *Anna in the Tropics* by Nilo Cruz, for example, a woman and her daughters wait at a Florida seaport for the arrival of a new hire for the family's cigar factory: a handsome lector from Cuba who will read to the workers. As the women study his photograph and speculate on what he will be like, we wait in suspense with them to find out how this newcomer will change their lives.

Plant. A plant is a character trait, speech, action, image, or object that will make a future story development understandable and credible to the audience by discretely paving the way for it. The plant does this by introducing information that will become important in retrospect when the development occurs. Unlike pointers, which draw attention to themselves, plants conceal their true purpose when they first appear. Plants are especially critical when a dramatic event is so unusual, difficult, or extreme that the audience may have a hard time understanding or believing it.

In *The Little Foxes* by Lillian Hellman, for example, a woman watches her wealthy husband having a fatal heart attack but does nothing to help him because she knows he is planning to cut her out of his will. We are prepared for her coldhearted response because of several plants earlier in the story that establish her ruthless greed, such as forcing her husband to discuss a lucrative business opportunity even though he is in poor health and obviously exhausted.

Whether the preparation process involves a pointer or plant, it has two basic steps: setup and payoff. In each case, the setup is what makes the payoff work. More often than not, the payoff then becomes the setup for another payoff later on.

■ **DOUBT: A PARABLE**
Examples of pointers

Provoking statement. In scene 2, as Sisters Aloysius and James discuss school business, Aloysius reveals that there may be a problem brewing at the school but will not explain what it is: "I'm sorry I'm not more forthright, but I must be careful not to create something by saying it. I can only say I am concerned, perhaps needlessly, about matters in St. Nicholas School." This provoking statement is a pointer that generates suspense by raising questions about what might be wrong and why she is being so secretive.

Revelation about the past. In scene 4, James reports that she may have smelled wine on an eighth grader's breath after he visited Father Flynn in the rectory. This revelation about the past creates suspense by raising questions about whether something inappropriate happened between the priest and the boy. It is not until the end of the play that we realize the question will never be answered with certainty. In the meantime, our anticipation of an answer is one of the driving forces that keeps us engaged.

Statement of willful intent. At different times in the story, Aloysius suggests future story developments by announcing what she intends to do. These statements of willful intent are pointers that raise questions about what will happen next. In scene 4, for example, after learning that Flynn may have given wine to an eighth grader, Aloysius says, "I'm going to invite Father Flynn to my office on an unrelated matter." This statement signals that a meeting between Aloysius and Flynn is imminent and prompts us to wonder what will ensue.

Examples of plants

Trait that will motivate future behavior. *Doubt* focuses on a nun's campaign to drive away a priest who may be a child predator. The campaign is based on circumstantial evidence rather than tangible proof that abuse occurred. The character who launches such a campaign must have a suspicious nature and a view of the world that does not bend to doubt once a conclusion has been reached.

These defining traits of Aloysius are planted in scene 2, when her first response to a student's nosebleed is not concern but, rather, the insinuation that the boy purposefully induced the bleeding to get out of class. As Aloysius lectures James about how to manage students, the scene also establishes her authoritative and rigid belief system. Such plants prepare us for the end of scene 5, when Aloysius refuses to believe Flynn's claim of innocence or to interrogate a caretaker who might corroborate Flynn's story. When she leaps to the conclusion that Flynn is guilty, we are prepared to believe that this is how this particular character would respond and to know that she will not change her mind.

Loaded object. In scene 5, when Aloysius brings Flynn to her office on the pretext of discussing the school Christmas pageant, their differences escalate into an openly adversarial relationship. Several factors, large and small, contribute to this divide. For example, when Flynn takes out a ballpoint pen to write in his notebook, we know without any words of explanation that he has just given Aloysius another reason to dislike him. Our insight is the result of a plant three scenes earlier when we learned that Aloysius blames ballpoint pens for the destruction of American penmanship and has banned them from the school.

Trait with hidden significance. In scene 5, when Aloysius is about to drop a lump of sugar into Flynn's tea, she notices the length of his fingernails. She says only, "Your fingernails." The stage direction goes further: "She is appalled but tries to hide it." The subtext suggests that she views his idiosyncrasy as a sign of vanity and perhaps something far worse. We are prepared to understand her reaction because of a plant two scenes earlier when Flynn bragged to the basketball team about his fingernails and we learned that they are unusually long.

Statement with hidden significance. In scene 4, after James reports her concerns about Flynn, Aloysius begins to plot a way to incriminate the priest. James reminds her that she is supposed to report problems to Monsignor Benedict, but Aloysius rejects the idea of going through regular channels. We understand her decision because of plants earlier in the scene, such as Aloysius's reference to the monsignor's erratic walks through the garden and her description of him as a senile man who is "oblivious" and "otherworldly in the extreme." It is no wonder that she does not see him as a reliable ally to help her deal with Flynn.

Ritual that will be important later. In scene 8, Flynn storms into Aloysius's office and slams the door, leaving the two of them alone. While such an entrance might be disturbing under any circumstance, it has added impact here because of certain plants earlier. In scene 4, Aloysius decided to ask Flynn to her office so she could interrogate him about his relationship with Donald Muller. In demanding James's presence, Aloysius introduced the rule that governs meetings between priests and nuns: "I can't be closeted alone with a priest. Another Sister must be in attendance." In the next scene, when Flynn arrived for the meeting, the third-party rule was reinforced: we saw that he could not set foot in the office until James arrived. All of this set up the showdown in scene 8 that begins with Flynn's door-slamming intrusion.

Examples of pointers

Provoking trait. Among the pointers that generate suspense, the character names—Lincoln and Booth—are foremost. With echoes of Abraham Lincoln and his assassin, John Wilkes Booth, the names suggest a violent end to the story even before it begins. When Lincoln appears in scene 1 dressed as the former president, it becomes clear that this choice of names is not arbitrary.

Provoking action. When Lincoln first enters in his Abraham Lincoln outfit, his startled brother pulls out a gun and nearly shoots him. The image of Booth pointing the gun at Lincoln makes a lasting impression that leads us to expect violence later.

Loaded object. The gun itself is a pointer that adds to our anticipation of violence between the brothers, especially since we are reminded of the weapon throughout the play, as in scene 3, when they discuss guns as a requirement for card hustling, and scene 5, when Booth reveals that he always keeps his gun on him.

Provoking statement. Throughout the play, Booth says things that reflect his violent nature and suggest trouble ahead. In scene 1, when he scolds Lincoln for wearing his Abraham Lincoln outfit home, Booth warns, "You pull that one more time I'll shoot you!" Later, after declaring his new name to be 3-Card, he offers another warning: "Anybody not calling me 3-Card gets a bullet." In scene 3, as he helps Lincoln practice his work routine, Booth pretends to be an arcade customer shooting the president and in jest says, "I am the assassin! *I am Booth!*" The menace of his declaration is underscored moments later when the brothers discuss the phony pistols used by arcade customers to shoot at Lincoln. "You ever wonder if someones gonna come in there with a real gun?" Booth asks. "Someone with uh axe tuh grind or something?" He thus unknowingly forecasts his own actions in the final scene.

Revelation about the past. In scene 6, as the rivalry between the brothers grows, Booth reveals that he slept with Lincoln's wife, Cookie, while they were still married and that this betrayal occurred in the very bed beside them now. The revelation raises questions about how Lincoln will respond and foreshadows an escalation of the conflict.

Examples of plants

Traits that will motivate future behavior. In a story that leads a man to murder his girlfriend and brother, certain character traits need to be planted so that these tragic outcomes ring true. Such traits include a penchant for violence, a possessive view of women, and an intense need to win at any cost. While Booth's near shooting of Lincoln in scene 1 works as a pointer that generates suspense, it is also one of many plants that establish his violent nature. His controlling attitude toward Grace is introduced in the same scene when he brags about giving her a ring too small for her finger so that she will be unable to take it off. His need to win is likewise introduced in scene 1—for example, when he competes with his brother over a petty issue: who will cross the room to get the Chinese takeout food so they can eat dinner.

Statement with hidden significance. In scene 5, Lincoln reveals that he has lost his job at the arcade. Plants earlier in the story have prepared us to accept this turning point as a credible development. In scene 2, Lincoln mentioned first that "Theyre talking about cutbacks at the arcade" and later that "theyre talking about cutting me." In scene 3, he expressed the fear that "they gonna replace me with a wax dummy." References to his unfair treatment at work—being underpaid and overly scrutinized by his boss—also foreshadowed his impending layoff.

Loaded object. Booth's impulsive decision to kill Lincoln is triggered by the sight of his brother about to cut open a tied-up nylon stocking with $500 inside. Several plants have established the importance of this money stocking to Booth. He first referred to it in scene 1 as his "inheritance," and Lincoln acknowledged Booth's reverence for the gift by describing it as cash he would never spend. In scene 5, we learned how Booth secretly received the stocking from his mother on the day she left. In scene 6, we further learned that he has never opened the stocking to verify its contents, a fact that adds to its status as a sacred object in his life.

■ **THE CLEAN HOUSE**
Examples of pointers
Provoking trait. In act one, scene 12, Lane returns home from work late at night and finds her new cleaning woman sitting alone in the dark. When Lane asks what she is doing, Matilde explains, "I was trying to think up a joke." Her dedication to humor is reinforced by other comments she has made about following in her parents's footsteps by thinking up jokes, particularly the perfect joke. This character trait raises questions about whether Matilde will succeed and, if so, what the perfect joke will be.

Loaded object. As Virginia irons the laundry of her sister and brother-in-law, she comes across a pair of women's underwear that clearly does not belong to Lane. This happens first in act one, scene 10, when Virginia finds black underwear in the laundry, and again two scenes later, when she finds red underwear. Since Lane only wears white, these physical items raise questions in the minds of both the characters and the audience. Whose underwear is it? Is Charles seeing another woman? Does he wear women's underwear himself?

Provoking statement and action. In act one, scene 13, Lane emerges from the kitchen with a bloodied dish towel around her wrist and claims to have cut herself accidentally. When she then reveals that her husband has gone off with a patient, her injury leads us to infer that she attempted suicide. This raises questions about how she will deal with her husband's betrayal and whether she will try suicide again. Questions about Lane's stability are revived later by other provoking actions, such as asking for hard alcohol when everyone else is drinking coffee (act two, scene 5) and launching into a tirade because her sister is vacuuming (act two, scene 9).

Revelation about the past. In act two, scene 7, Matilde informs Lane and Virginia that Ana's cancer has returned and that she refuses to go to the hospital. Two scenes later, Matilde reveals the further news that Ana is now alone because Charles has gone to Alaska. These revelations about the recent past raise questions about Ana's future and about Lane's response to the fact that her husband's soul mate is dying.

Statement of willful intent. In act two, scene 12, Ana tells Matilde, "I want you to kill me with a joke." Her request stems from Ana's knowledge that Matilde has been thinking up jokes and that, in the world of *The Clean House*, the perfect joke can cause one literally to die laughing. Ana's statement thus raises questions about whether Matilde will be able to grant her wish and, if so, how and when this extraordinary event will occur.

Examples of plants

Circumstances with hidden significance. In act one, scene 13, Lane confesses that her husband Charles has left her for one of his cancer patients. Certain plants in the story have prepared us for this news. Two scenes earlier, for example, while having coffee with Virginia, Lane revealed that she and Charles have both become so busy they rarely have time for each other. In the next scene, Lane arrived home late from work and discovered that Charles was not here and had not called to explain his whereabouts.

Traits that will motivate future behavior. In act two, scene 13, when her cancer has become unbearable, Ana asks Matilde to help her die. This impulsive, no-nonsense approach to problems was foreshadowed in act two, scene 4, when Ana first learned that she has breast cancer and demanded an immediate mastectomy, with no willingness to consider other treatment options.

In act two, scene 9, Matilde reveals that Charles has left for Alaska to search for a yew tree that might help treat Ana's cancer. His decision to embark on an ill-timed and questionable journey was foreshadowed by plants that established his sometimes childish behavior. In act two, scene 5, he displayed a sudden change of personality by extolling the virtues of apple picking and going to exotic places like Machu Picchu. Two scenes later, we learned that he was neglecting his responsibilities at the hospital so he could spend the day in bed with his soul mate. In the next scene, he tried to read Ana's mind and insisted on joining her in the sea even though he couldn't swim. His childishness helps explain his misinterpretation of Ana's needs, as she herself explains after he is gone: "I want him to be a nurse and he wants to be an explorer."

Revelation about the past that paves the way for future developments. In act two, scene 13, Ana literally dies laughing at a "cosmic joke" that Matilde tells at her request. While this cause of death might seem far-fetched in other stories, we are more likely to accept it as credible in the world of *The Clean House* because of certain plants earlier in the script. That one can literally die laughing was established in act one, scene 4, when Matilde revealed that this was how her mother died and offered the theory that she may have choked on her own spit. We have since been reminded of this fact a number of times, as in act one, scene 13, when Matilde expressed her concern to Virginia that thinking up the perfect joke might kill her.

ANALYZING YOUR STORY

Explore how pointers and plants can help prepare the audience for the key events of your story.

POINTERS

- For any event that you want the audience to wonder or worry about in advance, what pointers are you using to prepare them for this story development?
- What question does each pointer raise?
- For each pointer, how and when does the payoff occur?
- How does this payoff answer the question that the pointer raised? Does this answer include anything the characters or audience didn't expect?
- Before the payoff occurs, have you given the audience enough time to think about the pointer and anticipate the range of outcomes that might result? If not, how can you delay the payoff to increase the audience's investment in it?

- What other pointers, if any, need to be inserted into the script to raise additional questions in the audience's mind. To increase suspense, for example, can you highlight any:
  - Provoking statements?
  - Provoking actions?
  - Provoking traits?
  - Revelations about the past?
  - Statements of willful intent?
  - Loaded objects?

PLANTS

- If any story event may be difficult for the audience to understand or believe, what plants prepare them for this development?
- For any big emotional events, what plants prepare the audience to feel the full impact of what will happen?
- What is the apparent purpose of each plant when it is introduced? Its true purpose?
- How well have you hidden the true purpose of each plant? If it is an obvious plant that draws attention to itself, how might you change or replace it?
- Before the payoff occurs, have you given the audience enough time to accept the planted fact as true? If not, how might you delay the payoff to increase its credibility?
- What other plants, if any, need to be woven into the script to prepare the audience for important developments later in the story? For example, can you plant any:
  - Traits that will motivate future behavior?
  - Traits with hidden significance?
  - Statements with hidden significance?
  - Circumstances with hidden significance?
  - Revelations about the past that pave the way for future developments?
  - Rituals that will become important later?
  - Loaded objects?

A reversal is an event that turns the dramatic journey in a significantly new direction. Whether positive or negative, this turning point may be something that the character does or something that happens to the character due to outside forces, such as other characters, nature, or chance.

In Martin McDonagh's *The Cripple of Inishmaan*, for example, Billy wants to rise above his status as the village cripple on a remote Aran island and become a movie actor in America. He eventually succeeds in making it to Hollywood, but his quest for respect suffers a setback when he fails a screen test and ends up sick and alone in a squalid hotel room. As a result of this reversal in his dramatic journey, he realizes that Inishmaan is where he belongs and returns to his island home, not knowing that more trouble awaits him there.

Reversals create complications that cause the conflict to rise by introducing new problems or by making current problems worse. Such turning points make the quest more difficult and often require the character to deploy new resources and take greater risks. In plays with more than one act, each act usually ends with a major reversal that leads to the new territory of the next act.

While plot twists can add variety to a story and keep it from growing predictable, too many changes can have a diminishing effect. To feel the dramatic impact of a reversal, the audience needs to understand what has been happening in the character's life, what new developments have arisen, and what changes will result from these developments. Time is needed to flesh all of this out. If there are too many turning points or if they occur too closely together in the play, the audience may not have time to accept them as credible. The effect may be melodrama, where exaggerated conflicts come and go without emotionally engaging the audience.

■ **DOUBT: A PARABLE**

Once Sister Aloysius's quest has been incited, she encounters certain turning points that test her commitment to her goal and lead to her final showdown with Father Flynn. Each of these twists increases the conflict, but none reverses the action enough to divide the play into separate acts.

Aloysius receives disturbing news about Flynn

Aloysius experiences her first reversal in scene 4, when Sister James reports the possibility of an inappropriate relationship between Flynn and eighth grader Donald Muller. Her concerns stem from the boy's unusual behavior after a visit to the rectory and the possible smell of alcohol on his breath. "I don't have any evidence," James admits. "I'm not at all certain that anything's happened." For Aloysius, who already mistrusts Flynn, the suggestion of wrongdoing is all she needs to take decisive action. Her journey changes from mistrust to investigation.

Aloysius and Flynn square off

Another reversal occurs in scene 5, when Aloysius openly confronts Flynn about his relationship with Donald. With this, her suspicions about the priest become public and he finds himself unexpectedly having to defend his integrity. While Flynn easily persuades James of his innocence, he fails to convince Aloysius and, angered by her insinuations, leaves with a threat to have her removed from the school. She telephones Donald's parents to request a meeting, a sign that she wants to intensify her campaign against the priest. The scene thus ends with the battle line drawn between Aloysius and Flynn. Her journey has changed from investigation to attack.

Mrs. Muller sides with Flynn

Another reversal occurs in the first half of scene 8, when Aloysius meets with Donald's mother in hopes of enlisting her as an ally. Instead Mrs. Muller turns against her. The tipping point comes when, in reference to the possibility of an inappropriate relationship between Flynn and her son, Mrs. Muller says, "I think I understand the kind of thing you're talking about. But I don't want to get into it." It is an unexpected and devastating setback for Aloysius that contributes to her doubts at the end of the play. As a result of this setback, she must now face Flynn alone and resort to such tactics as lying to accomplish her goal.

■ TOPDOG/UNDERDOG

As they compete for topdog position, the dramatic journeys of Lincoln and Booth undergo reversals that lead ultimately to murder. The biggest reversal is the loss of the brothers' dreams, which begins at the end of scene 4 when Lincoln returns to the cards. The reversal peaks in scene 5 when it becomes clear that Lincoln has lost his job and Booth has lost Grace.

Lincoln returns to the cards

A major change in the dramatic journeys of both brothers occurs at the end of scene 4 when Lincoln succumbs to his inner demons and begins to throw the cards again after several years of resolutely avoiding them. He thus changes from one who resists card hustling to one who embraces it. This development in Lincoln's life also affects Booth's journey, since Lincoln will now become more involved in his brother's three-card monte scheme.

Both brothers lose their dreams

In scene 5, Lincoln reveals that, due to cutbacks at the arcade, he has been laid off from his job as an Abraham Lincoln impersonator and will be replaced by a wax dummy. This development shatters his dream of maintaining a legitimate lifestyle. He changes from one who wants to work within the system to one who is willing to work outside it. As a result, he will return to the world of three-card monte and eventually use his card hustling skills to con his brother out of his inheritance.

In the same scene, Booth, after making elaborate preparations for a dinner date with his ex-girlfriend Grace, must face the fact that she will never show up. This realization shatters his dream of winning her back. He changes from one fueled by hope to one driven by loss and despair. As a result, he will go to Grace's home later and kill her, a reckless act of violence that in turn will lead to the murder of his brother.

Lincoln and Booth play three-card monte "for real"

Another key reversal is the brothers' decision, in scene 6, to play three-card monte, with Lincoln as the dealer. Unlike earlier displays of the game, this one is "for real," with each brother risking $500 cash. For Booth, the stakes are particularly high, since his money is the inheritance he received from his mother two decades ago. The decision to play for this treasure changes the relationship of the brothers from reluctant allies to deadly foes.

■ THE CLEAN HOUSE

The dramatic journeys of the protagonists—Lane, Matilde, and Virginia— each undergo reversals that cumulatively lead the three women to a common bond. The biggest reversal is the collapse of Lane's marriage, which ends the first act and affects all of the characters in important ways.

Virginia and Matilde make a secret pact

Once the story has been set into motion, the first reversal occurs in act one, scene 7, when Virginia convinces Matilde to let her secretly clean Lane's house. This development has an impact on all three protagonists. Matilde gains more time to think up jokes. Virginia acquires a task to distract her from her empty life. Lane gets a clean house. The secret pact also begins a friendship between Matilde and Virginia that will deepen as the story unfolds.

Lane loses her husband

In act one, scene 13, Lane returns home from work distraught and reveals that her husband has gone off with a patient. This turn of events is a catalyst for multiple new story developments. Lane tries unsuccessfully to slit her wrist. Virginia gets so upset that she compulsively rearranges the objects on Lane's coffee table and, in doing so, inadvertantly reveals that she is the one who has been cleaning Lane's house. As a result, Matilde gets fired and ends up living part-time with Ana and Charles.

Ana's cancer returns

In act two, scene 7, Matilde returns from her stay with Ana and Charles with disturbing news: Ana's cancer has returned and, though she is in pain, she refuses to go to the hospital. This reversal eventually affects all five characters. Charles leaves for Alaska to search for a yew tree that might help treat the cancer. Ana is left alone and in need of medical assistance. Matilde becomes Ana's caretaker. Lane is challenged to forgive Ana and tend to her medical needs. Virginia is given an opportunity to help both her sister and Ana through a crisis.

Matilde agrees to kill Ana with a joke

In act two, scene 12, Ana asks Matilde to free her from the pain in her bones: "I would like you to kill me with a joke." The unusual request is the result of knowing that Matilde is a comedian and that her mother died from laughing. Matilde agrees to help and becomes an active participant in Ana's death. Ana is freed from pain. Lane performs an act of love and washes Ana's body. Virginia helps the others say farewell to the friend who brought them together.

ANALYZING YOUR STORY

Explore the key twists in the dramatic journey between the inciting event and the climax.

REVERSALS

- After the quest has begun, what are the major turning points in the dramatic journey?
- Where and when in the story does each of these reversals occur?
- How similar or distinct are these reversals?

- If any reversals feel too similar, what changes would add more variety to the throughline?
- Is there enough playing time between reversals to show the full effects each has on the world of the story? If not, what plot changes might you make?
- If your play has two acts (or more), look at each end-of-act reversal. Is the change big enough to create a new act with a different focus or direction?

FOR EACH REVERSAL . . .

- What triggered this development?
- How does it affect the main character physically and emotionally?
- Right or wrong, how does the character view this turning point?
- What new actions does the character take as a result of this change?
- Who else, if anyone, is affected by this experience, and how?
- What are the most important results of this event in the short term? In the long term?

CRISIS DECISION

The heart and soul of a dramatic story is the crisis that the main character faces near the end of the journey. This is usually when the character must make the most difficult decision of the story and it is the ultimate test of his or her commitment to the quest.

In Bryony Lavery's *Frozen*, a middle-aged, middle-class woman has been emotionally paralyzed with grief and anger for twenty years due to the murder of her young daughter by a serial killer. The mother's dramatic journey ultimately brings her to a decision point where she faces two unthinkable alternatives. One is to remain emotionally frozen with no hope of ever changing. The other is to meet the killer, who is now in prison, and forgive him so that she can move on with her life.

A decision like this is a "crisis decision" because it is not a choice between good and evil. Such a choice would be easy, since characters always choose what they perceive to be good at the time, even if their perception is incorrect or short-lived. Rather, a crisis decision forces the character to choose between two evils that cannot both be eliminated (by choosing one, you enable the other) or between two goods that cannot coexist (by choosing one, you lose the other). The task of the story is to bring the character to this point with compelling reasons to choose either way, so that the decision will be neither simple nor predictable.

■ DOUBT: A PARABLE
Aloysius's crisis decision: Lesser of two evils

Sister Aloysius must make many difficult decisions in her struggle to protect the children of St. Nicholas from Father Flynn. The most difficult occurs in scene 8, during her final showdown with the priest. Despite her efforts to extract a confession and force his resignation, he continues to profess his innocence and threatens to use his influence with the monsignor to have her removed from the school. She now faces a decision between two evils:

ALOYSIUS'S CRISIS DECISION

Option	Why do this	Why not do this
Admit defeat and end her campaign against Flynn	She might save her job and thus protect the school from further harm	She would fail to honor her duties as principal and an evildoer would go unpunished

196

Option	Why do this	Why not do this
Use deception to scare Flynn away	She might succeed in forcing him to resign	By telling a lie, she would be taking a step away from God

Final decision. Aloysius chooses to lie. This shows that she is willing to do anything, even risk being "damned to Hell," to fulfill her duties as a guardian of students.

■ TOPDOG/UNDERDOG

The most difficult decisions for Lincoln and Booth occur in scene 6, when they play a high-stakes game of three-card monte. At risk for Lincoln is the $500 he won tonight on the street by throwing the cards. At risk for Booth is the $500 he inherited two decades ago from his mother.

Lincoln's crisis decision: Greater of two goods

As a card hustler, Lincoln knows how to use sleight of hand and hypnotic patter to control who wins the game. When he plays three-card monte with his brother in the final scene, therefore, he faces a decision between two irreconcilable goods:

LINCOLN'S CRISIS DECISION

Option	Why do this	Why not do this
Win the game and prove that he is still a master dealer	He would protect his topdog status and net an easy $500	He might sever his relationship with his last remaining family member
Cheer up his brother by letting him win	He would safeguard his family ties and living situation	He could be subjected to further humiliation from Booth, who has been taunting him about his lost job and failed marriage

Final decision. Lincoln opts for the win. This shows that, after losing his dream of honest employment, his need to be topdog outweighs his need for family and his love for his brother. His decision also displays a selfishness that has often influenced his approach to the world.

Booth's crisis decision: Lesser of two evils

Booth's most difficult decision occurs after he has lost his prize possession: the money stocking he has guarded since his mother's departure and never opened. With Lincoln now threatening to look inside the stocking to see if it really does contain cash, Booth faces a choice between two evils:

BOOTH'S CRISIS DECISION

Option	Why do this	Why not do this
Accept his loss and let Lincoln cut open the stocking	He would preserve his relationship with Lincoln, on whom he relies for rent money, card hustling advice, and companionship	He might discover that his mother lied and that there has never been any money inside the stocking
Shoot Lincoln	He could reclaim his inheritance and keep the stocking intact	His brother could suffer serious injury or death

Final decision. Booth impulsively chooses to shoot Lincoln. This shows that, after losing his inheritance as well as his dream of reuniting with Grace, he feels he has nothing left. He will commit murder to vent his rage and avoid the possibility that his mother lied to him.

■ THE CLEAN HOUSE

All three protagonists must make difficult decisions as they pursue their individual goals. Each character's most difficult decision occurs at a separate point in the story.

Lane's crisis decision: Lesser of two evils

Lane's most difficult decision occurs at the end of act two, scene 9, when it becomes clear that the dying Ana needs a doctor but won't go to the hospital. Lane faces a choice between two evils:

LANE'S CRISIS DECISION

Option	Why Do This	Why Not Do This
Make a house call to the woman who ruined her marriage	Lane could stay true to her physician's oath to care for the sick	It would be an emotional ordeal she might not be able to handle
Let Ana suffer the consequences of refusing to go to a hospital	It would free Lane from the messiness of caring for her husband's lover	She would be abandoning a dying cancer patient in need

Final decision. Lane chooses to make the house call. This shows that, despite the devastating setback of a failed marriage, her moral principles remain intact. She wants to do the right thing even if it is painful.

Matilde's crisis decision: Greater of two goods

Matilde's most difficult decision occurs in act two, scene 12, when Ana asks Matilde to tell her a joke that will literally make her die laughing. Matilde faces a choice between two irreconcilable goods:

MATILDE'S CRISIS DECISION

Option	Why Do This	Why Not Do This
Tell Ana a cosmic joke	Matilde could free a dying friend from unbearable pain	Telling the joke could make her a participant in Ana's death and endanger her own life as well
Retreat to her peaceful inner world	She could avoid life's messes and cling to idyllic memories of her parents	She would be denying a dying friend her last wish

Final decision. Matilde chooses to tell the joke. This shows that she has become more involved in the real world and that she likes Ana enough to risk life-threatening danger to help her.

Virginia's crisis decision: Lesser of two evils

Virginia's most difficult decision occurs in act two, scene 9, after Lane has accused her of having a "weird obsessive dirt fetish" when Virginia was only trying to help. She faces a choice between two evils:

VIRGINIA'S CRISIS DECISION

Option	Why Do This	Why Not Do This
Submit to Lane's insults as usual	It would help keep the peace and preserve their tenuous sisterhood	It would be another humiliating defeat at the hands of a thankless sibling
Fight back and make a mess	It would enable Virginia to reclaim her dignity	It would be difficult to stand up to her domineering sister

Final decision. Virginia chooses to fight back. This shows that she has reached the end of her rope and gained enough strength from her friendship with Matilde to do what she really wants.

ANALYZING YOUR STORY
Explore the most difficult decision your main character(s) must make.

CRISIS DECISION
- Ideally the crisis decision occurs near the end of the story. Where in the script does your character's most difficult decision occur? Does it need to happen later?
- Where and when in the world of the characters does this crisis occur? How does this place and time affect the crisis?
- Who else, if anyone, is here now? How does their presence affect the crisis?
- What specific alternatives are available to your character?
- Is this a choice primarily between two goods or two evils?
  - If it is a choice between goods: Why can't the character have both? What makes these goods irreconcilable?
  - If it is a choice between evils: Why can't they both be eliminated? How does eliminating one enable the other?
- From your character's perspective, right or wrong, what are the most compelling reasons to choose each alternative? To not choose it?

MAKING THE CHOICE
- Which alternative does your character choose?
- How easy is this choice from your character's perspective?
- How predictable is this choice from the audience's perspective?
- If the crisis decision is too easy or too predictable, there is no suspense surrounding it. What changes in the character, the story, or the decision itself would make the choice more difficult for the character or less predictable for the audience?
- What does this choice reveal about your character?
- How has your character changed since the quest began?
- In what important ways has your character not changed?

CLIMAX AND RESOLUTION

The climax is the most intense part of the dramatic journey. It's when a man facing the gallows for witchcraft risks his survival by refusing the court's order to incriminate others (*The Crucible* by Arthur Miller). It's when a father disowns his son and throws him out of the house in a confrontation that leads to physical violence (*Fences* by August Wilson). It's when a brilliant but coldhearted academic in the final stages of ovarian cancer reaches her last chance to permit kindness into her life (*Wit* by Margaret Edson).

Traditionally defined as the peak of action, the climax is typically triggered by the crisis decision and leads to the end of the quest, where the character finally succeeds or fails. In most plays, the climax is followed by a resolution, in which final outcomes are shown and loose ends wrapped up. Such elucidations tend to be brief, since the dramatic journey has essentially ended and the intensity of the action is now in decline.

In some plays, there is no resolution, as in John Steinbeck's *Of Mice and Men*, which ends with the climactic action of a migrant worker euthanizing his mentally disabled partner, who has accidentally killed someone and now has a lynch mob after him.

■ DOUBT: A PARABLE
Climax: Aloysius vs. Flynn

Sister Aloysius's decision, in scene 8, to fabricate evidence against Father Flynn fuels the final showdown between them. The civility that governed their earlier meeting is gone. Threats, insults, and demands fly back and forth. During this battle, Aloysius threatens to do whatever is necessary to bring Flynn down: "I will step outside the Church if that's what needs to be done, though the door should shut behind me! I will do what needs to be done, Father, if it means I'm damned to Hell!"

The result of this climactic action is that her tactics partially succeed. Though she does not elicit a confession of wrongdoing, she does convince Flynn to request a transfer from St. Nicholas. The scene ends with him calling the bishop's office. The final stage direction is "Lights fade." It is one of the few times that the script specifies a fade-out at the end of a scene. The visual effect of light falling into darkness suggests that a conclusion has been reached. Indeed it is the final onstage moment of Aloysius's campaign against Flynn.

Resolution: Aloysius vs. Aloysius

Doubt ends with a short scene in which we learn through exposition the aftermath of Flynn's phone call. He has left St. Nicholas but he has been promoted to pastor of another parish. We also learn that Aloysius went to the monsignor and tried unsuccessfully to stop the promotion. With Flynn gone, the only demons left for her to battle are her own. By the time Sister James finds her in the garden, Aloysius is profoundly unsettled. Either she has enabled a child molester to seize greater power in another community, or she has damaged the reputation of an innocent man and run him out of his job, home, and community.

Either outcome would signal a failure of the belief system that has governed her life. Regardless of which is true, she has committed the sin of lying and violated her vow of obedience to the Church. We never learn what questions flood her mind as she admits to James that she is overwhelmed with doubts. We know only that she feels unsure and that, for the first time in the play, she is making a personal connection with someone else. It is a display of the bond that Flynn described in his opening sermon: "Doubt can be a bond as powerful and sustaining as certainty."

■ TOPDOG/UNDERDOG
Climax: Fratricide

The climax of the play occurs when Booth, holding his gun to the left side of Lincoln's neck, pulls the trigger and kills him. This action is the result of each brother's crisis, with Lincoln's decision to con Booth out of his inheritance leading to Booth's decision to retaliate. The murder echoes Lincoln's earlier description of his job at the arcade, where his "Best Customer" would always stand behind him and shoot on the left. That description of a fake shooting, in scene 3, foreshadows the real shooting, in scene 6: "The gun is always cold. Winter or summer thuh gun is always cold. And when the gun touches me he can feel that Im warm and he knows Im alive. And if Im alive then he can shoot me dead."

Resolution: A contest with no winner

The climactic killing of Lincoln is followed by two opposing beats, or units of dramatic action. Booth's first response is to justify what he has done. As he paces beside the body, he rages at his dead brother: "You stole my *inheritance*, man. That aint right. That aint right and you know it." His anger fuels his renewed pledge to become a three-card monte dealer named 3-Card and, in a last declaration of jealousy, to be as well known as his brother for his skill at throwing the cards: "And 3-Cards gonna be in everybodys head and in everybodys mouth like Link was."

Booth's second response to the murder is catastrophic grief. The transition occurs when he retrieves the money-filled stocking that triggered the shooting, but lets go of it so that he can reach out to his brother instead. The stage directions state, "Booth holds Lincoln's body, hugging him close. He sobs." His final action is a loud wail, which ends the play. It is the conclusion of a long-standing competition in which neither brother was able to rise above the sins of the past to be topdog.

■ THE CLEAN HOUSE

Each of the three protagonists' journeys has a separate climax and resolution. These outcomes affect one another and contribute to the play's climax—Ana's death by laughter—and the resolution of Matilde coming to terms with her parents' death. In the end, each woman is able to bond with the others and heal from her problems by accepting that life is not perfect.

Virginia

Climax: An operatic mess. The high point of Virginia's dramatic journey occurs in act two, scene 9, when she rebels against her sister's hostility and her own cleaning fetish to mess up Lane's house. The rebellion begins with a plant dumped onto the floor and soon leads to an "operatic mess." During this rebellion, Virginia has an epiphany, described in a stage direction: "She realizes with some surprise that she enjoys this." Her liberation is reinforced when Matilde asks if she's OK, and Virginia replies, "Actually. I feel fabulous."

Resolution: A meaningul life. Virginia gains the strength to deal with Lane as an equal, forces her to admit that she needs help, and then provides that help in different ways, such as counseling Lane to care for the dying Ana and then helping her do so. As a result, Virginia succeeds in making a meaningful connection with her sister as well as her new friends Matilde and Ana.

Lane

Climax: An act of forgiveness. The high point of Lane's dramatic journey occurs in act two, scene 10, when she breaks down emotionally in front of Ana, acknowledges that Charles loves Ana more than he ever loved her— "you're like two glowworms"—and forgives Ana. In doing so, Lane accepts the mess that her life has become. Her quest to regain control of her universe thus fails, but she is happier for it.

Resolution: New connections. Lane becomes Ana's doctor, invites her to move into her house for her last days, and washes Ana's body after she dies. Meanwhile, Lane bonds with Matilde and Virginia, whom she had previously kept at an emotional distance, and makes peace with Charles, who, in the end, asks her to hold his yew tree and prompts her final affirmation: "Yes."

Matilde

Climax: The perfect joke. The high point of Matilde's dramatic journey—and the high point of dramatic action in the play—occurs in act two, scene 13, when she tells Ana the perfect joke so that she can die laughing. It is a theatrically climactic moment, accompanied by a change of lights, sublime music, and a subtitle that reads, "The funniest joke in the world." The stage directions then describe Ana's death: "Ana laughs and laughs. / Ana collapses. / Matilde kneels beside her. / Matilde wails."

Resolution: A start to healing. After Ana's death, Matilde takes charge, guiding Virginia to pray and Lane to wash the body. The play ends with Matilde's last imagining: her birth in laughter under a tree. She acknowledges in this remembrance both the joy and pain of being alive: "I laughed to take in the air. / I took in some air, and then I cried." In experiencing Ana's death and then imagining her own birth with Ana as her mother, Matilde starts to heal from her loss. The stage directions indicate that there is "a moment of completion between Matilde and her parents."

ANALYZING YOUR STORY

With your main character(s) in mind, explore the climax and resolution of your story.

CLIMAX

- Where and when in the world of the story does the climax occur? Who is involved?
- What does each character want here and now? Are these the right objectives for these characters at this time in the story? If not, how would you change the objectives?
- What obstacles does each character face here and now? Are there any opportunities to increase the conflict? If so, how?
- What is at stake for each character? Is it possible to raise the stakes? If so, how?
- What happens during the climactic action?
- Does this event feel like the peak of action in the play? If not, how can you change the story to make this event more intense or a previous event less intense?
- How does the climax affect each character physically? Psychologically? Socially?

- What does the climax reveal about each of the characters involved?
- Has your main character succeeded or failed to achieve his or her goal, and why?

RESOLUTION

- Think about what has been resolved and not resolved as a result of the climactic action. What else, if anything, should happen before the play concludes?
- If any loose ends need to be tied up, have you focused only on what matters most?
- Where and when in the world of the story does this resolution occur? Who is involved?
- How does each character feel as the story draws to a close?
- Can you make better use of imagery to reduce the need for explanation? If so, how?
- What thoughts and feelings do you want the audience to experience as the play ends?
- Everything after the climax is literally "anticlimactic." Can the story end sooner without sacrificing something important? If so, what would the new ending be?

ACKNOWLEDGMENTS

Thank you to John Patrick Shanley, Suzan-Lori Parks, and Sarah Ruhl for writing plays. I have learned much about dramatic storytelling from reading, seeing, and studying your work.

Thank you as well to the University of Chicago Press and the staff who encouraged and supported the development of this guide, particularly Paul Schellinger, who was the first to champion the project; Christie Henry, who later helped steer it in the right direction; my editor, Mary Laur, who helped move it to publication; and my copy editor, Joel Score, who helped refine the words. Special thanks also to the theatre experts who, through the Press, were generous enough to review my materials and offer invaluable suggestions and insights: Arthur R. Borreca, Drew Brody, and Megan Monaghan Rivas.

In addition, I would like to express my gratitude to Emmi Hilger, Dana Lynn Formby, Helen Valenta, and Mary Parisoe, each of whom contributed in an important way to my story analyses in this guide.